Euro Crash

Euro Crash

The Exit Route from Monetary Failure in Europe

Second Edition

Brendan Brown

palgrave
macmillan

First published 2010
Second edition published 2012 by
PALGRAVE MACMILLAN

Palgrave Macmillan in the UK is an imprint of Macmillan Publishers Limited, registered in England, company number 785998, of Houndmills, Basingstoke, Hampshire RG21 6XS.

Palgrave Macmillan in the US is a division of St Martin's Press LLC, 175 Fifth Avenue, New York, NY 10010.

Palgrave Macmillan is the global academic imprint of the above companies and has companies and representatives throughout the world.

Palgrave® and Macmillan® are registered trademarks in the United States, the United Kingdom, Europe and other countries.

ISBN 978–0–230–31923–3   hardback
ISBN 978–0–230–36849–1   paperback

This book is printed on paper suitable for recycling and made from fully managed and sustained forest sources. Logging, pulping and manufacturing processes are expected to conform to the environmental regulations of the country of origin.

A catalogue record for this book is available from the British Library.

A catalog record for this book is available from the Library of Congress.

10   9   8   7   6   5   4   3   2   1
21   20   19   18   17   16   15   14   13   12

Printed and bound in Great Britain by
CPI Antony Rowe, Chippenham and Eastbourne

To the memory of Irene Brown

Contents

Acknowledgements

Elizabeth V. Smith, a graduate from University College London, provided invaluable help in research, in toiling through the manuscript at its various stages of preparation and in checking the proofs.

Introduction

In that wonderful cartoon of Jacques Faizant depicting the historic ceremony in January 1963 at which the Franco-German friendship treaty
was signed, President De Gaulle says to Chancellor Adenauer (in their
70s and 80s respectively) 'hurry up Conrad, you are not immortal'.
Adenauer's hesitation stemmed from concern that de Gaulle was trying
to wean Germany away from its close alliance with the US. The real
pity of that moment emerges now, almost a half-century later. If only
the two heads of state had agreed then on a monetary union between
France and Germany. And it would have been so simple given that both
countries were on the dollar standard meaning that the exchange rate
between the Deutsche mark and French franc was already fixed.

Those photos of President Mitterrand and Chancellor Kohl clasping
hands in the First World War cemetery of Verdun (1984) stir the same
sense of historical regret. If only the two heads of state in their desire to
make war impossible again between France and Germany had resolved
on a quick Franco-German monetary union. The contours of such a
deal would have included a Franco-German central bank with an equal
number of board members from each country, operating under a constitution of monetary rules applying monetarist principles.

Instead a generation of French politicians (spanning say 1973–98)
strove to end German monetary hegemony in Europe and to advance
multi-polarism (replacing US geo-political dominance with multi-poles
including China, Russia, the US and of course 'Europe in France') by driving forward the project of European Monetary Union (EMU). Mitterrand
seized the moment of the Berlin Wall coming down (November 1989)
and Germany's Second Re-Unification (1990) to negotiate a Grand
Bargain. In exchange for France fully supporting German political
union and the extension of the EU to include the central European

countries, Germany would join the drivers' seat in a rapid train journey towards EMU, accepting the eventual loss of monetary power by the Bundesbank.

Mitterrand had already famously realized that the way to push the EMU project forward at the EU level was to exclude the EU Finance Ministers. In 1988 he had got Kohl's agreement to the blueprint for EMU being drafted by a committee of central bankers headed by Jacques Delors, his close political ally and by then EU Commission President. The central bankers would rule over the new union with virtually complete independence from political authorities and with a vast amount of discretionary power.

Milton Friedman and Friedrich von Hayek would have been aghast at the idea of basing a new monetary 'order' on an absolutist central bank, answerable virtually to no one, and with no set of constitutional rules (determining crucially a pivotal role for a monetary base and how this would be expanded over time) established in advance of its birth so as to keep it on the rails of pursuing monetary stability. Friedman in his writings had been steadfastly critical of the Federal Reserve and by extension of central bankers. At every significant stage as analysed in his *Monetary History of the US* (jointly authored with Anna Schwartz) the Federal Reserve had added to the extent of monetary instability compared to what would have occurred without its meddling. Both Friedman and Hayek argued that monetary stability depended on the observance of strict monetary rules. If political necessity or accident of history meant that there had to be a central bank, then strict rules in place should limit the scope for discretionary decision-making, which almost inevitably would turn out badly.

Friedman might have favoured a European Monetary Union in which the central bank was constitutionally mandated to follow a fixed rate of monetary expansion, leaving all interest rates to be market determined, whilst eschewing any price level or inflation target. Hayek might well have argued for a version of the gold standard to be implemented within the context of a wider international return to gold. Both Friedman and Hayek would have been horrified at the vision of an authoritarian central bank setting its own monetary framework and not even constructing a 'monetary pillar' as it had promised in its architectural designs, instead adopting a form of quasi-inflation targeting.

Hayek's understanding of monetary stability turned out to be much more insightful than Friedman's as the first decade of European monetary union unfolded. Hayek, in the tradition of J. S. Mill, viewed the concept of monetary stability as including the key dimension of temperature level in asset and credit markets. Hayek cautioned against defining monetary stability as short- or medium-term stability of the 'price level'. For Hayek fluctuations of prices both up and downwards over the short or medium term were fully consistent with long-term monetary stability and indeed were essential to the capitalist economy continually re-finding balance along a long-run path of progress. Friedman's concept of monetary stability belonged to the time-warp of contemporary macro-economics with its emphasis on tame business cycles and continuously low or even zero inflation as the twin aims of sound monetary policy. In reality it was a wild rise in asset and credit market temperatures occurring in the context of apparent macro-economic stability and low inflation (through the years 2002–7) which proved to be so lethal for European Monetary Union.

The monetary instability which emerged through the first decade of EMU caused ultimately intense pressure to build up inside the whole edifice, threatening a fatal explosion. The pressure was exacerbated by the uneven pattern of asset and credit market temperature rise and fall across the monetary union. A group of periphery zone members where temperatures had been particularly hot during the boom found their anchoring to EMU severely weakened by the intensity of temperature downswings suffered into the bust phase. In particular, the gathering clouds of insolvency over the banking systems and government debt markets in the periphery zone countries (where temperatures had been hot during the boom phase) triggered episodes of capital flight as depositors moved their funds into the EMU core countries. Such capital flight had the potential to force one or more of the periphery zone countries out of the union unless it was checked by a massive offsetting flow of funds from the European Central Bank (ECB) or by a big injection of bail-out funds from governments in the euro-core. In fact, both means of resisting the forces of disintegration involved aid transfers from the financial stronger countries to the weaker.

The ECB in making massive loans against dodgy collateral to likely insolvent banks in the periphery (sometimes the national central banks as in Greece and Ireland acted as intermediary by extending 'emergency liquidity assistance' against the full nominal amount of collateral offered by their member banks, in effect obtaining ECB permission to print euros for this purpose) or in accumulating weak sovereign debt as part of its 'securities market programme' and financing these operations by issuing deposits or money market securities has been drawing on the implicit guarantee (or actual revenues) of governments in the financially strong core member countries. And so the bizarre situation has developed in which the central bankers in Frankfurt issued more and more contingent or actual claims on taxpayers in the strong countries (in that they effectively stood in as guarantors of ECB liabilities) towards sustaining the continuing membership of the troubled periphery. No democratic authority in those strong countries vetoed or even attempted seriously to block such transfers.

Professor Axel Weber, President of the Bundesbank, fought from Spring 2010 a rearguard action to block or slow the flow, but without the strong backing of the German government and evidently without shining success. His successor as Bundesbank President, Jens Weidmann, had no backing either (from the German government) when he dissented in late Summer 2011 from an ECB Board decision to accumulate further periphery government debt (this time aimed at conducting a bear squeeze operation against short-sellers of Italian and Spanish government debt). The ECB argued that its bad bank operations were only transitory in nature, undertaken so as to 'normalize the monetary transmission mechanism' (utterly meaningless!) and on the assumption that its loans would be taken over by the governments in the financially strong countries (most plausibly via the EFSF (European Financial Stability Facility), the new EMU bail-out fund which according to a July 2011 Summit decision was due to gain considerably enhanced powers). But no such undertaking was given to the ECB in advance.

The transfers of aid within EMU as determined by EU decisions (as against 'emergency' actions via the ECB) occurred on an intergovernmental basis, at first via make-shift agreements (as in the case of Greece) and then via decisions regarding the newly created EFSF. The German government took the lead in restraining the extent of such direct transfers by insisting on IMF involvement and on case-by-case consideration under conditions of unanimity amongst the government shareholders (in the EFSF). IMF involvement, though, could add to the ultimate burden of the EU bail-out on taxpayers in the financial strong EMU member countries, in that the Washington institution's claims would be senior to all other outstanding debts.

If German or French citizens had been told back in the early 1990s that the formation of European monetary union could leave them liable for huge transfers of aid to weaker members or to investors and banks with loans outstanding to those, it is all but certain that they would have rejected (with an overwhelming majority) the whole project. In Germany, citizens were never in any case given an opportunity to vote in a referendum, and in France the referendum (in September 1992) only came down in favour of EMU by a tiny margin. The question of

huge potential bail-outs just did not surface at all in the French referendum campaign. Under a more enlightened debate than that which
occurred, the possibility should surely have come to the forefront
of public awareness. And it is even possible that to counter public
concerns during the campaign the French government would have
pressed for a commitment from its EMU partners to the Maastricht
Treaty being amended so as to strengthen no bail-out clauses and to
correspondingly set out a clear legal exit route for any member which
could not otherwise (without bail-out) survive inside the union.

In retrospect if German negotiators (in the EMU process) had been
seriously competent in making sure that monetary union remained a
union of sovereigns with no fiscal transfers or other related burdens
on their fellow (German) citizens, they would have insisted on much
more stringent conditions under which the ECB could undertake loan
operations. There should have been no question of the ECB at its own
discretion setting eligibility criterion for collateral against which it
would lend and this collateral should not have included government
bonds of any description. And any so-called lender of last resort function should have been strictly curtailed or non-existent. Emergency
liquidity assistance (ELA) in the form of national central banks obtaining permission from the ECB to print a certain amount of money for
lending to their member banks under stress would have been out of
the question. If financial crisis erupted then the ECB would have been
able to increase the supply of base money (bank reserves and cash) in
line with increased demand as is typical at such a time. But any loans
made to stricken financial institutions, whether to tide over liquidity problems or threatened insolvency (and in the crisis moment it
is notoriously hard if not impossible to distinguish the two) should
have been possible only on a direct basis by the relevant member
government (and any other government which wished to help). Each
national finance ministry would have at its disposal an instant reaction force to deal with such situations.

If such rules had been in place, then the ECB could not have turned
itself into Europe's Bad Bank and then sought a partial metamorphosis
back into a good bank by imploring governments to take over its bail-
out operations. If a member country found itself at the storm centre
of financial crisis with its banks in a funding emergency (unable to
replace fleeing deposits), its government unable to issue bonds under
its own name to overcome this and governments of stronger countries
unwilling to help out, there would have been no alternative to withdrawal from EMU. A resuscitated money printing press in the exiting

country would have created a burst of high inflation in the process of re-establishing (via a levy on creditors equal to the erosion in the real value of their claims, whether bank deposits or bonds) bank solvency along with other aims (including fiscal crisis resolution). As a group of sovereign countries joined in monetary union with no transfer union, the constitution of EMU should surely have included a section dealing with how an exit and reincarnation of the national money should take place in such an emergency including some provision for transitional loans from the remaining EMU.

These rules prohibiting the ECB from changing itself into a bad bank and EMU becoming a transfer union were one big omission from the Maastricht Treaty and were incredibly overlooked even by those German politicians most concerned at the possibility of free rides by the fiscally profligate countries at the expense of the German taxpayer. The second big omission was a monetary constitution which would restrain the ECB from going down the path of creating monetary instability. If the founding governments of European Monetary Union had determined a set of monetary rules to be followed for the achievement of monetary and long-term price stability, defining that concept in a truly comprehensive form (rather than stipulating a dangerously fuzzy aim of stable prices), then the whole history of massive credit boom (including such aspects as investor appetite for periphery government debt at tiny margins over core government debt and for bonds issued by rapidly expanding banks in the periphery backed by exploding issuance of mortgage paper stemming from hot real estate markets) and bust would surely have been less wild. The founders would also have had to make clear that monetary stability for the union as a whole could mean some episodes of 'good deflation' (a fall in prices not due to monetary shortage but such factors as productivity surge or cyclical downturns) even at the level of the union as a whole and more frequently in some member countries, including the largest (Germany).

For such a large economic area as the European Monetary Union, monetary stability should have always taken precedence over any exchange rate stabilization aims. Indeed the attempt of the ECB in the period of currency warfare initiated by the Bernanke/Greenspan Federal Reserve in the early mid-2000s (2003–5) to keep a lid on the euro at the cost of allowing the proverbial monetary monkey wrench to get inside the euro area economic machinery should have been outlawed under the founding monetary constitution. After all a main objective stated by the lead advocates of EMU was that this should be a zone of monetary stability insulated as much as possible from the repeated pattern of US monetary turbulence. But for that ambition to be realized the dollar–euro exchange rate could not be a significant factor determining how the ECB set monetary policy. If the ECB sought to prevent the euro soaring at times when the Federal Reserve lurched into monetary instability (with its symptom eventually appearing, most likely after a considerable period of time, in the form of either asset or goods price inflation or both) then it would simply import this instability.

The reader might have imagined that when the immensity of the bubble-bursting process and its costs became evident to all, public opinion in the countries where taxpayers were called upon to bear the brunt of 'burden-sharing' (albeit in some cases to salvage the domestic banking system which had recklessly lent to the periphery zone countries) would have swung behind politicians (and political parties) pressing an agenda of reform to make good the defects listed above in the initial design. In general, though, no such agenda has emerged in mainstream political debate. There have been specific controversies about specific bail-outs, but no calls for a thorough revision of the monetary treaty (backed up by the potential bargaining power of one or more lenders to the bail-out funds). And the ECB itself has escaped all criticism. There is no Senator Bunning yelling at ECB President Trichet or Draghi 'you are the systemic risk', or a Representative Paul unafraid to call monetary incompetence to account, and no public opinion poll showing that the ECB has become even more unpopular than the tax collectors (as is the case for the Federal Reserve).

Instead of putting forward a comprehensive agenda for reform based on a monetary constitution, no Bad Bank expansion by the ECB, and provisions for EMU exits, the demands of the German government have been lodged in terms of long-run strict rules for budget balances in each member state together with toughened up sanctions for their disregard and wider economic reforms (in terms of no indexation of wages for example). Evidently the policymakers in Germany have not determined a viable programme for undoing the initial mistakes in the construction of monetary union which in any case they have still failed to indentify fully. Berlin has composed no blueprint for turning EMU fully into a monetary union of sovereign states without transfers and of which the fundamental aim is monetary stability. Those deficiencies could be explained in part by a lack of vision, but also no doubt by the perceived limits of what by 2011 was 'politically feasible' or 'politically correct' in terms of the euro-zone as a whole.

There is also the dilemma of the starting point – a version of the Irish joke about the man who asked the way to Dublin, to be told that 'you should not be starting from here'. In the situation of early 2012 it may well be that the first task should be to decide which countries are indeed fit to 'start from here'. Indeed that should have been the first task already in early 2010 when the Greek sovereign debt crisis erupted. Instead the nonsense 'euro contagion' hypothesis gripped euro-officialdom (defined to include key policymakers in France and Germany, at the ECB, and more broadly) – if Greece were forced out of EMU or into default (or both), a tsunami of capital flight would quickly break the defences of other less weak EMU members. But was it not more plausible that if Greece were denied aid (except on the basis of traditional IMF funding in the aftermath of a mega devaluation having first exited EMU) then the key member country of Italy would be in a more secure position. If German taxpayers had not been called upon to pay for huge transfers related to the threatened Greek insolvency then they might have willingly accepted the justification for a Franco-German solidarity loan to Italy at a later date. 'Solidarity' could take the form of a German equity participation in the ailing Italian banking system.

When it comes to defending a monetary union the same law might well apply as in military science – strength comes from a limited retreat first. The process of retreat would include re-incarnating sovereign monies in the periphery (a procedure which would involve re-denominating loans and liabilities of those countries exiting EMU, official support from the IMF and EU for the transition so that there would be confidence in the new devalued or floating monies) and governments in the financially strong countries dealing with banks (within their political jurisdiction) unable to re-capitalize themselves in the private markets in the wake of losses on their loans to the now exited periphery.

But how could the financially strong countries start the journey of limited retreat for EMU? One conceivable way would be for a Franco-German secret summit to take place. A historic opportunity came and went on that weekend in early May 2010 when Chancellor Merkel was dragging her feet about joining in a bail-out for Greece (or more exactly for lenders to Greece) and President Sarkozy threatened that France would withdraw from EMU in the absence of an immediate agreement. If Chancellor Merkel had said, 'OK go!' it is surely likely that President Sarkozy would have crawled back within 24 hours and begged for Germany's terms for holding monetary union together. The terms which Chancellor Merkel could have offered then would have included a secret undertaking that both countries would come to the support of Italy, but before that line in the sand had been reached there would be no bail-outs except in the context of conventional IMF post-devaluation arrangements (for members which had exited EMU). And Chancellor Merkel could have insisted on a joint Franco-German commission to recommend treaty amendments for monetary union in line with the agenda of reform discussed above.

In reality, however, 'Frau Maus' (as German Chancellor Merkel was described by one tabloid) would have had no menu of terms ready to hand and nor were any of her advisers at all minded to put one together. And in fact she came round to agreeing to the bail-out for Greece before that fateful Saturday evening in early May 2010 was out.

The most likely future of EMU is one of no monetary reform but of continuing rancorous negotiations between the financially strong and weak members about the terms and conditions for limited transfers through the front door (intergovernmental arrangements as through the EFSF) whilst the ECB continues to make huge 'temporary' transfers through the back door (without any explicit political agreement but nods from Berlin and Paris) as required to deal with any funding crisis in the periphery or indeed potentially within the core. There will be a lot of continuing pressure from Berlin in particular towards tighter rules with respect to members' budgetary policies and penalties for ignoring these.

This focus on creating a better and tighter fiscal straightjacket is in contradiction to the historical record. The debt crises in the periphery zone were fundamentally monetary in origin. Without the giant monetary disequilibrium created by the ECB there would not have been those armies of irrational investors (banks and their shareholders or long-term debt holders were prominent amongst these) ready to buy Greek bonds or Spanish mortgage backed securities or a whole range of other dubious securities (including Spanish government bonds given the likelihood of government revenues collapsing once the construction boom turned to bust) at such tiny margins above the yields on prime quality bonds.

The purpose of rancour over bail-outs from the viewpoint of say the German government will not be to focus on historical truths but to demonstrate to German taxpayers (and also to taxpayers of other financially strong countries) that they will not be funding open-ended transfers. Cynically EMU officialdom will continue to turn a blind eye to liquidity loans through the ECB back door (the expansion of its Bad Bank operations) keeping Humpty Dumpty together. A big question is whether markets also will continue to ignore the floods at the back door or at some stage begin to weigh the prospect that the financially strong members of EMU will be saddled with large extra debts (relative to their economic size) towards an eventual re-capitalization of an insolvent ECB. (This re-capitalization will be hidden most likely from public view.)

Humpty Dumpty's future is likely to be short-lived. Bank insolvency in the periphery zone is set to get worse. Many banks there hold portfolios of loans whose quality is still deteriorating. And these banks have investment portfolios which are highly concentrated in government debt issued by the local sovereign. Why would depositors continue to lend to weak banks in the periphery holding such portfolios (stuffed with periphery government bonds alongside dubious private sector loans including mortgage-backed securities) except at rates which are well above those in the core countries of EMU? Yet how could banks pass on higher costs to borrowers in an already enfeebled economic and financial environment? It is dubious that the weak banks could raise equity capital in the markets on viable terms and meanwhile the overall economic climate would be burdened by the lending squeeze. Add to this combustible mixture an element of political instability (in the periphery zone country) and an episode of capital flight could force one or more of the periphery zone countries to exit EMU. The route to that exit featuring occasional giant transfusions of further aid is likely to be much more costly for taxpayers in the financially strong countries than the alternative routes of a quick slimming down (of EMU) to an inner core or a lightning consummation of a Franco-German union with a reformed monetary constitution.

1
Euro Indictment

The global credit bubble and its bursting during the first decade and beyond of the twenty-first century set off a search for the culprits. The investigation is fundamentally historical rather than criminal. The actions and flaws of institutions and individuals are coming under scrutiny. The investigators are also turning to wider social and economic forces which in combination might have been responsible for the disaster.

A search for the causes of economic and financial breakdown has some similarity with the pursuit of blame for the eruption of war. The analogy is only partial because investigations into the breakdown of peace can lead to indictments of war guilt. The identified person or organization could be due for punishment (sometimes posthumously in a purely hypothetical court process) for crimes against humanity or lesser charges. Crime and punishment is not at issue in the investigation of economic debacle.

In general, blundering central bankers and finance ministers did not deliberately or knowingly stoke up the possibility of economic calamity in a wager from which there could have been handsome national (and personal) gains. Perhaps some of the economic policymakers at a rare moment during the phase of stimulus might have had a fleeting insight as to how things might all go very wrong. Maybe they should have acted on those insights by the exercise of greater caution. Even so there was no target for their recklessness – no designated victim to pay for the potential gains, no enemy to be vanquished.

The main purpose of the investigation into economic calamity – and this is also an important purpose in war investigations – is the exposure of frailties and fault lines which allowed the catastrophe to occur. The hope of many investigators is that a better understanding of what went wrong can lead on to a set of remedies which will prevent anything similar happening in the future.

Historical investigations are decentralized. There is no chief prosecuting counsel. Rather, experts, politicians and commentators, undertake their own research and analysis, sometimes alone, sometimes in organized groups. In the example of such investigations into the global credit bubble of the mid-2000s and its subsequent bust, the areas of suspicion have included half-baked or downright false monetary doctrines, regulatory regimes with no safeguards against the regulators falling asleep and which inadvertently overrode and distorted potential disciplinary mechanisms operating in the marketplace, financial intermediation based on systemic underestimation of risk and perverse standards of remuneration, severe inefficiencies in capital market pricing – embracing the crucial topic of how to value bank equities, Confucian tradition in East Asia and many others.

In reflective moods, investigators have raised important concerns about inherent flaws in the functioning of Adam Smith's 'invisible hands' – in particular those guiding the production and dissemination of reliable and insightful financial information, whether by stock market analysts or investigative business journalists.

Many of the eventually identified culprits and their defenders have responded by attempting to demonstrate that others were to blame.

A sampling of the literature and media on the subject of blame would reveal that 'indictments' handed out so far by the decentralized investigation are far-reaching. In some 'trials' or pre-trials, the targets (of the indictment process) have been prominent central bank officials, all the way down from Alan Greenspan and Ben Bernanke (where the charge list starts with inducing severe monetary disequilibrium).

In other trial processes, it is collective entities or groups which stand accused – the government of China (for its exchange rate policy), East Asian households and businesses for saving too much, regulators – including prominently the SEC, BIS and central banks in Europe and the US – for being blithely unaware of what was occurring in the areas they were regulating, innovators for producing flawed financial products, business managers or clients who failed to spot the problems, analysts or journalists who failed to discover or uncover what was really going on (especially in terms of leverage and broader risk-taking) within the financial sector, investors who were blind to or in a state of delusion concerning the risks of leverage and who put an extraordinarily high probability on one particularly favourable scenario (without rationally making appropriately high estimates of probability weights for less favourable scenarios, or even thinking about these clearly).

A big omission in the list of potential suspect areas has been the new monetary regime in Europe which replaced at the end of 1998 the previous regime headed by the Deutsche mark and the Deutsche Bundesbank. Correspondingly there has been no indictment either against European Monetary Union (EMU) or against the European Central Bank (ECB), or any leading euro officials. Also remarkable has been the complete silence of governments or mainstream oppositions in EMU countries with respect to monetary failure (whether in monetary framework or ECB policy actions) and its contribution to the European debt crises which in reality were a part of the global credit bust following the preceding bubble. The Japanese publisher of this book noted that the apparent political consensus to shield the ECB from criticism put it in a position comparable to the Emperor of Japan.

The central theme of this book is that the launch of the euro unleashed forces which played a critical, albeit not exclusive, role in generating the global credit bubble and in making the post-bubble period unnecessarily painful and wasteful, most of all in Europe. A succession of bad policy choices by the ECB is an integral part of that case.

As we shall discover in the course of the narrative, structural flaws in the new monetary union – some of which might have been reduced in size if the founders of the union had not handed responsibility for designing the framework of monetary policy to the just-created ECB (within which the secret committee in charge of the design project, headed by Professor Otmar Issing, newly appointed Board Member and Chief Economist, was given only a few weeks to complete the task) – and policy mistakes by its operatives (including crucially those at the ECB) combined to make the outcome so much worse. (The distinction between structural flaw and operating error cannot be hard and fast in that there are grey areas where the two are inseparable.)

In this first chapter a set of accusations is levelled at EMU and specifically its central bank (the ECB) as the prime culprits. This forms the indictment. In the rest of the book the evidence to support the indictment is presented in full and so are the claims in defence of the accused (much of which takes the form of diverting blame to other targets). A balancing of accusation and counter-claims leads to a hypothetical judgement as to the best way forward for monetary union in Europe. This judgement includes an outline of remedies to contain the dangers posed by EMU both during the painful continuing bust of the great bubble and far into the distance beyond.

Let us start with the summary indictment.

Summary indictment

The launch of European Monetary Union (in 1998) set off a *sequence of monetary and capital market developments* in Europe which seriously contributed to the global credit bubble and subsequent burst through its first decade (and beyond). The European dimension of the bust was perhaps less obvious at first than the US dimension. Whereas mainstream opinion in the global market-places had already adopted a plausibly harsh analysis about the extent of US damage from the bust by early 2009, the reckoning was delayed in Europe. Realistic estimates of the European fall-out from the period of high speculative temperatures (affecting markets in real estate, sovereign debt, financial equities and credit generally) emerged in stages well into 2010 and 2011 as the sovereign debt crises erupted amidst a continuous process of market discovery. Eventually it came to light just how rampant irrational exuberance had become amongst European investors including financial institutions during the bubble period.

Though the European Central Bank (ECB) undoubtedly faced big challenges and was handicapped by essential flaws in the architecture of monetary union, its poor design of monetary framework (even recognizing constraints due to public scepticism regarding its mission of achieving price level stability) had played a key role in fermenting the bubble and bust. The bad mistakes in its policymaking, which magnified greatly the economic damage, were avoidable.

We proceed to the charges in detail.

Faulty instrument board

The *sequence of developments* from the launch of the euro to the credit bubble-and-burst started with an almost total unreliability of the instrument board to be used by the pilots of monetary policy (the central bankers) in the newly created union.

A key problem with the instrument board was the lack of basis for confidence that any chosen definition of money supply in the new union as constructed would be a reliable guide for policymakers seeking to achieve the aim of price level stability as mandated by the founding Treaty of Maastricht.

This absence of confidence stemmed from the fact that little was known about either the extent of demand (in equilibrium) for the new money (in the form of banknotes and bank deposits) or the dynamics behind its supply (how vigorously the overall stock of bank deposits would expand for any given path of monetary base).

Even the best monetary engineers under skilful instruction could not have fully fixed that problem. We shall see later (Chapter 5), though, how enhanced monetary base control together with modestly high reserve requirements might have partially fixed it.

With the passage of time the problem might have been expected to become less severe as learning took place. And it was reasonable to hope, moreover, that policymakers would devise extra checks and balances to contain the extent of monetary instability caused by the unreliability of the instrument board and thereby the ultimate damage which might result. Such hopes were dashed.

Flawed monetary framework and incomplete mandate

Right at the start of the monetary union, and indeed even in the half-year before its formal start (from mid- to end-1998), the founder members of the ECB Council took a series of ill-fated decisions regarding the design of the monetary policy framework.

In seeking to understand how these mistakes occurred, we should not underestimate the difficulty of the task awaiting the founding policymakers of the ECB, especially in view of the defective instrument board.

The ECB Council, in the short time from the EU Summit of May 1998 (where the heads of state took the formal decision to proceed to the final stage of EMU) until the last date possible to have worked out a fully operational plan (autumn 1998) ahead of the euro's launch (1 January 1999), had to decide how to interpret and implement the key Article 105 of the Maastricht Treaty with respect to the new monetary union.

Article 105 states:

> *The primary objective of the European System of Central Banks (ESCB) shall be to maintain price stability. Without prejudice to the objective of price stability, the ESCB shall support the general economic policies in the Community with a view to contributing to the achievement of the objectives of the Community as laid down (in article 2).*

The treaty left it to the ECB to interpret carefully what price stability should mean and how this could be achieved. As it turned out, the feasible time for deliberations stretched only over a few weeks. All of this was unfortunate.

The treaty writers should have composed a clear set of guiding monetary principles. The guiding principles in the Treaty (the monetary clauses) should have included the goal of *monetary stability* alongside the aim of *price level stability in the long run.*

Monetary stability means that money does not become a source of serious disequilibrium in the economy (the proverbial monkey wrench in the complex machinery of the economy – see p. 21).

One key aspect of money becoming a source of disequilibrium is the driving of market interest rates (as quoted for that range of short and medium maturities most relevant for business and household decisionmaking) far out of line with the neutral or natural rate level (distinct for each given maturity). The neutral level refers to a span of market rates (across the different maturities) which would be consistent with the economy following that path in which all markets (for goods, labour, etc.) would be in equilibrium through time (allowing for frictional costs of adjustment).

Monetary instability can occur without any symptom suggesting the possible presence of monetary inflation in goods and services markets. Instead the symptom which first appears (and this may be with a considerable lag behind the initial emergence of monetary instability) might be speculative temperature swings in asset and credit markets (high temperatures mean a lot of irrational exuberance and very high temperatures can bring about bubbles). As illustration, a temperature rise might be driven in considerable part by the central bank first manipulating money conditions so as to steer market interest rates far below neutral in a period of time when the economy is recovering (after a recession-shock) and later in similar fashion weighing down market interest rates with the intention of force-feeding the pace of economic expansion. (The *neutral* level of interest rate is the *natural* rate plus the average annual rate of price increase expected over the very long run; in the gold standard world, that rate of increase was zero, and so economists originally made no distinction between the two terms.) The tools which the modern central bank typically uses for influencing market rates (predominantly for short and medium maturities) are an official peg to short-maturity money market rates and strong hints as to how the peg is likely to be adjusted over the short and medium term.

Monetary stability and *price level stability in the very long run* are partly overlapping concepts and are sometimes not mutually achievable. The goal of monetary stability has to be missed (to a moderate degree) over some medium-term periods so as to achieve the aim of long-run price stability.

The element of trade-off between the two aims here – monetary stability and price stability in the very long-run – shares some appearances with the trade-off in the much discussed dual mandate of the Federal Reserve, which is charged by Congress to pursue price stability and full employment. But that dual mandate is in main part phoney, based on a Keynesian notion of higher employment rates being attainable via the engineering of inflation. As we see below, the dual mandate of monetary stability and price stability in the long-run, though harder to grasp, is of greater substance.

The friction between the requirements of monetary stability and long-run price stability is an essential and perennial source of disturbance in the modern economy. The Treaty makers should have provided some guidelines for the ECB to manage the friction.

The friction arises from the fact that the aim of *price level stability over the very long run* might require the deliberate creation of some limited monetary instability. Moreover the pursuit of monetary stability should involve sometimes the emergence of short- and medium-term price level instability even though this might induce some concerns about the likely attainment of price level stability in the very long run. In a stable monetary order these concerns would not be validated.

For example, during a spurt of productivity growth or terms of trade improvement, the price level should be allowed to fall. If by contrast the central bank tries to resist the forces driving down prices it might fuel a credit-and-asset bubble (symptoms of severe monetary disequilibrium).

Similarly if the central bank resists price level rises driven by real sources, such as sudden energy shortage, an abrupt fall in productivity or in the terms of trade, it would generate monetary disequilibrium with the symptoms of asset and credit deflation (among other symptoms also).

Moreover some price level fluctuation up and down with the business cycle coupled with expectations of price level stability in the long run is instrinsic to the benign process by which the capitalist economy pulls itself out of recession or truncates periods of unsustainable boom and should not be resisted by a central bank mistakenly zealous about achieving price level stability over too short a time period. It is not possible, though, to exclude totally some episodes of monetary instability in a system of control designed to achieve as one aim price level stability in the very long run.

It may be that the price level has drifted through time well above or below the guidelines consistent with long-run stability, even though there has been no serious episode of monetary instability. For example, most of the real shocks (such as productivity growth, terms of trade improvement) may have been in the direction of driving the price level downwards.

In that case there has to be some deliberate injection of controlled monetary disequilibrium towards achieving the long-run price level target. This can be done in a context of decades rather than years – as was indeed the case with the functioning of automatic mechanisms under the gold standard (see Brown, 1940).

No attempt to construct automatic money control mechanism

In our monetary world outside the golden Garden of Eden (a romanticization of a complex reality!) from which we were expelled in 1914, a replacement-stabilizing mechanism (for fine-tuning the extent of monetary disequilibrium to be created towards attaining price stability in the very long run), as automatic as possible, has to be constructed. The likely delicate mechanism has to be capable of allowing a limited degree of monetary instability to emerge sometimes in the form of a speculative temperature swing in asset markets so as to achieve price stability in the very long run.

The drafters of the Treaty did not mention at all the fundamental juxtaposition of monetary stability with the aim of long-run price level stability. They did not specify how the best automatic mechanism should be designed for limiting the essential degree of monetary instability required for long-run price level stability. This big omission left the way clear for fatal errors in design of the monetary framework and in subsequent policymaking.

The Treaty should have provided for a much more comprehensive review surrounding the design of monetary framework and for this to take place in an open, not secret, forum. There should have been ample time (perhaps one year between the EU Summit deciding to proceed with EMU and on which countries would be founder members to the actual start, rather than just six months) for the design process and even longer to allow for needed institutional modifications (especially as regards reserve requirements) to occur towards creating the best possible money control system.

There was a wide range of suggestions available from the well-known literature of monetary economics for the ECB framework-design committee (under Professor Issing) to take on board in the course of their work.

Botched output from the secret 'Issing Committee'

No available evidence indicates that the ECB at the start undertook an appropriate review of alternative ways in which the Treaty's albeit imperfect specification of price level stability as the ultimate aim should be made operational, even if an impossibly short time-framework for final decisions on monetary framework was amply to blame.

One possibility (choice 1) would have been the targeting of a trajectory for money supply growth over time at a low average rate (deemed to be consistent with the price level being 'broadly stable' over the very long run, albeit with considerable swings possible up or down over multi-year periods and also with considerable short-term volatility). The 'central path of the price level' (abstracting from white noise and transitory disequilibrium) would be determined by equilibrating forces (which would balance supply and demand for money as for all other goods in general equilibrium). The price level would be one variable among many to be solved in the process of achieving general equilibrium. In the short-run, there could be considerable disequilibrium!

This monetary targeting might have been coupled with the setting of a quantifiable guideline for price level stability in the very long run (say a ten-year average price level – calculated for the present and previous nine years – which is 0–10% higher than the previous ten-year average for the period 10–20 years ago) so as to monitor that this ultimate aim is indeed likely to be achieved. (Perhaps the broadest of all price indices, thoroughly revised on the basis of new evidence about the past, the GDP or private consumption deflator, would have been used in this calculation). Signs that the price level path might be going astray relative to the aim of stability in the very long run would lead to a twigging of the monetary targeting – meaning a revision in particular to the rule specifying the expansion rate.

Monitoring signs of potential difficulties in meeting the aim of price level stability in the very long run whilst achieving monetary stability in the present was bound to be challenging in the new monetary union given the lack of knowledge about the nature of the demand for money (technically the money demand function). The accumulation of evidence that the aim (of long-run price level stability) might well be in danger or that monetary instability was forming would feed back to a review of the rule used to determine the targeted path for the chosen monetary aggregate. There would be the key issue of what particular definition of money to select, with the possibilities ranging from narrow to wide.

Later in this book the argument is presented that the narrowest of definitions would be best, subject to a revamp of reserve requirements (so as to foster a more stable demand for reserves which would be non-interest bearing – see Chapter 5).

In effect the target would be set for high-powered money (reserves plus cash in circulation) – alternatively described as monetary base – and not for any wider aggregate. The revamp of reserve requirements, however, which would be essential towards the success of a monetary base targeting system, was not feasible, even if deemed as optimal, in the rushed circumstances of summer 1998. (The UK, so long as it kept open the option of being a founder member of EMU, had blocked all discussions of this issue. But in May 1998 the UK had made the final decision against becoming a founder member.)

Choice 1 (of method to make the Treaty's ultimate aim of price stability operational) would have been consistent with the propositions of Milton Friedman (even though he did not recommend that his famous $x\%$ p.a. expansion rule should apply to monetary base but to a wider – yet still narrow – aggregate and he would have been cool to the suggested variation of including a guideline for the price level in the long run), who in his famous collection of essays under the title of *The Optimum Quantity of Money* (Friedman, 2006) had rejected the setting of a price level target in favour of a money supply target. (In technical jargon the money supply would be the intermediate target selected so as to achieve the long-run aim of price level stability.)

Choice 1 might also have found favour with the Austrian School economists, providing that the process for setting money supply targets was sufficiently flexible.

The 'Austrians' (see, for example, Hayek and Salerno, 2008) argued that the price level consistent with monetary stability (including money performing its function of reliable long-run store of value) could vary up or down by significant amounts over the short- or medium-run as for example in the situation of big shifts in productivity growth or the terms of trade. Also the price level should fluctuate in accordance with the business cycle, with a wide span of prices (most of all in the cyclically sensitive industries) falling to a low point during the recession phase and picking up into the recovery phase.

This pro-cyclical movement of prices is indeed in principle a key automatic stabilizer – inducing consumption and investment spending by the financially fit households and businesses during the recession (as they take advantage of transitorily low prices) and in encouraging some households and businesses to postpone spending in the boom phase of the cycle (in the expectation that prices will be lower during the cooler next phase). These cyclically induced changes in the price level should not be interpreted as signifying monetary disequilibrium. These key insights of the Austrian School were referred to earlier in this indictment (see pp. 16).

According to the Austrian School (see Hayek and Salerno, 2008, and von Mises, 1971) the overriding principle of monetary management should be that money does not become the 'monkey-wrench' in the economic machinery (the phrase attributed to J. S. Mill and famously re-quoted by Milton Friedman – see Friedman, 2006). This means (as highlighted in an earlier indictment above – see p. 16) in particular that monetary conditions should not shift in a way such as to cause market rates (illustratively for those maturities which are key to household and business decisionmaking) to get far out of line with neutral or natural levels (which in turn fluctuate through time according to such influences as range of investment opportunity or propensities to save). Monetary stability is defined by money not becoming the monkey wrench 'in the machinery of the economy'.

A big question for the Austrian School is how practical policymakers should implement this prescription when the span of neutral or natural rates (across a range of maturities) might vary considerably over time and be hard to estimate with any precision. And what meaning should be given to 'far out of line'. When an economy is in severe recession, ideally the normal self-recuperative forces in a capitalist economy should produce a path for interest rates which for some time would (with long-run money supply growth firmly anchored) be well below the neutral or natural level which would prevail in long-run equilibrium. The solution is to give markets as big a role as possible in the estimation of the neutral interest rate (as specified for varying maturities) and where this lies relative to long-run norm during a period marked by considerable economic disturbance. The authorities should not engage in such practices as rate pegging in the short-term money markets which might get in the way of this process.

By contrast, the well-known 'Taylor rule' stems from an attempt to discover the optimal path for a central bank in its pegging of short-term money rates. In the world of the Taylor rule there is no notion of market revelation. Instead there is the all powerful black box of econometrics and optimal control theory. Application of the rule requires that the monetary authority knows the neutral rate of interest and the exact degree of slack in the economy. The econometrics assumes stability of the underlying relationships estimated.

The Austrians could concur with those monetary economists from other schools who argue that the most practical way forward would be to target high-powered money (defined as the total of bank reserves and currency in circulation; high-powered money is the same as what is sometimes described as monetary base), while allowing as much scope as feasible for markets to determine even short-term interest rates (which would be very volatile).

ECB architects destroy pivot role for monetary base

A key argument for targeting high-powered money (the monetary base) is grounded on the belief that, given a firm monetary anchor (in this case a target for high-powered money growth), the market would do a better job of steering interest rates close to the ideal equilibrium path (and in discovery of the natural or neutral interest rate level – a crucial element in the auto-piloting process) than the monetary bureaucracies (central banks).

Very short-term money rates would be highly volatile as was the case under the gold standard regime. The volatility would stem from passing shortages and excesses in the market for bank reserves. The average level of these rates, though, over several weeks or months, should be fairly stable. Anyhow it is the rates for medium-term and long-term maturities which would have the greatest information content and be most relevant to business and household decisionmaking.

The Austrians would be in favour of discretionary twigging of the monetary expansion rule to take account of new information regarding the likely profile through time of the real demand for money (especially high-powered money) consistent with overall equilibrium. And some deliberate controlled overshoots or undershoots of the rule could be required to attain long-run price level stability even though that means some monetary instability.

Essential to the operation of monetary base (high-powered money) targeting is first, unrestricted scope for the differential between the zero rate of return on excess reserves (beyond the legal minimum) and on other risk-free assets to fluctuate so as to balance supply and demand in the market for bank reserves. Second, an institutional structure must have been designed in which demand for monetary base is likely to be a stable function of a few key identifiable variables, including in particular real incomes.

The first requirement is achieved where the rate of interest on reserves (and excess reserves) at the central bank is fixed at zero throughout. The second requirement is satisfied by a high level of reserve requirements on the public's transaction deposits with the banks.

The ECB in its design of monetary framework jettisoned both requirements for the operation of monetary base targeting or for any fulcrum role for monetary base in policymaking. Moreover its scheme for paying interest on reserves had the potential to become an infernal destabilizing force during a severe financial crisis, as in fact was to occur in 2007–8 (see p. 90).

High reserve requirements were rejected in part to meet UK objections (see p. 20) but also in line with current fashionable views of not cramping banking industry competitiveness by imposing a tax on transaction deposits sold by resident banks as against other near-alternative assets including offshore deposits.

In the mid-1990s the Bundesbank had reduced reserve requirements substantially already towards countering competitive pressures for German banks from Luxembourg in particular. But it continued with payment of zero interest on reserves right up to the end of its sovereign existence.

Such concerns about competitiveness were doubtless a factor (albeit mitigated by Luxembourg becoming a part of EMU and thereby subject to any reserve requirements) in why the architects of EMU's operating system decided in favour of paying interest on deposits with the ECB at only a modest margin below official repo rates. But another newer factor was the concern to reinforce the new central bank's power to control short-term interest rates within tight limits of the chosen official peg (adjusted, typically by micro-amounts at a time, in line with monetary micro-policy decisions).

Professor Issing rejects advice from Vienna and Chicago

There is no evidence from any published material or from any other source that Professor Issing's secret committee designing the monetary policy framework (in summer 1998) gave weight to the Austrian School's arguments.

'Giving weight to' does not mean comprehensive endorsement. The committee could have raised important practical reservations. In particular, in view of the newness of EMU and public scepticism about the ECB's likely success in avoiding inflation, there had to be an easily understandable target to measure (this success). Austrian 'poetic' concepts of monetary stability might have jarred with that purpose.

It can well be doubted whether a sceptical public would have had patience with the sophisticated argument that monetary inflation need not show itself up as rising prices for goods and services but as rising asset prices, or that a rising price level for goods and services might not be symptomatic of monetary inflation.

It would have been possible in principle for Professor Issing's Committee to include the concept of monetary stability (defined to include absence of asset price inflation in the general sense of speculative fever) alongside a goal of long-run price level stability even though this (concept) had not been specified in the founding treaty.

In so far as public scepticism meant that such a dual mandate (stable price level in the very long-run plus monetary stability) was impractical, then creation of a new monetary union was likely to incur a considerable cost in terms of potential monetary instability.

The omission of an overriding concept of monetary stability along Austrian School lines played a key role in the global credit bubble-and-bust which was to follow.

Under its self-imposed code of secrecy, the ECB has never released transcripts or other documentary evidence of key discussions between its policymakers – including their chosen external advisers – in the critical months before the euro's launch. Perhaps if these officials had known that all evidence, including the transcript of the discussions would be published, the deliberations on this key issue would have been fuller and more efficient.

The ECB's first chief economist and founding board member Professor Otmar Issing writes (see Issing, 2008) that he did discuss within his research team the concern that severe monetary disequilibrium capable of eventually producing credit and asset bubbles could coexist with observed price level stability (as defined by a target average inflation rate over say a two-year period set at a low level).

And there is also some autobiographical evidence (from Professor Issing) to suggest that there was a passing informal review of something similar to the Friedman proposal for money supply targeting without an explicit short- or medium-term numerically expressed aim for the price level.

None of these deliberations, however, which occurred in a necessarily very short period of time during summer and early autumn 1998, translated into any impressive design features of the monetary framework. Yes, there was the sketch of what was subsequently described as the 'monetary pillar', but this remained little more than a blurred section of the original architectural drawing. The main and clearest section of the architectural drawings was filled with what most economists would recognize as a system of inflation targeting even though Professor Issing repudiated that description.

Indeed, the second possible way in which to make the Treaty's specification of price level stability operational, policy choice 2 (for outline of policy choice 1, see pp. 19–20), was for the ECB to reject definition of the ultimate aim in terms of a very long-run price parameter (as in choice 1). Instead the ECB would stipulate a medium-term (say two years) desired path for say the overall consumer price index (CPI), expressed as an average annual rate of change. A practical problem here, amid the many theoretical problems already discussed on the basis of Chicago and Vienna critiques, would be that the so-called harmonized index of consumer prices (HICP) hammered out in committee by the EU Statistics Office excluded altogether house prices or rents and once estimated remained unchangeable even if subsequent re-estimation revealed past error.

In seeking to achieve this two-year path for the price level, the central bank could set a target for growth in a selected money supply aggregate (choice 2a), adjusting the target on the basis of any serious new evidence concerning the relationship between money and inflation. Its tool for achieving the money target could be either strict pegging (adjustable) of a key money interest rate (for example, overnight) or the setting of a subsidiary target for so-called high-powered money growth (reserves and cash) while allowing even the overnight and other short-term rates to fluctuate within a wide margin as determined by conditions in the money market.

Or alternatively the central bank (in its pursuance of the two-year path for the price level) could set no target for money (choice 2b), and instead rely on forecasts for inflation based on an array of econometric tools to be applied to a whole range of variables to be monitored, one of which could be money supply. In this case the central bank would adjust repeatedly the peg for very short-term rates so as to forge a path for these and for longer-term rates that would (hopefully) achieve the ultimate objective for the price level (over a two-year period).

(Rate-pegging is a 'fair-weather' operational policy. If continued during a financial crisis it becomes a catalyst to a vicious cycle of instability (see pp. 110–12).)

A variation of choice 2b (let us call this 2ba) would be to give money supply a special place amid these monitored variables and set an alarm to ring if ever money supply growth estimated over a given stipulated interval strayed outside its specified range. In principle, the alarm would not be turned off even if the monitors determined that no danger existed in the form of the price level target being missed over the 'medium-term' (meaning in practice two years) unless they were also satisfied that there were no other dangers present (for example, inflation in the long run or a bubble in the credit market).

Response to the alarm would include a change in the official interest rate (normally specified with respect to a very short maturity in the money market), which under all versions of policy 2b is set on an entirely discretionary basis in line with policymakers' views about how changes in short-term money market rates influence the actual inflation outcome.

The fantasy of the monetary pillar

The ECB policy-board ratified the Issing Committee's proposals in October 1998 and announced 'the main elements of its stability-oriented monetary policy strategy'.

The Committee had in effect decided in favour of option 2ba above. It stipulated the price level aim in terms of the rise in the euro-area HICP over the 'medium-term' (with subsequent practice demonstrating that this meant around two years), stating that this should not be more than 2% p.a.

There was no indication that the policy board had any realization that rate-pegging under its choice 2ba would have to be suspended or implemented in an abnormal way under conditions of financial crisis (see p. 101).

It was left unspecified (until spring 2003) as to how the ECB would respond to inflation outcomes well below 2% p.a. But early policy-rate decisions implicitly filled that gap (see p. 30).

The ECB board in reaching its decision as regards the definition of price level stability including its selection of numerical reference value betrayed the trust put in it by the founders of monetary union (albeit that the founders were wrong to have staked such an important issue for future economic prosperity of their peoples on a small group of central bankers holding discussions entirely at their discretion in secret and instead of bringing in a wider range of decision makers in an open process with much more time in which to implement their architectural plan).

The announced construction (by the ECB) of an alarm system based on money supply monitoring which would be sensitive to danger over a long-run frame of reference transcending the two-year definition of price stability was largely fantasy. And in particular there was no careful specification of one such danger – temperature swings in credit and asset markets which culminate in severe economic disequilibrium and related waste (sometimes described as 'mal-investment').

The decision on policy framework as described put at great risk the achievement of monetary stability. Serious monetary disequilibrium – full of damaging consequences for the real economy – could result from an over-strict pursuance of the price-level aim as defined.

The ECB board appears (from the evidence available) to have been at best complacent about the possibilities (as raised for example by the Austrian School) that a positive productivity shock coupled with price level path targeting over medium-term periods (say two years) could lead to a credit bubble or that a negative terms of trade shock (in particular a big jump in the price of oil) similarly coupled could lead to depression. Nor did ECB policymakers realize that monetary instability could be symptomless in terms of goods and services price inflation whilst manifesting itself already in dangerous fashion via asset price inflation (temperature rise across a broad range of asset and credit markets). And there could be notoriously long lags between monetary disequilibrium and when the symptom of asset price inflation (or goods and services inflation) was at all apparent in convincing form.

The evidence reveals no awareness on the part of the ECB about the possibility of benign pro-cyclical moves of the price level (see p. 20). In consequence the ECB became inclined to spot illusory threats of inflation falling 'too low' (as in 1999 and 2003) and to suffer more generally from 'deflation phobia'.

All these deficiencies in official perceptions explain how the ECB in its first decade became the engine of huge monetary instability.

No shelter from 'English-speaking' monetary instability

The ECB, in following a quasi-inflation targeting regime as instituted by the Issing Committee, was in great company. (The term 'quasi' is used to acknowledge that the ECB's formal description of its policy framework includes a 'monetary pillar' even though this has never become a well-drawn component of any detailed drawing).

The Federal Reserve and Bank of England were committing very similar types of errors.

That was no excuse for failure.

The ECB as a new institution driven by the idea of setting a high standard of monetary excellence and carrying out the mission of sheltering the new monetary union from 'English-speaking instability' (francophone writers use the term 'Anglo-Saxon') should have done better than its peers.

The Bank of England, after all, had been at the bottom end of the scale (in terms of monetary policy performance) during the decade of the Great Inflation (1970s) (it enjoyed less independence then from the government than in the recent past), so it did not make history in being the worst performer (in terms of inducing credit bubbles and burst) during the debacle of monetary policies around the world wrought by 'inflation targeting'.

Professor Issing does show some possible disquiet about the company in which he found himself in stating (see Issing, 2008) that his secretly deliberating committee decided against following a monetary framework in any significant way embracing the strict inflation targeting pursued by the Bank of England. In writing about the work of his secret committee, Issing comments:

> Of particular value to us (the committee) were the visits by prominent experts who combined an academic background with central bank experience. For instance, we were able to discuss the whole spectrum of issues relating to inflation targeting with one of its proponents, Bank of England Governor Professor Mervyn King.... Inflation targeting was well on the way to becoming the 'state of the art' in central bank policy-making. What could have been more obvious than to follow the example of these central banks (which had adopted inflation-targeting) and the urging of leading economists? There are persuasive reasons why the ECB at the time took a different course.

Professor Issing mentions UK and New Zealand by name but is too politically correct to refer to the quasi-inflation targeting of the Federal Reserve. In any case it was only four years later, in 2002, that the leading academic proponent of inflation targeting, Professor Bernanke, was appointed by President Bush as Governor of the Federal Reserve Board. The irony is that practice did not match intention!

The new event from a historical perspective was that the ECB, as successor to the Bundesbank in the role of leading European monetary authority, followed by its actions (but not fully by its announcements) the crowd of popular (and deeply flawed) monetary opinion, even though its senior officials appreciated some of its fallacies (though not in terms of a thoroughgoing Austrian School refutation!). The protests of the ECB's chief policy-architect through the early years, Professor Issing, that his institution remained distant from the crowd were largely meaningless.

How different the ECB's performance during the monetary madness of the early twenty-first century was from the Bundesbank's stellar record in distinguishing itself from the crowd of popular monetary opinion during the Great Inflation (of the 1970s)! Would the old Bundesbank (before bending before the imperative set by Chancellor Kohl of attaining the EMU destination on schedule), operating counter-factually without the encumbrance of EMU, not have remained nearer to past performance?

Milton Friedman had warned long ago that setting the aim of monetary policy in terms of a stipulated price level outcome over a two-year period (or any other short or medium-term period) would reduce the accountability of the central bank (see Friedman, 1966). For the outcome in any such period could be attributed only in part to central bank policy, given the range of white noise and non-monetary factors outside the control of the central bank which potentially affects short- and medium-term measured inflation rates. Hence there would be a wide range of plausible excuses for failure to achieve the aim. Instead, central bankers should be made responsible for something over which they have a considerably greater degree of control – the path of the money supply (and in the case of the monetary base control is 100%.)

In fact the ECB had a fair degree of success in meeting its stipulated 'medium-term' target for the price level during its first decade, with the average rate of inflation barely above 2% p.a. And so Milton Friedman's warning about lack of responsibility amid a plethora of excuses did not in fact become relevant during that period. It would have been better if the ECB had missed the price target (in the direction of prices undershooting) and its officials had discovered why this should be broadcast as good news!

Indeed more relevant in practice than Friedman's concern about responsibility was the Austrian critique that price level targeting especially over short- *and* medium-term periods, even if successful in its own terms, could go along with the emergence of serious monetary disequilibrium (one key manifestation of this could be asset and credit bubbles on the one hand and severe recessionary deflation on the other). The Austrian School economists would accept that a price level aim should be set over the very long-run (as occurred endogenously under the pre-1914 international gold standard). But their 'very long-run' was far and away beyond the medium-term as conceptualized by Professor Issing's secret committee and even further beyond the medium-term as implemented in practice by ECB policymakers.

The Austrian critique leads on to a further accusation in the present indictment.

Faulty monetary framework leads to three big policy mistakes

In choosing to define price stability as inflation (measured by HICP) at *not more than 2% p.a. on average over the medium-term* (in practice policymaking during the first decade of EMU is wholly consistent with medium-term meaning a two-year period despite the existence of many textual references in official publications and speeches to longer time-horizons) – supplemented by a further 'clarification' in spring 2003 that too low inflation, meaning more than a tiny margin below 2% p.a., would be contrary to the aim of monetary policy – the ECB substantially raised the likelihood of serious monetary disequilibrium ahead (defined to include the symptoms of rising temperature in asset and credit markets).

Indeed, allowing for 'good' price level fluctuations up or down related simply to the business cycle in which a recessionary phase might well last as much as two years, the notion of a two-year period for measurement purposes was palpably absurd.

In practice the ECB Board followed what was to prove disastrous monetary fashion in the US and UK (albeit that the Federal Reserve did not adopt explicit inflation-targeting, mainly out of concern that this could become a point of leverage for greater Congressional control over its policy decisions). ECB officials who pretended that the small actual differences between their own policy framework and that of the Federal Reserve were more than technical or linguistic and that the 'money pillar' component of its monetary alarm system had any operational capability were at best in a state of self-delusion.

As a matter of semantics, as we have seen, the ECB denied right from the start it was following the fashion of inflation targeting. In subsequent refinements (of its communication regarding the framework) the ECB stressed that its policy decisions are based on two pillars (first, medium-term inflation forecasts based on the highest quality of econometric work carried out by its staff and second, money supply developments considered in a long-term time frame including possible implications well beyond a two-year period) and so distinguishes itself from some other central banks which target a given low inflation rate over a similar time-period (two years) without any separate cross-check to money supply growth.

Crucially, however, in common with all inflation-targeting central banks, the ECB stipulates a precise formulation of a stable desired average rate of rise in the price level over a fairly short period of time (it is mainly semantics whether this is a two-year period as officially for the Bank of England or the 'medium-term' as for the ECB) rather than acknowledging that the price level should fluctuate by a considerable amount over the short- and medium-run consistent with price level stability in the very long-run. Indeed that is what happened under the international gold standard – when there were occasional way-out years in which the price level rose by 5% or more, as in the UK during the Boer War, and long stretches of price level rises or falls, but in the very long run, price stability reigned.

Some ECB officials, including notably Professor Otmar Issing, were undoubtedly aware of the dangers in pursuing price level targets over short-term or medium-term horizons and realized that monetary disequilibrium could indeed manifest itself in asset price inflation and credit market over-heating well before any goods and service price inflation might emerge (and emergence might never occur if the bubble burst first). In practice, however, ECB policymakers (including Professor Issing) were not sufficiently sensitive to these risks.

The unreliability of any monetary indicator in the new world of EMU including the framework of monetary control designed by the Issing Committee threw the policymakers off the scent (of credit and asset bubble in the making). This unreliability was one factor in the failure to specify a serious long-run dimension to monetary policymaking.

In the first decade of EMU, three episodes of monetary disequilibrium – first, 1998 Q4 through 1999 (see p. 61), second, 2003 to 2005/6 (see p. 68) and third, 2007 H2 to 2008 Q3 (see p. 101) – were to result from the ECB's adoption of a 2% p.a. inflation target (in official terminology a price level path over the medium-term).

Each episode of disequilibrium was grave in its own way, with the third entering the competition for the worst monetary mistake in European or global financial history since the early 1930s.

The monetary error of 1998–9

Right at the start of EMU, the official aim of the price level rising by 2% p.a. (or a little less) over the medium-term came in for some immediate practical clarification, in a deeply unsettling fashion. When the ECB opened its doors, inflation in the euro-area was down at 1% p.a. If seeking to minimize monetary disequilibrium, the ECB would have done better to aim at first for a continuing level of price increase around that level rather than immediately seeking to breathe in a higher rate of inflation. And if medium-term meant five to ten years rather than two, then there was nothing to worry about in inflation now being at near zero!

After all, with the IT revolution in full swing, oil prices at a two-decade low and terms of trade improving rapidly as cheap imports from Eastern Europe and China ballooned, a policy of driving inflation back up to 2% p.a. was surely wildly expansionary by any Austrian definition! ECB officials remained perma-bears on euro-area productivity even in a period of IT revolution, perhaps because the data available in several European countries almost certainly failed to pick up the full extent of its contemporary spurt. That statistical failure, however, did not apply to Germany in particular, where the statistics office by this point in time practised 'hedonistic accounting', according to which the prices of goods and services were adjusted downwards in line with quality improvements including those now emerging in consequence of the IT revolution.

In addition there is the general point that the price level should move pro-cyclically even under a monetary regime which specifies the aim of absolute price level stability in the very long run. This (1998) was a year of recession or near-recession in the euro-area. The German economy in particular was suffering the headwinds from the emerging market debt crisis which had erupted first in South and East Asia the previous year and then in Russia.

During the boom periods, manufacturers in the highly cyclical industries (especially automobiles) should be charging high margins to compensate in part for the loss which they incur in business recessions. Indeed in a well-functioning market economy firms in highly cyclical industries should tend to have relatively low debt and high equity in their capital structures so as to contain the danger of bankruptcy during recession. Vital equity is attracted to cyclical industries on the basic premise of extraordinarily high profit during boom-time and such equity in effect insures labour and bondholders against recession-destruction of income and capital. And during the recession, the fall of prices in the highly cyclical industries to below normal levels are an inducement to contra-cyclical spending by financially fit firms and households who take advantage of low prices now compared to when prosperity returns.

Inflation below 2% p.a. in 1998 should not have been construed by the ECB as a reason for exceptional monetary ease. Benign cyclical fluctuation of prices on its own could explain a dip of the recorded rate of price increase below the long-run average rate aimed at as the anchor to inflation expectations. The monetary decisions of the ECB at that time hinted at the extent to which the newly constructed monetary policy framework was indeed flawed.

There is some evidence (see Chapter 2, p. 61) to suggest that the ECB in early 1999 was concerned that inflation had already fallen into a 'dangerous low zone' – dangerous in the sense that if the next recession (beyond the cyclical recovery generally forecast for 1999–2000) were to become severe, the central bank would very quickly find that conventional monetary policy reached its limit to provide any stimulus (once risk-free nominal rates fell to zero).

If the ECB were indeed greatly concerned on this score, there were three ways of dealing with it boldly. The first way was to aim for a considerably higher inflation rate (say 3–4% p.a.) during the next economic recovery and expansion phases (of the business cycle). If successful, then in a subsequent severe recession deeply negative risk-free rates could be reached in real terms even though under conventional monetary policy money market rates (even risk-free) could not fall below zero.

This option (aiming for steady-state inflation at say 3–4% p.a.) is discussed further in Chapter 2. Its suitability to the circumstances of EMU is rejected (see pp. 62–3). And in practical terms there was surely no great likelihood of such an inflation rate being reached in just one cyclical recovery. There are also more general grounds for rejection.

One of these grounds has been hinted at already. The higher the long-term average inflation rate which is taken as reference benchmark by monetary policymakers, the more paralysed becomes the inbuilt recovery mechanism during recession of a transitory fall in many prices coupled with the expectation that these will re-bound in the upturn (that expectation justifies spending in the depths of the recession, when cyclically sensitive prices are at their lowest, by the financially strong – see p. 20). There is no evidence, though, that anyone in the ECB gave any attention to this mechanism, let alone believed that it could play a role in driving the economy out of the recession or near-recession of 1998.

The second bold option (for the ECB in confronting a hypothetical danger of monetary policy paralysis in severe recession) was to draft a contingency emergency scheme which would be on the shelf ready in time for possible use were the next recession to prove severe. This scheme would allow risk-free rates to fall to deeply negative levels in both nominal and real terms and yet be consistent with aiming for very low inflation or absolute price level stability over the very long run.

The third bold option – and the wisest according to subsequent analysis here – was to shake off deflation phobia and realize that a pro-cyclical move of prices (reaching a low-point in the depths of the recession, then expected to rise back to normal level) could stimulate economic recovery even in the situation where the use of the conventional monetary tool (adjust-ing nominal interest rates downwards) were no longer feasible due to the proximity of the zero rate boundary. The ECB would help educate euro-citizens that in the new stable monetary order there could be some periods of time during which the price level would fall but that subsequently the price level would recover in line with the stipulated objective of long-run price stability. Expectations of price level recovery would mean that low nominal interest rates would become negative in real terms and stimulate spending.

No contingency planning, no boldness

The ECB did not draft any contingency plan for deep recession or financial panic. Instead right at the start of monetary policymaking (in late 1998 and early 1999) it sought bureaucratic safety in seeking to lift inflation a little from the then 'low level' (relative to the aim for the price level over the 'medium-term').

Inflation, though, running at 2% p.a. instead of 1% p.a. makes only a small potential difference to the extent that risk-free rates in real terms can fall below zero. So long as the zero rate barrier remains firmly in place the path followed by short-maturity risk-free rates during a severe recession or panic would be constrained still at a well-above optimal level. The continuous state of inflation gets in the way of the key pro-cyclical price level mechanism (price cuts during the recession together with the expectation of price level rebound afterwards) which potentially plays such an important role in generating a subsequent recovery. (In general, the lower frequency of big price cuts would mean less of a spending response.)

Given the problems (instabilities) which accompanied getting inflation up from 1% p.a. to 2% p.a., it is just as well the ECB was not bolder on that particular score (aiming for a higher inflation rate than 2%)!

Monetary policy blunder triggered 1999–2000 euro crisis

A consequence of the ECB's implicit decision in 1999 to drive inflation higher (the euro-area CPI was then rising at around 1% p.a.) towards 2% (put into operation by reducing the officially pegged money rates to very low levels and so driving short- and medium-maturity market rates well below neutral level despite the absence of any severe economic disequilibrium in a recessionary direction) was to bring about the huge overshoot downwards of the euro, fuelling a later troubling increase in inflation (to above the target level) which crippled euro-area economic recovery in the early-2000s.

ECB policymakers puffed and fumed about many subjects during the precipitous decline of the euro in 1999–2000. President Duisenberg in Don Quixote fashion took on the title of Mr Euro shooting in all directions. But there is no evidence to suggest that the ECB top official and his policymaking colleagues realized even in part they were largely to blame through the pursuit of a destabilizing monetary policy (breathing a higher rate of inflation into the euro-area economy).

At a time when the euro was a totally new currency, incipient weakness could be interpreted by anxious investors as revealing only feeble fundamental demand for the euro as a store of value given its potential flaws. Hence a monetary blunder by the ECB in triggering an initial fall (of the euro) could become the source of a confidence crisis in the new currency (which is what occurred!).

ECB follows astrology (econometrics based on dubious data)

Also real estate markets in some countries did begin to warm (most of all in Holland at this early stage of EMU but also elsewhere) around this time (1999–2000). In most cases, though, the temperature rise was from low temperate or even cool levels (as for France). In any event, the ECB in choosing to target the movement of a particularly simplistic definition of the price level (euro-area CPI), which excluded almost altogether the price of housing (whether in capital or rental terms), removed itself one stage further from housing market developments.

ECB policymakers realized the problems of definition with euro-area CPI (and how it would fail to pick up a rise of residential space occupancy costs, surely an important component of the overall price level for goods and services) but made no urgent effort in the following years to bring about an improvement.

Yes, there were research papers, speeches and working groups (including national statistical office representation) on the issue, but no strong direction from Frankfurt to get things moving! The hesitancy to back intuition (admittedly in short supply, it seems, around central bank policymaking tables, including that in Frankfurt) about the big picture and instead following statistics of evident low quality (as in the case of euro-area productivity and indeed of CPI), whilst emphasizing the output of the 'high-quality and high-powered econometric model' constructed within the Economic Research Directorate, are flaws in policymaking by the Frankfurt-based monetary bureaucracy which appear repeatedly (and most dramatically in 2007–8, see pp. 30–1).

Monetary error of 2003–5

Then there was the second 'breathing in inflation' error when in spring 2003 the ECB indicated its concern that year-on-year rises in the consumer price index (HICP) might soon fall significantly below 2%. Yet considerations of overall monetary equilibrium at the time suggested that observed price level rises should have fallen well below 2% and that such a fall would still have been consistent with 'price level stability' in the very long-run (not the misleading 'medium-term' of the ECB official-speak), even where this were defined as a path where prices on average, say over a ten-year period, were around 15–25% higher than over the average of the prior ten-year period (the equivalent of an average price level rise at 2% p.a.).

It is true that ECB officials remained dubious about the hypothesis of a secular increase in productivity growth. This hypothesis was the basis of the Austrian critique that the rate of price level rise, appropriately adjusted for quality improvements as in Germany (but not in several other smaller member countries of EMU, for several years should be well below any very long-run aim for this.

The big picture was still one of IT revolution in progress and even cheaper imports from China and other emerging market economies whether in East Asia or Eastern Europe. Together these should have gone along with a period of euro-area inflation below the long-run aim of 2% p.a. (though the extent of undershoot might be under-estimated in so far as statistics offices in the smaller member countries failed to practise hedonistic accounting and these latter were actually sharing in the productivity spurt so recognizable in Germany). And nowhere in the ECB analysis published at the time does there emerge the notion of a benign cyclical swing downwards in the price level (or of the rate of price level increase falling below the long-run average aim for this). The cyclical situation, though, was evolving from 2003 onwards, as the euro-area economies in aggregate started to re-bound from the recession of 2001–3.

The spring 2003 re-affirmation and tightened specification of an explicit 2% p.a. inflation target (forward-looking over a two-year period) by the ECB coincided with dramatic monetary news in the US.

The Federal Reserve under the special prompting of Professor Ben Bernanke (appointed a governor in 2002) decided in favour of a policy of 'breathing inflation back into the US economy' for fear of inflation falling too far (towards zero rather than near the unofficial target level of 2% p.a.). This was the first time in US monetary history that the Federal Reserve shifted policy towards deliberately raising the rate of inflation (from an already positive level).

The key role of Ben Bernanke in pushing for the implementation of this policy is found in the transcript of policy discussions of that time published in full in May 2009. Professor Bernanke was particularly impressed by the 'paralysis of deflation' in Japan, evidently unaware of the possibility as highlighted later by Professor Sakakibara that this country never suffered monetary deflation (defined as a fall in the price level driven by monetary disequilibrium) at all in the 1990s – see p. 68. The alternative explanation – to monetary deflation – for the episodes of a falling Japanese price level during the 'lost decade' and beyond was the combination of first a benign cyclical fall in prices during recession and second a good deflation driven by both rapid economic integration between Japan and China and the IT revolution.

The doomed 2003 revision of ECB monetary framework

The ECB's announcements in spring 2003 (in effect a clarification that the ECB would seek to forestall any significant dip of the price level path as measured over two-year periods significantly below 2% p.a. and would be as vigilant in this as preventing any rise above) got less media notice (still substantial!) than the Federal Reserve's. This was at least in part understandable as the rate of increase in the euro-area CPI was coasting at around the target level (albeit that the price level in Germany was virtually stable in underlying terms – see below). Hence the policy shift was less obvious in Frankfurt than in Washington (where it was not a question of forestalling a possible decline in inflation below its present level in line with target level – as in the euro-area – but of pushing up the rate of price level increase from a rate – around 1% p.a. – already deemed to be too low).

The ECB in effect reiterated (in spring 2003) that it would block the equilibrium forces emanating from accelerated productivity growth, terms of trade improvement, and business cycle weakness, which were pressing the rate of price level increase down below 2% (as would have happened if market rates were following a path closer to neutral level rather than being driven far below by present and expected future rate-pegging in the money market). Yet this was a period when the IT revolution was still in full swing, even if its effects were not being fully registered by most statistics offices in the member countries outside Germany. Hence yet again (as in its opening formulation in 1998 as described above) the ECB, in revising in spring 2003 its monetary framework, totally failed to distance itself and tread a different path from the flawed policies being adopted on the opposite side of the Atlantic (and the English Channel).

The 2003 decision to resist any fall of inflation seriously below 2% p.a. was a critical factor in the creation of the credit and real estate bubbles.

The 2003 decision was taken in a situation where on some measures (excluding the price of public goods and services) the underlying price level in Germany was actually falling slightly. The IMF, headed by an ex-senior finance official in the German government (Horst Koehler), and advised by Chief Economic Counsellor (Kenneth Rogoff), was warning ominously about the dire state of the German economy and about 'deflationary dangers' there.

The coincidence of a dark mood concerning German economic prospects with a monetary blunder at the level of the euro-area as a whole is one piece of evidence (among many others) in support of the next point in the indictment.

ECB makes policy for Germany, not for euro-area

At several critical junctures for ECB monetary policymaking, German-centric factors have influenced decision-making to an extraordinary extent (well beyond the weight of the Germany economy in the total euro-area economy).

Professor Mundell's quip that in monetary union policy is made for the largest member (for example, New South Wales in Australia, Ontario in Canada) applies also to the euro-area despite all the protestation of European political correctness. Further evidence is reviewed in detail in subsequent chapters to support this charge at three crucial periods. (It is too early at the time of writing to analyse in full a possible fourth period when the ECB started tightening monetary conditions in spring 2011 – a time when the German economy had been recovering strongly under the very positive influences of boom in China and in the commodity exporting countries on German exports.)

The first (of these three periods) was on the eve of the euro's launch and during its first year (1998–9) when one influence behind the decision to ease monetary policy despite overall solid economic expansion amid a golden low rate of inflation at the euro-area level was the underperformance of the German economy. This underperformance was in part due to the continuing slump in the construction industry there following the post unification boom (bubble) and in part to the repeated upward adjustments of the Deutsche mark within the European Monetary System, well beyond what could be justified by differential inflation.

The second period encompasses the reformulation of monetary framework in spring 2003 already described and the subsequent three years or so experience of over-stimulatory (non-neutral) monetary policy continuing despite symptoms of monetary disequilibrium such as real estate and credit markets heating up in Spain, France, Italy and several smaller economies.

These events occurred when Germany was still experiencing a construction sector downturn and its real estate markets were still soft. From a business cycle perspective, Germany was in a relatively weak situation compared to the other euro-area countries. There was concern (within Germany) about business investment remaining weak overall due to the re-location of production into cheap labour countries to the East (most of which were soon to come into EU). Inflation as measured in Germany was at the bottom end of the range for euro-area members. German banks were with the benefit of hindsight getting heavily drawn into the warming up global credit markets, but that was not registering on any market or official monitoring device.

The third period during which German economic conditions assumed over-proportionate influence on policymaking (with the Bundesbank President, Professor Axel Weber, and the ECB chief economist, Professor Jürgen Stark – himself an ex-Bundesbanker – both very influential) was in the aftermath of the first big credit quake of summer 2007 and continuing into almost all of 2008 (except possibly for the last few weeks of that year). It seemed then to the Bundesbank (and to the main forecasting institutes) that the German economy was still in a strong growth phase despite the big slowdown elsewhere in the euro-area (and beyond).

In the first quarter of 2008 coincident economic indicators (these lag somewhat behind reality!) suggested Germany was in a boom driven by exports to the oil-exporting countries (including Russia) and other commodity exporters (in the midst of a commodity bubble), Eastern Europe, and China in particular. (Later events and data were to show that the Bundesbankers were remarkably slow in realizing the downturn of German overall business conditions which set in already in spring 2008. And their concerns about the oil price bubble spilling over into wage–cost inflation – a perennial fear among the Bundesbankers – turned out to be fantasy).

More generally what has been perceived by Bundesbankers, ex-Bundesbankers and their allies within the ECB policymaking council, as the best monetary path from a German-centric viewpoint has not always turned out to be so when Time has made its full revelation. And this applies in particular to the failure of the ECB to realize the extent of the credit bubble which was building up in the euro-area from 2003 onwards, the particular role in that of the rapidly expanding inter-bank market, and the fact that German banks were becoming dangerously exposed even though the real estate market in Germany remained cool or cold.

German savings surplus swamped infant euro-credit market

It would be wrong to put all the blame for the euro-roots (there were strong US roots also!) of the global credit bubble at the door of the ECB or even more narrowly of the Bundesbankers and ex-Bundesbankers and their allies who have sat around its policymaking table.

Some part of the blame can be attributed to flaws in the very essence of EMU.

The coming together into monetary union in 1999 of Germany, where the savings surplus was set to bulge (a corollary of continuing construction sector wind-down and transfer of some stages of manufacturing production to the newly opened-up cheap labour countries to the East), with large countries (especially Spain) where construction activity was set to boom and savings deficits widen (households there responding to the historic opportunity of low interest rates superseding the high interest rates which had been associated with pesetas, liras and until recently French francs) was bound to create testing conditions for central bankers, bankers and financial markets. All three failed the test. The biggest failure was monetary. The invisible hands of market forces can be counted upon to distribute efficiently surplus savings in one area of a monetary union to deficit areas (whether inside the union or outside), but only in the context of monetary stability. In fact the ECB presided over growing monetary instability.

The one-fit-all monetary policy meant that the price level would climb fastest in those countries which were now in the swing of construction boom and where savings deficits were expanding. The rise in price level would be at a much lower rate (if even positive) in the main country (Germany) moving in the opposite direction (savings surplus rising). Correspondingly real interest rates (as measured with reference to relevant national price level expectations) in the economies in construction boom and widening savings deficits could fall to significantly negative levels. This fall of real rates in Spain and other savings-deficit economies exposed them to the danger of violent business cycle fluctuation (at first boom, later bust) along the route to full integration with Europe.

The formation of monetary union in itself was virtually pre-programmed to increase the potential divergence of savings surpluses and deficits between Germany and the other countries. Without union, a lower level of interest rates in Germany than elsewhere, coupled with exchange risk between the German currency and the currencies of those European countries in big savings deficit, would have kept the divergence (in equilibrium) between savings surpluses and deficits within tighter limits.

Those tighter limits are not self-evidently a 'good thing'. In terms of neoclassical economic modelling, the removal of barriers (including exchange risk) to capital flows leads to a more efficient allocation of resources between the countries participating in the union. Scarce capital goes to a greater extent towards the biggest investment opportunities. (On the other hand such benefits might be outweighed by the costs of sacrificing monetary independence).

In fact the emergence of recycling in the form of German savings surpluses being channelled into the savings deficit countries (the largest of which by far was Spain) inside and outside EMU (especially Eastern Europe) went along with a growing potential credit problem.

Were the lenders to (including depositors), or equity investors in those intermediaries who were active in the transfer of capital (out of the savings surplus countries, especially Germany, into the savings deficit countries) taking sufficient note of the credit risks involved (related to the capacity to service debt of the borrowers in the savings deficit countries)? Were the intermediaries charging sufficiently for assuming the credit risk and controlling their exposure to this risk adequately? And was the ECB – or any other authority with responsibility within EMU – on due alert to the dangers of potential malfunctioning, especially overheating of credit markets in the euro-area, related to this recycling process and thereby even more determined to foster conditions of monetary stability?

An important element in the flow of capital was German banks lending surplus funds (excess of deposits over loans) into the Spanish banking system – sometimes on a secured basis (via the purchase of so-called covered bonds where the loan from the German financial institution to the Spanish bank was secured by a portfolio of mortgages on Spanish real estate).

Subsequent events starting with the credit quake of summer 2007 revealed that the banks and investors in or lenders to the banks, under the 'warming influence' of monetary instability, underestimated the risks and overestimated the likely returns related to such 'inter-bank loans' within the euro-area context or indeed as between the euro-area and EU countries outside the euro-area (in the latter case this had nothing to do with the transfer problem generated directly by the coming together of savings surplus and deficit countries in monetary union). The largest of the latter group was the UK.

Under the complex rules which described the procedures for ECB money market operations, the new central bank's secured lending operations extended to subsidiaries in the euro-area of non–euro area banks and the security could take the form of eligible assets in any EU country, even if not a member of monetary union (by far the biggest example was the UK). Hence a British bank subsidiary in France (or any other euro-area country) could present parcels of asset-backed paper based on UK residential mortgages for discounting at the ECB.

British banks became huge borrowers in the exponentially growing euro-money markets towards financing the UK real estate and credit bubbles. They covered the currency mismatch (between euro borrowing and Sterling lending) by entering into sterling–euro currency swaps (buying pounds spot for euros and selling the pounds forward for euros).

The ultimate buyers of pounds in the forward market (from the British banks) were most plausibly in many cases the carry traders who were shorting the yen (and sometimes Swiss francs) against high coupon currencies (in this case the pound) so as to gain thereby from the large interest rate spread between the two currencies. The counterpart sale of pounds in the spot market came to a considerable extent out of the mega-trade deficit of the UK.

No diagnosis of monetary disequilibrium despite rising credit market temperature

There is no evidence from ECB statements (including speeches by its Board members) during the years of booming euro-credit business in all its forms that officials realized that the temperature in euro-credit markets was climbing fast and likely to culminate in a bubble or burst. And there is no evidence that officials realized the importance of monetary stability in its widest sense towards reducing the danger of temperature rise, or the particularly high level of this danger which emanated from the starting situation of European Monetary Union.

Nor is there any evidence that the ECB was monitoring the particular credit risks which emanated from the huge savings divergence between Germany on the one hand and the countries in construction boom (and real estate boom) on the other (including the UK, via the channels described).

Of course ECB officials could claim that monetary policymakers had no role in spotting bubbles in advance and should come in only to clear up afterwards. That after all was the so-called Blinder doctrine followed by the Federal Reserve under Alan Greenspan and subsequently Ben Bernanke. But the doctrine was flawed. Even if central bankers were no better than anyone else at spotting possible bubbles they should by profession realize that monetary disequilibrium is the fuel to possible rises in speculative temperature many of which do not end up in bubble but nonetheless result in considerable economic waste. And in the pursuance of monetary stability the central bankers should allow market forces to operate freely in determining market interest rates, without continuously hectoring as to where they intend to peg money market rates over time. The invisible hands would tend to pre-empt violent temperature rises even before central bankers or anyone else could be sure that these have occurred.

The ECB should have done better than the Federal Reserve.

One aim of the EMU was to conduct monetary policy in a superior way (to what was possible before union) given the new degree of freedom from external influence (attributable to an enlarged monetary area). No independent European well-designed and well-tested monetary doctrine emerged.

Instead the ECB in practice largely copied the flawed US framework of monetary control, and to such an extent that critically it failed to react to growing symptoms of severe monetary instability in the form of temperature rise in credit and asset markets.

The ECB had no power to directly cool credit markets via raising margin requirements or minimum loan to value ratios, in contrast to some such authority (albeit very clumsy and never used in modern times) possessed by the Federal Reserve. Much more importantly (than blunderbuss control actions), the ECB could have been vigilant that the 'machinery of money' was not getting out of control, taking account of the danger that credit markets could be warming up, even though overall inflation was still running at 'no more than' 2% p.a. ECB Board Members could have given speeches highlighting the dangers of the situation and remonstrating with private capital markets to use more acumen in judging the value of bank equity and debt; or they could have remonstrated with the national central banks to raise margin requirements on risky real estate lending.

None of this happened. One reason was what we might describe as *euro-nationalism* (defined p. 45) and euro-euphoria.

ECB officials wrongly diagnosed many of the symptoms of rising temperature in credit markets as indications that the euro was indeed taking off as international money and that euro financial market integration was flourishing.

This wrong diagnosis was not limited to the ECB.

Capital markets – and especially equity markets – applauded (and rewarded in terms of share price) banks which were rapidly expanding on the assumption that they were seizing the opportunities in a brave new world of euro-led financial integration, rather than realizing that hidden leverage and growingly risky and under-priced credit positions were being assumed. Banks and investment houses which piled into the government debt markets of Portugal, Greece, Ireland and Spain, to earn a little extra income (compared to what they could get on German government bonds) and in many cases did so on a highly leveraged basis gained popularity with their stake-holders (as reflected in their share market performance or in the new client business which flowed to them). There was little room in markets fired by monetary disequilibrium for long-term doubts about future solvency to affect present prices.

Euro launch spurred irrational exuberance about banks

The launch of EMU did not make it inevitable that such inefficient use of knowledge and bad judgement (as just described) should occur in European capital markets concerning the apparent successes of rapidly expanding bank groups and the quality of credit. But such dangers rose with the launch.

The creation of a new monetary regime, EMU, just when the temperature in global credit markets was about to start rising under the influence of growing US monetary disequilibrium, and its accompaniment in the form of drum-beating (whether by officials, analysts, journalists) about the big new opportunities which financial market integration in Europe would bring, increased the danger of various psychological behaviour patterns becoming prevalent. These are described by behavioural finance theorists and summarized under the well-known catch phrases of speculative displacement, irrational exuberance, learning processes. They help power credit bubble formation.

ECB officials out of misguided pride became cheerleaders in the credit warming process. They were too ready to read euro success and broadcast this rather than first examining more sinister explanations for the apparent good news. A particular illustration of this was the unqualified praise which ECB officials gave to the outward signs of rapid financial market integration in Europe – whether fast growth in the inter-bank and wholesale overnight money markets, or the growth of a euro-denominated corporate bond market, or in the rapid diversification of government bond portfolios (for example Dutch or German investors disposing of domestic government bonds and buying slightly higher yielding government bonds issued by the periphery zone countries).

In praising uncritically the take-off of the euro-denominated corporate bond market (on one occasion the claim was that new issues were now outpacing those in the US), ECB officials failed to realize that an extraordinarily large share of such paper was being issued by banks (flashing red as regards leverage ratios) and the extent to which the bonds were being bought by highly leveraged non-bank financial intermediaries (especially hedge funds) at remarkably low credit spreads. In effect their search for evidence of euro-success led them astray in their monitoring of temperature (and solvency risks) in the euro-area financial system.

The integration of two big countries into EMU right at the start – Italy and Spain – where typically high interest rates and other restrictions had held back mortgage credit growth for decades before set the stage for financial intermediary institutions in those countries to experience rapid business growth. In turn the high profits growth for the leading banks in Spain and Italy helped fuel the temperature rise in their equity markets which allowed them to become (by aggressive merger and acquisitions) leading euro-wide institutions.

There is no evidence that the ECB or capital markets became wary about the risks implicit in the rapid ascent to euro-area (and indeed global) stardom of Spanish or Italian banks. Instead the capital markets fell into the trap (in part created by monetary disequilibrium) of reading rapid expansion of domestic banks in Spain, Italy or elsewhere in the euro-area as evidence of a genuine renaissance in the 'European financial space', applauding the emergence of newly efficient and profitable global players.

Such exaggerated optimism in the context of 'speculative displacement' (the term is found in the Aliber–Kindleberger analysis of bubbles followed by their bursting and refers to a big change in the economic or political environment which is followed by a jump in Knightian uncertainty which sometimes eventually stimulates various forms of irrationality), always in part fuelled by monetary disequilibrium, is a well-known feature recognized by students of bubbles through the ages (see Aliber and Kindleberger, 2005). In this case, the replacement of various second-order high-coupon currencies by the low coupon euro was the speculative displacement.

Euro-nationalists and Quai d'Orsay gain control

The excitement created by the new money and the opportunities which it could bring to financial institutions in the integrating European space was distinct from *euro-nationalism*. This latter phenomenon features in particular the enthusiasm about the reduction in US hegemony – economic, financial and geo-political – which EMU might bring.

Euro-nationalism, perhaps an inevitable outgrowth of EMU, has led the ECB into expensive errors with respect to its G-7 diplomacy and has also gone along with a systematic under-estimation of European economic vulnerability to US economic and financial developments.

In fact euro-nationalism, with its evident pitfalls, was pre-programmed as a feature within the ECB by the virtually pre-arranged appointment of M. Trichet as the second President.

According to the deal between French President Chirac and German Chancellor Kohl at the May 1998 EU Summit, Germany's strong preference as President, Wilhelm Duisenberg, was to be succeeded by Claude Trichet with the change-over to take place well before the end of the eight-year term of office.

Already identifiable as a euro-nationalist from his long career as top French economic diplomat, it was predictable that he would use his office to push forward an agenda long popular in the Quai d'Orsay (French foreign office) of combating US monetary hegemony.

(This agenda was a component of the wider French policy aim described as multipolarity, evident for example in the special relationship – albeit intermittent – between Paris and Beijing.)

M. Trichet's big opportunity to push forward the euro-nationalist agenda came with the Dubai G-7 summit (autumn 2003). In the context of an already weak dollar against the euro (which the ECB was attributing to the US mega current account deficit and its counterpart in 'too low US savings' rather than to the fundamental source of over-stimulatory US monetary policy), M. Trichet embraced the case (suddenly being put forward by the Bush Administration responding to protectionist pressure in Congress most of all vis-à-vis China) for East Asian currency appreciation.

The idea of breaking up the dollar bloc in East Asia was superficially attractive also from a trade viewpoint for Europe, which could gain competitiveness (in Asia) from the 'inevitable' (in the view of M. Trichet and his economist advisers at the Banque de France) appreciation of currencies there. He formed an unholy alliance with the currency populists in Washington to demand a break-up of the Asian dollar bloc, meaning in particular that Beijing should unpeg its currency against the US dollar and make sure it climbed – far from inevitable if all exchange restrictions were to be lifted and official intervention halted simultaneously!

In dealing with China, M.Trichet had to be duly sensitive to Paris's special relationship to Beijing. In consequence, he and his colleagues in French diplomacy presented themselves as forging a middle way – advocating a milder path of currency adjustment than what the Washington neo-mercantilists were putting forward!

ECB joined fateful Washington assault on Asian dollar bloc

There is no evidence to suggest that any serious debate occurred around the ECB policymaking table about whether it would be of overall benefit to the euro-area for the Asian dollar bloc to disintegrate. And even if there had been a debate, there is no record of a strong alternative view within the ECB. No policymaker there was publicly taking issue with the mantra about global imbalances and the prescription that Asian surplus countries should take steps to lower their savings surpluses whilst the US took action to raise its level of savings and arguing instead that the fundamental malaise was US monetary disequilibrium as generated by the Greenspan Fed now under the influence of its new board member from Princeton University (Ben Bernanke). That is disappointing in terms of the ECB's policymaking record.

The whole episode is another illustration of the flaws of an independent central bank so insulated from the political arena – particularly in the context of a monetary union unaccompanied by political union.

What was the alternative view which could have been considered, and might well have entered the policy debate, in a more open system?

A robust and frictionless capital outflow between the huge savings surplus countries of East Asia and the biggest savings deficit country the US – such as would occur within the context of a dollar bloc where exchange risk was only slight – was beneficial also for Europe. The break-up of the dollar bloc in itself would introduce huge new uncertainties into the global flow of funds. In principle the emergence of exchange risk between East Asia and the US would mean a fall in the equilibrium level of interest rates in the former and a rise in the latter together with a rise in the East Asian currencies and fall of the US dollar.

Who, though, had the least idea of where the new equilibrium levels would be? In the interim there was likely to be an extended learning process in the marketplace, such as accompanies any such major 'speculative displacement' (in the Aliber–Kindleberger sense of a huge change in the economic, financial or political environment – see p. 42). Surely the danger loomed of this process fuelling speculative runs (especially in the dollar exchange rate)?

Was there not enough monetary uncertainty in the world already through the launching of EMU and the change of monetary frameworks announced by both the ECB and the Federal Reserve in spring 2003 without adding the break-up of the Asian dollar bloc to the list?

Dollar plunge leads ECB policy astray in 2004

The further plunge of the dollar which developed as a consequence of the 'successful' ECB–Washington demarche at the Dubai summit (towards breaking up the Asian dollar bloc) and of the growing US monetary disequilibrium (as the Greenspan/Bernanke proceeded to raise its interest rate peg at a glacial pace from an abnormally low level) led ECB monetary policy seriously astray and laid the seeds of a future global force of instability – an explosive bubble in the yen carry trade.

There is an accumulation of evidence to suggest that one factor at play around the ECB policy board which delayed any tightening of monetary stance already in 2004 despite evidence suggesting excess monetary ease (including the heating up real estate markets) was the strength of the euro against the dollar, itself exacerbated by the break-up of the Asian dollar bloc.

During the episode of intense dollar weakness in 2003–4, the ECB put too much weight on the exchange rate (primarily of the dollar against the euro) in terms of judging the overall appropriateness of its monetary stance and not enough on other factors (for example monetary data, evidence of – or perceived danger of – temperature rise in credit or real estate markets).

The break-up of the Asian dollar bloc also laid the seeds of the future yen carry trade bubble. The Bank of Japan, out of fright at the super-strong yen triggered by the Dubai summit (on top of over-stimulatory US monetary stance), decided to introduce (in early 2006) its own anaemic and abridged form of inflation-targeting. This was used to justify holding interest rates in Japan at sub-neutral levels rather than boldly adopting a framework of monetary stability untarnished by contemporary fashion in the US and European. The engendering of monetary disequilibrium in Japan in turn stimulated powerfully the yen carry trade into the zone of irrational exuberance.

The overheated yen carry trade became one of the catalysts to credit market temperature rise not just in many East Asian countries (especially South Korea) but also in Europe (in hot real estate markets and private equity markets) and in particular in the emerging market economies of Central Europe.

European banks, riding a wave of enthusiasm in the equity and debt markets about their long-term profit outlooks as enlarged in particular by euro-induced financial integration in Europe, became aggressive participants in a new emerging market loan business (of which Central Europe was the epicentre, but also including East Asia), an area (of business) which US banks were avoiding this time round. In addition, European banks became huge participants in the US credit boom – including a whole range of what were to become 'toxic assets'.

This was the first time since the late nineteenth century that European investors had got sucked into a US credit bubble. With no natural dollar deposit base to match, European banks became critically dependent on funding themselves in overnight and very short-maturity dollar repo markets.

There is no evidence that ECB officials during this period (mid-2000s) were aware or pointing to the dangers related to European banks' high involvement in foreign – and especially US – credit booms. Instead they gave speeches about how in the new age of the euro, European countries had indeed gained a new degree of independence from US economic or financial shock. Exactly the opposite was the reality.

Not only did the ECB totally fail to recognize the extent of US–European financial interdependence that had grown up under its watch but it exaggerated the degree of economic independence that monetary union had brought.

ECB repeatedly underestimates danger (for Europe) of US recession

On the eve and into the early stages of both recessions in the first decade of monetary union (early 2001 and early/mid 2008), the ECB repeated the same error of assessing that the euro-area economy could avoid being dragged down by a sharp US downturn (or that indeed the euro-area economy was subject to the same forces that were pulling the US economy down). Policy at a critical cyclical turning point fell far behind the curve.

In the case of the recession which started in the US in November 2007, heralded by the US growth recession (defined as a period of below trend but still positive growth) from mid-2006 to early 2007 and later much more loudly by the global credit market quake of July/August 2007, the ECB at first denied that the euro-area economies would follow suit. During the growth-recession phase, the ECB was firmly on the side of the economic optimists (predicting no hard landing in the US nor severe downturn in its real estate market).

In late 2007 and early 2008 there may have been some divergence of view within the ECB about the economic outlook (with the Bundesbankers and ex-Bundesbankers remaining optimistic) but key officials could agree on a continuing tough monetary stance due to their common concern that sky-high oil and commodity prices would drive up inflation. That toughness is evident from the juxtaposition of the actual risk-free interest rate (as proxied say by the one-year yield on German government bonds) rising at the same time as the bursting of the credit bubble surely meant a big drop in the equilibrium risk-free rate (together with a much wider than normal spread of risky rates above the risk-free rate).

The ECB policymakers in deciding to toughen their monetary stance through the first three quarters of 2008 completely failed to put a substantial probability on there being an oil price bubble and on this bursting endogenously. That in itself is not the most serious criticism, as we should hardly expect that monetary bureaucrats are at the forefront of identifying bubbles. More seriously they should have considered the likelihood that the spike in oil prices was a late symptom of earlier global monetary excess which had now given way to a totally different situation of emerging financial panic and sharp temperature fall in credit markets (apparent to all).

Indeed the leap to the sky of oil and other commodity prices in late 2007 and early 2008 could have been viewed as most likely a late appearance of asset price inflation in one sector of the global marketplace (commodities) which had previously in this cycle remained temperate. The most likely underlying cause of the sudden temperature was severe monetary disequilibrium in the past rather than the present. Asset price inflation describes a powerful rise of prices (of assets) under the influence of growing irrational exuberance (fuelled by monetary disequilibrium). Even without monetary action, asset price inflation burns itself out and is followed by a price plunge. The question for monetary policymakers is whether by taking action against asset price inflation which has been long in appearing they actually make the subsequent downturn in the economy worse than it otherwise would be. Records do not show that any of this was a subject for discussion around the ECB policymaking table.

No consideration of alternative strategies in wake of credit quake

It seems that the credit quake of July/August 2007 took ECB policymakers to a large degree by surprise, even though they appreciated that credit markets had long been warm or hot in the sense of credit spreads being abnormally low. The biggest surprise (to ECB policymakers) was the extent to which European banks were participants in the US section of the credit bubble and how far this participation had been hidden in off-balance sheet entities (so-called structured investment vehicles or SIVs).

As the European inter-bank markets became suddenly submerged in crisis (many banks finding it impossible to roll-over borrowings in inter-bank market except in some cases at lofty premiums to normal rates – in other cases not at all) on August 9 in reaction to news of BNP Paribas freezing three of its investment funds and the rescue of Europe's highest profile sub-prime casualty IKB (with the high-risk debt in a SIV), the ECB ordered that the taps be opened wide open – meaning that the

ECB should offer unlimited funds (against eligible) collateral at the then overnight rate (of above 4% p.a.).

The ECB decision (of 9 August 2007) (reached by telephone conference between the policymaking officials with anecdotal evidence suggesting that the Bundesbank played a key coordinating role) to make massive secured loans to any bank on demand at a rate near to the actual unchanged official rate appears to have been taken without any consideration of the main alternative plan of action and without any consideration of the exit strategy.

It is also obvious (with supporting evidence) that those making the decision wrongly diagnosed the source of the crisis as a liquidity shortage rather than an eruption of insolvency danger. Yet any reading of financial history should have suggested to the ECB policymakers that a liquidity crisis is usually linked to a solvency crisis. Some of the institutions suddenly unable to borrow are indeed insolvent. If the ECB were to now make loans to a range of institutions which turned out to be insolvent it could find itself in effect acting as a transfer agent taking funds from financially strong countries in the union to bail out insolvent institutions in financially weak countries. As illustration, already in summer 2007 there was awareness of credit bubble in Spain and ECB officials might have imagined the possibility that part of the Spanish banking system might turn out to be insolvent. If the ECB used the strength of its own balance sheet as effectively guaranteed by taxpayers in Germany, France and Holland, to make massive loans to Spanish banks, it would have turned itself into transfer agent. That would be totally against the spirit of the Maastricht Treaty which had created a monetary union without any fiscal or wider political union. Moreover the ECB was not at all obliged under the Maastricht Treaty to act as so-called lender of last resort.

The alternative action plan would have been to immediately cut the rate on the overnight deposit facility at the ECB to zero (in response to the crisis in the inter-bank funding markets) while imposing a premium charge on secured lending above a given quota amount to any bank (and this charge would rise with the amount of excess over the quota subject to an overall limit related to the size of the bank). Larger premiums would apply to any extraordinary unsecured lending by the ECB (subject to limits on a case-by-case basis). Beyond the limits set for emergency lending (which would have been only modest), banks would have had to apply immediately for emergency assistance from their own national governments. The ECB would have resisted any pressure from governments to make loans in advance of such assistance out of justifiable caution that once having gone down that route its independence would become fatally wounded.

Under this plan, the yield on short-maturity high-quality euro-government bonds would have collapsed simultaneously to near zero under the pressure of those banks with excess reserves seeking any alternative risk-free outlet to leaving them at the ECB (where they would now earn zero). In the wholesale money markets, there would have been an instantaneous fanning out of rates – with those banks recognized as less weak being able to attract non-insured funds at very low rates (only a little above zero) while those seen as weak (or under suspicion) having to pay rates well above the official repo rate applicable to normal size borrowing from the ECB.

Given the wide spread which would have immediately developed between rates on low-risk deposits and higher risk inter-bank or wholesale lending, the banks with excess reserves or non-banks with an appetite for risk-arbitrage would have ploughed some funds towards the weaker banks or towards money market-type paper (on which the yields would be well above risk-free level).

There would have been a cluster of financial institutions which could not satisfy their funding needs even at high rates in the private markets – except to some limited degree in secured repo markets where a procedure for placing collateral including paper of so-called top quality backed by mortgages was already in place (this market itself froze up at the worst point of the crisis) – and who would have been borrowers at premium rates from the ECB up to the limits which it set for such assistance.

In turn, the ECB would have had to decide (in conjunction with national authorities in the member countries) whether to continue such emergency lending to the very weak institutions or to insist on restructuring. (The options would range from an injection of government capital to a liquidation process in which a government entity would take over the banks' loan assets while selling the deposits – the goodwill element – to another stronger bank while wiping out its shareholders and bondholders.)

ECB officials remained in a state of denial about the extent of insolvency risk related to the European home-grown credit bubble (hot real estate markets in Spain, UK, France, Eastern Europe, Holland) or to a more general participation in emerging market loans or private equity boom and well into 2008 continued to stress that there was a crisis of liquidity rather than potential insolvency among several major institutions. And as regards its money market operations, the ECB continued to defy any market solution in the form of allowing spreads between weak and less weak bank rates to widen (alongside a rise of rates on risk-credits to non-banks), which would have produced a profit incentive to re-capitalization.

In particular the less weak banks by issuing equity capital (a procedure which would have required full disclosure) and so reducing the riskiness of their (non-insured) deposits (in that depositors would now be protected by a larger equity cushion) would have been able to earn widened margins on their on-lending whether to other (weaker) banks or to non-banks.

Bogus separation principle

In their conduct of monetary policy from the quake of August 2007 through to the crunch of Autumn 2008 the ECB promulgated a bogus doctrine called the separation principle. This led policy far astray (from optimal).

According to this doctrine, there should continue to be virtually only one rate in the overnight market (rather than a span of rates applying to institutions of now starkly different credit risk) and this rate should continue to be pegged closely to the announced official repo rate. This rate should be set as in normal times in line with inflation-targeting requirements.

Separately, the amount of credit support operations (sterilized secured lending to the banks) should be determined so as to maintain 'liquidity' of the money markets and the rate applied on these operations should be uniform for all (and close to the official repo rate).

In fact, under the circumstances of inflamed risk perceptions and highly heterogeneous credit-risk of differing financial institutions relevant even to overnight borrowing, the separation principle aggravated disequilibrium.

In equilibrium, there would not in such circumstances be one rate in the overnight market for all institutions. In the absence of intervention to suppress differentials, there would be a wide span of rates – lowest for the strongest financial institutions, highest for the weakest.

In order to allow the markets to function in this way, the ECB would have abandoned the attempt to peg one overnight rate for all. Interest rates on overnight deposits with itself would have been cut to zero. And the ECB would have added reserves (on an unsterilized basis) through open-market operation such as to meet any increased demand for excess reserves and so prevent a shortage of high-powered money developing which would have manifested itself in a wide range of risk-free rates (such as short-maturity government bonds or repo rates secured on government bonds) rising far above zero.

Quite to the contrary, at the peak of the financial crisis in September 2008, the ECB moved to narrow the band between its deposit rate (paid on excess reserves placed with it) and its marginal lending rate, re-doubling its efforts to peg one uniform overnight rate for all. Unsurprisingly this action in defiance of market forces resulted in a huge round-trip, where stronger institutions with excess reserves parked them at the ECB and the ECB in turn became the only marginal lender to the weaker institutions.

In applying the separation principle, the ECB lost total sight of a fundamental shift occurring in the pattern of equilibrium interest rates across the marketplace and so acted in a direction contrary to equilibrium tendencies, thereby intensifying the financial crisis and economic downturn.

The ECB was also acting in contradiction of the well-established monetary response during previous financial panics in history. Under the gold standard, or under subsequent paper money standards where reserves paid zero interest (the norm until the ECB's creation), the central bank would allow (unless blocked by the overriding obligation to defend the gold parity now under attack) risk-free rates on near-money assets (for example, short-maturity government bills) to fall towards zero under the pressure of funds seeking a safe haven, while pumping extra monetary base into the system so as to prevent any temporary shortage of reserves (banks scrambling to increase excess reserves so as to protect themselves against panic withdrawal of funds) from developing (of which a manifestation would be a re-bound of risk-free rates of return on near-money assets such as T-bills or short-maturity government bonds).

In the presence of heightened risk aversion and grown credit risks, the equilibrium tendency was surely for the risk-free interest rate to fall relative to risky interest rates. On top, the overall lurching of the global economy towards recession (in fact US and Japanese recession already started in November 2007 unknown to contemporary economic observers) meant that the average cost of capital across all risk-categories should surely be falling (so as to balance an increasing propensity to save with a decreasing propensity to spend).

Even leaving that last consideration aside and taking at face value (without criticism) the ECB's intent to steer market rates above neutral level so as to defend the euro-area against 'inflation dangers', it should still have been the case that the risk-free rate as represented by short-maturity government bond yields and overnight money rates (as applicable to the least weak financial institutions) should have been falling to very low levels, whilst the risky rates applicable say to one-month or three-month inter-bank lending or re-po lending secured by non-tip-top paper would have been rising.

In resisting this tendency by pegging an overnight rate and setting a high floor to the government bill rates (by offering unlimited access to its deposit facility at near the pegged rate) – and by effecting massive intervention on a sterilized basis in the term-secured lending markets (so as to stop riskier rates rising there) – the ECB acted as a destabilizing influence on the euro-area economy.

In fact, by applying the bogus separation principle, the ECB not only acted as an economic de-stabilizer but it magnified the amount of dis-equilibrium in the credit markets.

By preventing a fan of market rates widening out in the context of heightened credit risks, the ECB magnified the perceived job of 'liquid-ity maintenance', the misnomer for the recycling of funds on a steri-lized basis (by the ECB) towards the weak institutions.

If the market had been allowed to operate freely, several channels of credit flow which in fact clogged up would have been kept clear under the power of much wider spreads.

Of course as on so many issues the ECB could claim that it was in good company. Other central banks, including the Federal Reserve, were following versions of the same separation principle, at least until late winter 2007/8 (when the Bernanke Federal Reserve embarked on further rate cuts, albeit inadequate). As already emphasized, though, in these indictments, should the ECB as a new institution not have aimed to be above the crowd and especially to outperform the Federal Reserve?

In fact at this time (until late autumn 2008), reserves at the Federal Reserve were still zero interest bearing and so some of the automatic stabilizing behaviour of risk-free rates did occur there (with T-bill rates in particular falling to zero). It was late in the day that Professor Bernanke resolved to follow the ECB in implementing a regime where interest would be paid on reserves so as to strengthen his institution's power to peg money rates.

There is another issue related to the flawed separation principle and the many other listed mistakes of the ECB in this indictment.

Lack of accountability

Flaws in the construction of EMU – in particular, the weak standards set for transparency and accountability set by the Maastricht Treaty – meant that major decisions in policymaking (such as how to respond to the 'liquidity crisis' of August 2007 and the subsequent enunciation of the separation principle; and earlier in 2003 or 1998 the design or re-design of monetary framework) were not subject to challenge from inside or outside in any effective way.

ECB officials have boasted throughout the lifetime of EMU that monetary policymaking is transparent and accountable. They cite the press conferences that follow on immediately from the monthly policy board meeting. On closer examination these provide no serious challenge to policymakers – most of the questions are about whether a rate increase (or decrease) was discussed or not discussed; and on the rare occasions that any difficult question is asked it is snuffed out by a filibuster of loquaciousness on the part of the President, frequently with some evidence of incomprehension of the exact point made by the questioner! There is no serious opportunity for follow-up questions and of course the President selects which journalists to ask the question!

Then there is the Monthly Report in which the ECB policymakers can explain the basis of their policy. That never reveals the nature of any debate or alternative policies which have been considered around the (policymaking) table. Yes, there is some disclosure of the macroeconomic forecasts and ECB members certainly take pride in the depth and sophistication of the econometric work. But by their nature these forecasts are mostly wrong and everyone knows they will likely be wrong. A central bank is not an economic forecasting institute.

The interesting facts to be discovered, when it comes to transparency or accountability, are the specific alternative scenarios and risks which were discussed together with the collective thought processes (including considerations of monetary principles) which led up to the key policy decisions. The ECB has never outlined these.

There are the regular testimonies of the ECB President to the EU Parliament. But a review of all the transcripts shows no seriously critical and well-founded questions on monetary policymaking or damaging challenges for the ECB which might change the course of policy or trigger a re-drafting of the monetary framework. Has any journalist or parliamentarian ever had the opportunity or the preparedness to ask the ECB President directly why his institution made the serious error of steering an over-easy monetary policy in 1999, 2003–5, and worst of all of imposing a monetary squeeze in late 2007 and most of 2008 when a recession had already set in the US and Japan and very likely had already spread or was spreading to Europe?

The answer is no.

More important even than these flaws in accountability is the absence of any such questions during the periods the policy mistakes were being made in the hope that the policymakers would realize their mistake or that democratic pressures would be brought on them to realize these!

ECB officials pride themselves on the transparency and accountability which stems from their annual ECB Watchers Symposium, where outside renowned economists deliver papers and partake in discussion related to live monetary issues. Apparently here is indeed an opportunity for outside challenge. Yet there is absolutely no hint of acrimony or even heated exchange to be found amidst the carefully crafted summary transcripts of proceedings. The symposium is put together by a Frankfurt research institute funded in part by the Bundesbank! Participation is by invitation of the institute. The tone as judged by material available is one of deference and polite exchange within a club. There is no chance of discomfort here.

In principle there could have been a national political dimension to accountability. The French government, in particular, could have appointed an intellectually provocative head of its central bank, willing to break the ranks of silent conformity in Frankfurt, to challenge policymaking consensus (see Marsh, 2009). That has not happened to date, perhaps because there has been no intention of undermining a French President (of the ECB). Italian governments, even those headed by Silvio Berlusconi, have similarly passed up any such opportunity. And in Germany it would be politically taboo to challenge the central bank, given the prevailing concern that any political interference would present serious dangers in the long run for monetary stability.

ECB abstains from key role in approving new EMU members

The ECB has strenuously sought to keep outside EU politics of any description, except to when it comes to lecturing national governments on their budgetary policies or lack of economic reform policies (such as to boost productivity) – neither of which are within its constitutional mandate.

Towards bypassing points of controversy, the ECB smothered one key issue of responsibility within its mandate. Under the Treaty of Maastricht, the ECB was to have an equal role with the European Commission in drawing up reports (each independent) on the eligibility of any applicant to join monetary union. Very early on, the ECB made clear that it had no intention of being drawn into such a political minefield, restricting its report to laying out the facts without any recommendation. In effect it passed the responsibility to the Commission and the EU Council.

The procedure which the ECB has ended up by following on issues of new members joining EMU has been entirely cynical.

In May 2000, ECB Vice-President Noyer (later to become head of the French central bank) held a press conference to announce the publication of its convergence report on Greece (and Sweden). Noyer's comments and the report's summary on Greece was bland. The vice-president announced that the decision on whether Greece could join EMU would be taken by the EU Council of Ministers, who would have to hand the convergence report prepared by the EU Commission staff and the recommendation of the EU Commission. There was no mention by Noyer of the widespread scepticism at large about the quality or correctness of the Greek data which went into the report. France was the main advocate of Greek entry into EMU just as it had been for its earlier entry into EU. In the event Greece joined EMU on 1 January 2001.

Five years later (2006), the ECB raised no objection to the EU Commission's verdict (2006) that Lithuania should not be allowed to join EMU despite this country just missing one entry test and then by only 0.1 percentage points on the inflation score (which was no miss at all if the inflation benchmark had been limited to other EMU countries rather than including an artificially low current inflation rate at the time in the UK). Rather it published its own bland factual summary on the matter with no conclusion. This was a bare-faced decision by the EU Commission, with no expert protest from the ECB, to allow Germany to get its way with its Russian policy (not worth hurting German interests by annoying Russia over extending the euro to the Baltics!).

As a matter of constitutional fact (according to the Maastricht Treaty) the ECB could have broken from the Commission's stance and produced an expert evaluation free of politics which could have been used by those in the Council inclined to favour European liberalism and democracy over sucking up to the Putin dictatorship.

Three years later (in 2009), the ECB and the European Commission might have been patting themselves on the back once the global credit crisis erupted for having either by omission or commission obstructed Lithuania's entry into EMU (even though there is no evidence that a possible credit bubble figured in the Commission's case for rejecting Lithuania or in the ECB's refusal to challenge that rejection). The Baltics with their massive real estate cycles (relative to the size of the economy) and critical dependence on large capital inflows via the banking sector fell into deep recessions.

If Lithuania had been in the euro-area, the ECB would have had to extend its rescue mission to domestic banks or Russian linked banks there (against the collateral of dodgy domestic credit assets) in order to counter and hopefully pre-empt a damaging run of capital out of that country on the fear of a forced withdrawal from EMU. Even so, any such rescue would have been tiny relative to the size of any of the big EMU countries.

In the event, in early spring 2009, the post-bubble crisis in the Baltic countries deepened with intense speculation that Latvia would be the first forced to engineer a huge devaluation of its currency. As the IMF was called in, replenished with the promise of vast new financing as negotiated at the April 2009 G-20 summit (where France obtained remarkable diplomatic success in spearheading multilateral aid for this institution now with Strauss-Kahn – an ex–French finance minister – at its head with the explicit intention of bailing out the emerging market economies in Eastern Europe and implicitly the weak euro-area countries) the speculation started to fade with respect to the immediate future amid savage public expenditure cuts and fantastically high interest rates.

Again the ECB played a role (by omission) in passing up a historic opportunity for the EU to use monetary union as a means of solidifying the economic and political future of a region bordering on Russia where the menace from the Putin–Medvedev dictatorship had become only too clear a year earlier.

Instead of devoting half his press statement on 4 June 2009, to the ECB's latest forecasts on the economic outlook, almost certain to be wrong again, President Trichet could have used his platform to float the historic proposal that the Baltics should be admitted immediately into EMU, subject first to a 40% devaluation of their currencies. That would have worked most likely a miracle, in that interest rates in the Baltics would have collapsed and the devaluation would have given a big impetus to economic recovery there.

M. Trichet, despite his literary idealism on the subject of 'Europe' (see Brown, 2004) implicitly decided not to risk taking on Berlin (where 'Russia first' was still the leading principle at the Foreign Office) over the issue of any bold move to buttress the position of the Baltics as safely outside the reach of the Putin–Medvedev dictatorship. Yet desperation of the Baltic governments to attain euro-membership had meanwhile reached a new pitch, not least in view of Russia's war against Georgia in summer 2008. Estonia was the first of the Baltics to demonstrate that it had met all the stringent conditions for entry – leaving not even a decimal point to the discretion of its EU judges as Lithuania had done in 2006 – and duly was admitted into EMU in January 2011.

Self-indictment of euro-complacency

As ECB officials showered their praise on EMU at its tenth anniversary (January 2009) in the immediate wake of the Great Financial Panic (for which the catalyst was the Lehman bankruptcy) the words of President Trichet provide the final self-indictment of complacency.

In an interview with Le Figaro Magazine (7 January 2009) he exclaimed:

> The euro is evidently an advantage for those democracies that have chosen to adopt it. It has proven its stability, its resistance to shocks and its resilience in the face of financial economic turmoil. Once again, I would say, the euro has been a key factor in providing a shield against international turmoil. [...] We were the first central bank to react immediately when the international financial turbulence first appeared (9 August 2007). [...] Europe was able to take decisions even in the most difficult circumstances. [...] The euro is a big success.

The editor of the European Wall Street Journal was on M. Trichet's side. In a lead article on 2 January 2009, he wrote:

> The Single European currency, born on New Year's Day in 1999, is a rare economic shining star of the past decade.

Evidently EMU and the ECB have had powerful officials within and friends without who would speak in their defence against any indictment. We discover in subsequent chapters how that defence could stack up and what the prosecution could respond.

2
Origins of the Euro-Bubble

How were such great hopes dashed?

Here was a new central bank and a new monetary union which started up at the end of the 1990s. Yes, there were the cynics right at the start, including Milton Friedman who warned that EMU would not survive the first serious recession. And as is often the case some of the cynics turned out to be partly right but for the wrong reasons. They had written much about misaligned business cycles and inflexible labour markets but little if anything about the potential dangers of monetary instability (including the key dimension of temperature rise in credit and asset markets) in a union presided over by a rate-fixing and inflation-targeting central bank unconstrained by constitutional monetary rules.

In contrast the euro-enthusiasts – and they were now in charge of Europe's monetary destiny – had boasted that a new financial economic and political future dawned. The boast proved to be empty of content. Just over one decade later the monetary union was submerged in the aftermath of a credit bubble which was as bleak – and on some accounts bleaker – than in the US! Political integration had made no progress at all (despite the claim of Jacques Delors that monetary union would be the catalyst to political union – see Brown, 2004) and in some respects had moved backwards. Financial integration had moved into reverse gear.

A flight of capital out of the government bond markets and banks in a range of financially weak member countries had brought the scenario of EMU break-up or shrinkage within the mainstream of investor vision around the globe. Embarrassed euro-officials who had been praising their own record at the official tenth anniversary events had to issue statements of denial, mainly to the pompous effect that anyone who argued for a strategic retreat of EMU into its core must be idiotic or deluded!

In this chapter the task is to study EMU in the years up to the peak of the bubble, say early 2007, and pick out the salient factors behind the ensuing malaise. In effect this chapter assembles the evidence from this period towards justifying the indictments of Chapter 1.

Historical observations of Otmar Issing

Let us start with the evidence provided by Professor Otmar Issing, founder member of the ECB Board and its first Head of Economics and Research.

Much of this testimony can be found in his book *The Birth of the Euro* (2008). There he states (written in late 2007?):

> Nine years on (from the run-up to the launch of EMU), the ECB can lay claim – virtually undisputed – to the success of its monetary policy. Those observers that remain sceptics at heart might at most add the qualification 'so far'. Over this period, the average annual increase in the HICP (euro-area CPI) has been 2.06 per cent. [...] Even the D-mark performed considerably less well over the period from 1950 to 1998, with a rate of 2.8%.

Well here is the statement of a single-minded general who achieved his self-selected target, which incidentally did not make much sense in terms of broad strategy, never mind the cost! As we saw in the previous chapter, the aim of monetary stability should not be interpreted as a stable inflation rate over the short- or medium-term but in considerably broader terms which includes temperature level in asset markets and also the possibility of 'good deflation'. And the bill for single-minded 'success' was soon to be presented in the form of an almighty bursting of a massive credit bubble. The historical comparison (with the D-mark) on close examination includes an element of fiction alongside fact (see p. 134).

Let us start with the first big policy decision in what Professor Issing claims was a decade of monetary policy success.

First big monetary policy decision was a big mistake (1998–9)

With inflation in the euro-area as a whole running at just 1% p.a. at the start of monetary union, the ECB decided in favour of monetary easing. In early December 1998 while the national central banks were still legally in existence as sovereign policymakers, the ECB (which had grown out of the European Monetary Institute, opening its doors on 1 July 1998) arranged for an across-the-board cut of official rates by all participating countries. Accordingly the official repo rate set for the start of EMU was at 3% p.a.

In a second policy move in April 1999 the Governing Council decided to reduce again all policy rates. The main refinancing rate and the deposit rate were both reduced by 50 basis points, to 2.5% and 1.5%, respectively.

Albeit with the benefit of hindsight, this sequence of monetary easing through late 1998 and early 1999 was deeply unsettling for the new monetary union. What was so bad about inflation for a time at one percentage point below the upper limit to the inflation target? The IT revolution was now in full swing, which surely would be ushering in accelerated productivity growth globally even if the official statisticians in some EMU member countries (but not Germany) were bound to do a bad job of measuring this. In itself, accelerated productivity growth would lower the path of the price level through time which would be consistent with monetary equilibrium.

Late summer 1998 had seen the eruption of the Russian debt crisis leading on to the brief long-tem capital management (LTCM)-related liquidity crisis of autumn 1998. In response, the Federal Reserve under Chairman Alan Greenspan embarked on a pre-emptive easing of monetary policy (taking a cue in part from a passing sharp fall in the equity market). All of that would have undoubtedly influenced sentiment around the policymaking table at the just-opened European Central Bank. But the degree of that easing by the FOMC (Federal Reserve Open Market Committee) and the slowness with which it was withdrawn has been widely criticized since – especially given its contribution to the final expansion of the NASDAQ bubble.

Could the ECB at its start not have done better than following the mood and monetary style of Washington? And in any case, in making a big rate cut in April 1999 the ECB was already six months on from the crisis action by the Fed and concerns about a possible growth recession in the US had dissipated.

Strangely Professor Issing in his book chooses to provide little insights into how the ECB might answer such criticism. He states somewhat lamely that

> [m]ajor foreign markets were still suffering the effects of the Asian crisis and the repercussions of the Russian crisis of summer 1998 were also still being felt. [...] The assessment of risks to price developments

as being on the downside underlay the ECB Governing Council's decision to reduce the interest rate on the main refinancing facility by 50 basis points to 2.5% at its meeting of 8 April 1999.

A similar non-plus analysis of the monetary easing of late 1998 and spring 1999 is found in *Monetary Policy in the Euro-Area* (2001) under the joint authorship of Issing, Gaspar, Angeloni and Tristani. This account was written nearer the event and stresses the so-called 'downside risks to inflation'. The authors write:

> [O]n April 8 (1999) the Governing Council was facing a situation in which all forecasts projected the euro area inflation rate to remain around levels well within the definition of price stability in the following two years. These projections, however, were in every case the result of a sequence of reassessments, always in a downward direction, which were by themselves the manifestation of a trend leading to downward threats to price stability. While there were no expectations of the euro-area facing deflation, there was the perception of a risk that this could happen, and the main risks to price stability remained on the downside. The risk could be taken particularly seriously in light of the dangers inherent in a situation in which monetary policy operates at very low levels of inflation.

Fear of too low inflation influences ECB policyright from start

We see from the quote above that already the ECB's monetary policy in early 1999 was being driven in part by fear that inflation would enter into a dangerously low zone (dangerous in that the ECB might become powerless to provide stimulus in an economic downturn given that the equilibrium risk-free rate could fall below zero). This was a few years before such fears became enunciated by the Federal Reserve (in early 2003). The lead of the ECB in revealing deflation phobia can be explained in part by the fact that US inflation at the time (late 1990s) was further above the 'danger zone' than euro-zone (and particularly German) inflation and in part to the timing of key appointments to the Federal Reserve Board.

The strong advocate of action against 'too low' inflation in the Federal Reserve – University of Princeton Professor Ben Bernanke – was appointed by President Bush to its Board in 2002. Even so, Alan

Greenspan had been already following for many years a quasi-inflation targeting policy (he would never admit this!), failing to acknowledge that monetary equilibrium is consistent with and even requires an uneven pace of inflation or a fluctuating price level (up and down) over considerable periods of time. In particular, a phase of accelerated productivity growth (as in the mid- to late-1990s under the influence of the IT revolution and related investment spending boom) should go along with a dip in the price level to be consistent with monetary equilibrium (see p. 30). And in a weak phase of the business cycle (as in 2001–3) a dip in the price level or a lower than normal inflation rate should be considered as an essential element in how the capitalist economy auto-generates a recovery out of recession (see p. 19).

One reason why the spectre of too low inflation (not a spectre to those economists aware of the key distinction between good deflation including benign cyclical dips in inflation or the price level and monetary deflation) first appeared in Europe was the extent of monetary savagery in the run-up to EMU. In proving their credentials to join the new union – and to resist the waves of intermittent currency flight during the early/mid-1990s – many of the national central banks (excluding the Bundesbank which was not in the position of having to prove eligibility and which in any case several years earlier during 1991–3 overdid its monetary cooling in response to the inflationary dangers evident during the post-unification boom) had pursued (earlier in the decade) disequilibrium monetary policies in a recessionary direction. Also in late 1998 Germany was in near-recession (driven there by first the global trade slowdown in the wake of the Asian crisis of summer 1997 and then the Russian debt together with wider emerging market debt crisis of summer 1998).

There is no evidence, either in the form of contemporaneous or subsequent testimony, that ECB officials – and crucially Professor Issing – considered seriously the hypothesis that the then feeble inflation rate (around 1% p.a.), even though well below the implicit 'medium-term' target of 2% p.a., might well have been consistent with monetary equilibrium (taking account especially of the benign tendency for many cyclical prices in the economy to fall in the weak phase of the business cycle and rise in the recovery phase). Nor is there any evidence to demonstrate that those officials were aware of the danger (especially in a new monetary union) that breathing in a significantly higher inflation rate (above 1% p.a.) could cause speculative temperatures to rise across a range of asset markets (including the euro currency markets) with economically troublesome consequences.

In practice, by aiming to push inflation very slightly higher from the then level of 1% p.a. (in 1999) the ECB could not realistically hope to gain significant extra margin of firepower should the spectre of deep recession and debt deflation become reality in the next cycle. And indeed if seriously concerned with reducing such dangers in the far distant future the ECB would have done much better to concentrate on building the still effectively missing monetary pillar in its overall policy framework.

In any event, it was not long before the chickens came home to roost from the ECB's decision (implicit!) in spring 1999 to breathe a little inflation back into the euro-area economy. The euro started to decline, with the pace of depreciation gathering pace. From a starting level of 1.18 US$/€ the euro had fallen to virtually 0.80 US$ by October 2000, and the decline against the yen was even greater.

As a new currency, the euro was doubly vulnerable to a policy of breathing in inflation. Each leg down seemed to demonstrate to the sceptics about monetary union that the new money could not earn the trust of international investors. In the language of the behavioural finance theorists, there was a negative feedback loop.

ECB in state of denial about monetary source of euro's plunge 1999–2000

One salient aspect of the official reaction in Frankfurt to the euro's slide is that no one there made the connection with the monetary decision to breathe a higher rate of inflation back into the euro-area economy. Instead, there were a series of explanations including why the euro was not undervalued by any long-run perspective or why the depreciation in fact stemmed from the strength of capital inflows into the US to take advantage of that country's pre-eminence in the IT revolution. Increasingly officials got drawn into a debate as to whether there should be official intervention to support the euro.

The ECB President, Wim Duisenberg, irritated by his colleagues' speeches studded with different nuances on the subject of the weak euro and the benefits or not of intervention, announced that he personally and no one else took responsibility for euro currency policy – 'I am Mr Euro', he told the assembled journalists. Mr Euro had no plan, though, to restore confidence by designing a solid monetary pillar (including automatic rules and automatic stabilizing mechanisms) to support the new construction of monetary union and prevent it from heading into crisis at some point in the not-too-distant future.

A bout of official intervention did take place eventually in autumn 2000, as undertaken jointly by Washington and Frankfurt. With the NASDAQ bubble already bursting, the US Administration saw an advantage (some cynics saw the looming Congressional and Presidential elections as a factor here) in providing some support for US equities by driving the dollar down from its elevated levels (versus the euro). But the effect of the intervention was short lived.

The strong bounce-back of the euro from winter 2001/2 went along with a reversal of relative stance between US and euro-area monetary policies. The ECB continued to be cautious about easing policy – not least because of an inflation overhang now emerging in consequence of the earlier big devaluation (on top of jumps in food and energy prices at the start of the new decade).

The Federal Reserve, in the wake of the September 2001 terrorist attacks on the US, moved at last to a stimulatory policy towards combating recession (in the previous year up to September 2001 the Federal Reserve had been significantly 'behind the curve' – albeit less so than the ECB – and had been very late in recognizing the onset of the economic downturn). Eventually in spring 2003 the Federal Reserve came out with its more explicit version of breathing inflation into the economy than the ECB had done in early 1999 or even than the ECB was doing simultaneously (in spring 2003).

The shift by the Federal Reserve to a stimulatory policy in autumn 2001 occurred six months after the start of recession and barely two months before the start of recovery (as dated by the National Bureau of Economic Research). Eventually in spring 2003, still disbelieving evidence of an economic upturn, the Federal Reserve came out with its aggressive version of breathing inflation into the economy. This was more explicit and focussed than the ECB's earlier version of the same policy enacted in the first few months of 1999. The Federal Reserve's new policy also struck contemporaneous observers as more radical (and expansionary) in its implications than the almost simultaneous shift in monetary framework announced by the ECB in spring 2003.

That is running ahead of our story. Let us return to how contemporary commentators viewed the weak euro of 1999–2000. The authors of the ECB's tenth anniversary edition of the *Monthly Bulletin* (June 2008) subtitle the period mid-1999 to end-2000 as 'Phase 2 – raising rates to contain inflationary pressures (mid-1999 to end-2000)'. There is (of course!) no mention of the fact that the inflationary pressures might have been a consequence of an earlier erroneous decision to breathe in higher inflation (an exercise which apparently got out of control) back in winter 1998/9 and spring 1999. Instead the authors blame extraneous events:

> Over this period, sharp increases in oil prices and a general rise in import prices (was this due to euro depreciation??) continued to exert upward pressure on prices in the short term. As these increases were larger and lasted longer than previously foreseen, the risks of indirect and second-round effects on consumer price inflation via wage-setting rose significantly in the context of robust economic growth. These concerns were compounded by the development of the euro exchange rate. Its trend depreciation continued over this period, gaining momentum in, especially, the second half of 2000 when it moved further out of line with the sound fundamentals of the euro-area. As a result, the balance of risks to price stability over the medium-term was shifted upwards.

The authors congratulate (no surprise there!) the ECB policymakers.

> It became clear that the downside risks to price stability identified at the time of the reduction of the key ECB interest rates in April 1999 no longer prevailed. With the ECB's economic and monetary analyses both pointing to upside risks to price stability, the Governing council raised the key ECB interest rates by a total of 225 bp in a series of interest rate hikes between November 1999 and October 2000, bringing the minimum bid rate in the Eurosystem's main refinancing operations to a level of 4.75% in October 2000.

The authors do not judge policy by the counterfactual – how much better would the outcome have been if the 200 bp rate rise had all taken place by the end of 1999, or if the starting rate cuts had not been made at all in late 1998 April 1999.

The counterfactual experiment should not be limited to euros and cents of lost GDP over the business cycle as a whole. There was also the damage in terms of the related plunge of the euro at its start (attributable to over-easy money) and higher-than-otherwise inflation slowing down the growth of trust among euro-area citizens in the new money.

As we shall see, this possible lack of trust played a role in restricting the freedom of choice of the ECB when it came to reformulating the monetary framework in 2003, making it more difficult to abandon quasi-inflation targeting and embracing sounder principles of monetary stability.

ECB's policy mistake of 1999–2000 handicaps response to 2001–2 recession

Reverting back from counterfactual to actual history, we arrive at the ECB's response to the global recession in the wake of the IT bubble bursting. Issing and his fellow authors (see Issing et al., 2001) describe this period as phase (3) 'Downward Adjustments to Key ECB Interest Rates – early 2001 to mid-2003'. They applaud the ECB's 'grand old duke of York tactics' (not a term used by the authors and stems from the English nursery rhyme 'he marched them up to the top of the hill and he marched them down again, and when they were up they were up and when they were down they were down!'):

> In the course of this period, the Governing Council lowered the key ECB interest rates by a total of 275 basis points, with the minimum bid rate reaching a historically low level of 2% in June 2003. This is the lowest level of interest rates seen in Europe since the Second World War.

It seems that the authors exclude Switzerland from Europe for the purpose of this statement.

One critical issue missed is whether the ECB's refusal to countenance a sharper fall of money interest rates during the period of the actual recession (2001–2) stemmed from the earlier mistake of having breathed in too much inflation during 1999–2000. The tone of contemporary official commentaries do reveal anxiety about dislodging the anchor to stable low inflation expectations already loose as a result of that earlier episode (and in particular the plunge of the euro) paralyzed decision-making.

The second critical issue is whether the ECB should still have been easing policy (as against tightening) in early 2003 given the then explosive growth of money supply which itself might have been seen as one indicator of incipient temperature rise in credit and real estate markets.

The authors slur over that second issue, admitting that the rapid growth of M3 (which was accelerating from mid-2001 onwards) was a source of concern, but pointing out that surge in the money supply was explicable by portfolio shift ('the incidence of sizeable shifts in private investors' portfolios away from shares and other longer-term financial assets towards safe and more liquid monetary assets included in M2'). The authors do not comment on the explosive growth of M1 (especially from mid-2002 on), driven in part by very rapid growth in the overnight inter-bank market – itself an early indicator of bubble trouble.

Without further ado they move on to a discussion of 'Phase 4 – No Changes to Key ECB Interest Rates (mid-2003 to end-2005)'. In doing so they pass over the monetary framework announcements of spring 2003 in which the definition of price stability was 'clarified'.

Long day's journey into monetary madness, spring 2003

Coincidentally, early 2003 was a watershed in US monetary history (see Broaddus, 2004) (and also in UK monetary history, with the Bank of England, albeit under closer government instruction but with no evidence of disagreement, shifting its policy framework in similar respects to the US and euro-area). At the conclusion of its May meeting (May 6), the Federal Reserve Open Market Committee had expressed concern for the first time that inflation might decline too far:

> The probability of an unwelcome substantial fall in inflation, though minor, exceed(ed) that of a pickup in inflation from its already low level.

For those in the know, the newly appointed Governor, Professor Bernanke, a specialist in the Great Depression (who had concluded that the blame for this lay primarily with lack of forceful enough monetary intervention to prevent a severe recession turning into depression) and ardent advocate of inflation targeting, had persuaded Chairman Greenspan and his colleagues that the US economy now (in the wake of the earlier NASDAQ bubble-and-burst) was in danger of entering a 'Japan-style' deflation.

Federal Reserve transcripts tell us that Professor Bernanke did not totally convince Chairman Greenspan in that his hints about the next step being the use of non-conventional policy tools – including creation of massive excess reserves – were not taken up, perhaps because the recovery of the economy became clear so soon afterwards.

In fact, Professor Eisuke Sakakibara was much later to argue that the very mild decline of the Japanese price level in the late 1990s and early 2000s was not at all bad depression-style deflation (what Austrian economists would describe as severe monetary disequilibrium in a deflationary direction) but instead good deflation attributable to jumps in productivity per man-hour and improvements in terms of trade related to rapid integration of the Japanese and Chinese economies.

Journeys into monetary deflations in history are characterized by an ongoing process of money creation lagging far behind money demand in real terms. In principle at a later point when expectations of price level declines continuing have become prevalent and are, matched by projections of persistent feeble growth or actual contraction in money supply, there may no longer be any present monetary shortage. Long-run price declines fully expected and matched by monetary developments in the same way as long-run price increases fully in tandem with monetary expansion are not evidence of monetary disequilibrium, but they are inconsistent with the aim of price level stability in the long run.

Many economists argue that there was indeed such a monetary journey into deflation in Japan during the period 1989–93 when Bank of Japan policy was extraordinarily tight (see Brown, 2002). But that monetary disequilibrium was not accompanied by an actual fall in the price level. It is plausible that the episodes of gentle decline of the price level many years beyond that could have been due in part to the good deflation forces described by Professor Sakakibara in his revisionist account of the so-called 'lost decade'. There were also short periods of good deflation related to cyclical downturns. The evidence does not support the emergence in Japan of extrapolative expectations of continuing price declines.

As regards the US situation in early 2003, the fall of recorded price level rises to around 1% p.a. was much better explained by normal (and economically efficient) pro-cyclical behaviour (dominated by prices in the highly cyclical sectors of the US and global economy – including commodities) than any hypothesis of sinister monetary developments. Critics argued that the new Governor from Princeton University had become 'obsessed' with the Great Depression to the extent of giving an unrealistically high probability to a recurrence and that moreover he had not learnt the most important lesson of all – about the Federal Reserve's mistakes during the boom period which preceded the Great Depression (see Lowenstein, 2008 and Brown, 2008 and below, p. 73).

Early 2003 was also a critical period for the evolution of the ECB's monetary framework. Two days following the critical May 6 FOMC meeting (after which an immediate press release detailed the decision), the ECB held a 'press seminar on the evaluation of the ECB's monetary policy strategy'. This consisted of a slide show by Professor Otmar Issing. The first and most important point was that the Governing Council clarified its quantitative definition of price stability.

Price stability shall be defined as a year-on-year increase in the Harmonized Index of Consumer Prices for the euro-area of below, but close to 2%.

The new element here was 'close to' whereas previously the degree of tolerated undershoot had been left unstated.

As before, price stability was to be assessed over a 'medium-term' horizon, but meaning in practical terms (though not expressly stipulated) around say a two-year period. Other points – less important – in the slide-show included semantics about whether the ECB was targeting inflation (according to Professor Issing no – but in practice yes); and semantics about the role of money supply path monitoring in the so-called 'two-pillar approach' to implementing (don't mention the word!) inflation-targeting.

Professor Issing's notorious slide show

There were two particular points of interest to come out of Professor Issing's slide show as regards the role of monetary analysis in the policy-making framework.

First, he repeated the assertion (so well-known since first public explanation of policy framework just prior to the start of EMU) that monetary phenomena deserve separate attention, from the econometric type analysis which formed the first pillar, as triggers to the raising of an alarm bell (in the corridors of the central bank). Conventional forecasting models do not capture fully the signalling capacity of monetary phenomena, whether within the two-year horizon relevant to econometric equations, or beyond. (This is a point of view on which Friedman and the Austrians would both agree – see p. 23) Monetary analysis provides a means of cross-checking from a longer-term perspective the shorter-term indications from the economic analysis which forms the 'first pillar'.

Second, Professor Issing commented directly on bubbles:

> Excess money may provide additional information for identifying financial imbalances and/or asset price bubbles, which ultimately may impact on price developments.

The impression from this second remark was that financial imbalances and asset price bubbles were not a problem in themselves except in so far as they had implications for the meeting of the long-run price objective (inflation target by any other name). That was far removed from the Austrian concept in which severe monetary disequilibrium could occur without emitting a symptom in the form of goods and services price inflation or deflation. Rather the symptom might be just asset price inflation (or deflation) – and by the time this symptom could be confidently diagnosed the disease might already by well-advanced. And for the Austrians severe monetary disequilibrium albeit without symptom in the form of goods and services inflation was not anything to be dismissive about. Its consequences were dire in terms of economic costs – including in particular the waste (misallocation of scarce capital, both physical and human) of the bubble-and-bursting process.

For example, the monetary disequilibrium in the US during the mid-1920s (evident, according to the Austrian analysis, in the strong temperature rise of credit and real asset markets, even though there was no symptom in the form of a rising price level for goods and services – see Rothbard, 1972), attributable to the Federal Reserve under the domination of Benjamin Strong holding down money rates well below the high neutral rate reflecting the contemporaneous technological revolution, had occurred alongside broad stability of the price level. Germany, the second largest economy in the world in the late 1920s, was also in severe monetary disequilibrium at the same time.

The German monetary disequilibrium (of a totally different nature from during the hyperinflation) stemmed from the fixed link to the US dollar of the Reichsmark as stipulated by the Dawes Plan (1924). This prevented German interest rates coming into line with the very high natural rate level which corresponded with the great investment opportunity to emerge in the aftermath of war and hyperinflation. US investors, stirred into irrational exuberance by monetary disequilibrium in the US, became avid buyers of apparently high yielding German securities. US banks, their appetites for risk fed by the sky-high price of their equities, were at the forefront of the lending boom to Germany. The overall result was a fantastic credit-and-asset bubble in both countries (Germany and the US) without upward pressure on the overall price level in either. And yet the bubble would inevitably be followed by a burst, meaning that monetary excess would never show up in goods and services inflation.

There are no references to the possibility of severe monetary disequilibrium without the accompaniment of an actual rise in the price level in Professor Issing's speech. Instead, there was much reference to the possibility of 'deflation'. Professor Issing emphasized (in his slide show) that there was a need for sufficient safety margin to guard against risks of 'deflation', hence the revamped wording of the price aim.

There was no comment by Professor Issing to suggest awareness of the key distinction between monetary-led deflation (initiated by a severe monetary disequilibrium in which money supply is growing well below the demand for real money balances) and various forms of non-monetary driven declines in the price level (related to terms of trade improvement, productivity growth acceleration and cyclical fluctuations) which could well be symptoms of a well-functioning capitalist economy with no monetary disequilibrium.

This re-vamped and expanded description of the monetary framework was disconcerting in several respects. Perhaps most disconcerting of all was the fact that the ECB was moving even further away from an ideal monetary framework which would recognize that the achievement of monetary stability transcended and could indeed be frustrated by an intense focus on price level changes over short or medium periods of time.

One might have hoped that now the ECB had been open for almost five years, it could build on the grown trust of euro-citizens concerning their new money to back away from such a concentration on movements of the price level over the short- and medium-term.

Instead, the policy framework reformulation made the medium-term profile of the price level an even greater focus with less room for flexibility than before (price level rises now had to be held close to 2% p.a., not falling significantly below that figure).

Yes, the mistake of the ECB (unrecognized of course in official statements) in pursuing excessively easy money policy in its first year or so had squandered some opportunity to build trust (in stability of the new money) among euro-citizens. Nonetheless, some progress had surely been made.

The innovation of setting an implicit lower bound to inflation (as well as the upper bound) implied a reinforcement of inflation-targeting (though Professor Issing denied staunchly that the ECB was an inflation targeter) which could increase the risk of severe monetary disequilibrium in the Austrian sense. If changes in real variables were driving the price level down (as for productivity acceleration or terms of trade improvement or passing cyclical weakness) or up (the reverse), the ECB by combating those pressures would induce monetary disequilibrium (of which a key eventual symptom could be asset price inflation or deflation, respectively, with all the associated misallocation and eventually waste of economic resources).

The ECB was evidently in the same intellectual culture as the Bernanke/Greenspan Federal Reserve (and Bank of England), in which temperature swings in asset and credit markets were outside the range of concern except in so far as they had implications for the inflation target. (This is one of the discredited 'Ten General Principles' of Professor Bernanke – see Brown, 2008.)

Perhaps there were nuances and throw-out remarks which suggested that Professor Issing had an understanding that monetary stability involved much more than what he revealed at the slide show. Nothing implied, however, that these reservations would seriously influence policymaking, notwithstanding the already accumulating evidence (for those who looked) of credit market temperature rise.

In the course of his presentation, Professor Issing made a point which unwittingly hinted at a further element in the deflation phobia afflicting both himself and his colleagues. He defended the lower limit to inflation (of close to 2%) not just in terms of avoiding the perils of deflation generally (in particular the zero rate trap) but also in terms of providing a margin for relative price fluctuation within the euro-area.

In the context of 2003, the margin to which Professor Issing implicitly referred was scope for the German economy to experience a relative price decline (vis-à-vis other euro-area countries) without suffering actual 'deflation'. This hypothesized equilibrium path of relative prices was in line with the widespread perception that sluggish domestic demand in Germany (relative to elsewhere in the euro-area), explained by the bursting of the post-unification construction boom and shifting of investment opportunity to cheap labour neighbours to the East, called for some gains in its competitiveness. Hence dynamism of exports could compensate for lack of domestic demand along the route back to overall equilibrium.

Professor Issing did not raise the possibility that the apparent relative sluggishness of domestic demand growth in Germany relative to several other countries in the euro-area could be in fact a symptom of underlying monetary disequilibrium. That would be the case if excess money was fuelling an uneven pattern of temperature rise across asset markets with those most affected concentrated in a few member countries rather than all equally. At this time the obvious causes for concern would have included the construction and real estate boom in Spain and the public spending boom in several small periphery zone countries.

In future it could be another member economy (than Germany) which would find its route back to prosperity conditional on an increase in its competitiveness (decline in its relative price level). For example, at some possibly distant stage the construction boom in Spain would come to an end. But Spain as a much smaller economy than Germany could surely not count on or expect other member countries to experience sufficient price level increases so that no general fall in prices would have to occur domestically. Professor Issing's analysis of safety margin (for inflation) was in fact remarkably German-centric. Indeed Professor Issing was hinting that one defence for the decision to breathe inflation higher in 1999 (notwithstanding its consequence of sharp depreciation of the euro) was the concern that the then current rate of rise in the euro-area CPI at around 1% p.a. was too low to allow for rapid relative price level adjustment downwards in Germany without an absolute fall in the price level occurring there.

IMF wrong again! It warns about euro-deflation in 2003

Deflation risks in Europe were certainly on the international conference agenda at this time. The IMF issued a much discussed research paper on deflation ('How to fight deflation in a liquidity trap; committing to be irresponsible', Eggertsson, Gauti, March 1, 2003). Kenneth Rogoff, Economic Counsellor and Director to the IMF Research Department, wrote:

> Our indicators suggest that the prospect of deflation cannot be entirely dismissed, and the same would be true for the euro-area as a whole; although there are higher risks for Germany. Interest rates and inflation rates will remain near or at fifty year lows throughout the globe, and a sufficiently strong negative demand shock could tilt the balance towards worldwide deflation (17 July 2003).

The IMF in its World Economic Outlook in Spring 2003, in a study put together by a special task force overseen by Kenneth Rogoff, warned that

> Germany is at high risk of deflation and Japan, Hong Kong and Taiwan are vulnerable to an accelerating pace of price declines. [...] There has been a clear increase in the vulnerability to deflation for a number of industrial and emerging market economies.

The IMF report stirred deflation phobia, warning that 'deflation is seldom benign and is difficult to anticipate'.

Professor Issing at his press conference understandably made no direct reference to the deflation-mongers in Washington who clearly had never read von Mises on 'good deflation'! Calmly Professor Issing went out of this way to say that little had changed in the monetary framework. The significance of the lower limit to inflation was high at the moment because real pressures (cyclical and secular) might be taking observed year-on-year CPI changes below the newly formulated lower bound. But the same situation had prevailed in 1999 – in fact even more so.

Why did you go to such trouble, Professor Issing?

In the question-and-answer session which followed the slide show, there was an inter-change between one journalist and Professor Issing which can be described as at best superficial, at worst smug.

Q: Professor Issing, you have obviously gone to a lot of trouble to produce this review, but could you explain exactly what difference it is going to make to the way you formulate monetary policy? Will it, for example, make it easier to cut interest rates? Or is it all really a matter of presentation?

Issing: First, it was no trouble. It was not always pleasurable, but it was fascinating and, for somebody with my background, it was a very challenging aspect of my work, and cooperation with our experts is always very enjoyable. The word 'trouble' is certainly not appropriate. But as the President has already said, even if we had had the same clarification back in 1998, our policy would not have been any different. So I do not expect – and there is no reason to expect – a different monetary policy on the basis of the clarification of the strategy, which was decided on today.

Q: What was the point of it then?

Issing: If you are married and after four years of happy married life, perhaps one evening you sit together over a glass of wine and think about why you are so happy all the time: nobody would say it does not make sense (laughter!!!).

What issues should have been discussed at the review but were not?

We will look at this in more detail during the trial process (Chapter 4). But already in spring 2003 the possible rise of temperatures in credit and asset markets and how monetary policymakers should respond – without simply copying the conventional wisdom at the Federal Reserve (or Bank of England) – might well have been on the agenda. This did not mean a proposal to target asset prices but rather to consider whether monetary instability in its widest sense (to include possible but not yet provable asset or credit market inflation) might be forming.

Also of relevance could have been a thorough look at the issue of whether the extra comfort provided against the risks of monetary policy paralysis by setting a floor to inflation of *closely below 2%* was at all significant.

After all in a serious financial crisis or deep recession (or both), the optimal path of real risk-free interest rates (in terms of a safe yet reasonably fast journey back to overall economic equilibrium) for say short and medium maturities would surely pass through substantially negative territory. Now if the prevailing rate of inflation at such a time were 1–2% due to the choice of an inflation target of 2% rather than 0–1%, then consistent with the zero rate boundary remaining in place real risk-free rates in the first case could fall to say –1.5% rather than –0.5% in the second. But is that difference really significant?

Surely the much bigger concern in any re-draft of the monetary framework should have been a re-look (not possible perhaps in the rushed preparation in summer 1998) at the whole question of inflation-targeting.

This re-look would have gone far beyond the tired semantic exercise to demonstrate that the ECB's framework was not an extreme example of the monetary madness associated with inflation-targeting in the UK or in the US. Rather there would have been a good look at the Austrian or Friedmanite critiques of inflation-targeting or quasi-inflation targeting (see p. 28) interpreted flexibly enough to include the reality of the ECB's policymaking process. The re-look should have extended also to the evidence already accumulating about rising temperature levels in European in credit and real estate markets.

What warning signs were flashing?

Warning signs of monetary disequilibrium already evident in 2003–04

We have already referred to the rapid growth of M1 (see p. 69) partly on the back of a booming overnight deposit market. (This was for banks and non-banks, but only non-bank deposits included in the definition of M1.) In addition there was the explosive growth of mega banks in the euro-area, which the ECB much later (December 2008 – after the definitive bursting of the credit bubble) came to describe as LCBGs (large and complex banking groups).

It could hardly have been expected that the newly appointed ECB President, Claude Trichet (autumn 2003), would side with the vanguard of analysts concerned about a rise of temperatures in European credit markets, not least given his own complex history regarding involvement or non-involvement in the Credit Lyonnais debacle. This had ended up with an acquittal in spring 2003 in a criminal trial where the charge was that M. Trichet as top Finance Ministry Official responsible for nationalized industries had signed off on misleading financial statements of Credit Lyonnais, no doubt influenced by the strong ties of his political chief, Finance Minister Bérégovoy, to its CEO – see Brown, 2004.

The blinding of vision extended far beyond the ECB presidency amid the rapture about the new age of financial integration in Europe ushered in by the euro.

ECB officials – and Professor Bernanke – cheer euro-banking boom

Some US 'friends of the euro' could not see the European credit bubble forming below the apparent good news of euro-driven financial integration. In the case of one 'friend', Professor Ben Bernanke, the cynic could say that his record of not spotting temperature rise in the US surely would suggest the same mistake when he turned to Europe! And indeed in a speech to the Institute for International Economics in Washington (26 February 2004), the then Federal Reserve Governor told his audience:

> The most important benefit of the currency union has been and will continue to be its strengthening of European financial markets. Traditionally, the efficiency and scope of these markets has been hampered by the costs and risks associated with the use of multiple currencies as well as by the fragmentation arising from international differences in legal structure, accounting rules, and other institutions. Given the rapidity and frequency of trade in financial markets, even small transaction costs can hamper efficiency and liquidity in these markets. The common currency, with ongoing efforts to harmonize financial regulations and institutions, has significantly reduced those transaction costs. Together with lower country-specific macro-risks arising from the adoption of the common currency (no mention of what these are!), this reduction in transaction costs has greatly improved the breadth and efficiency of European financial markets.

No doubt these words of praise, if he had remembered them, would have been one of the many embarrassments for Professor Bernanke when later the scenario of credit bubble and burst in the US and Europe became a reality. Just as Anna Schwartz was to accuse Ben Bernanke of having learnt the wrong lesson from her and Milton Friedman's history of the banking crises during the Great Depression (see Hirsh, 2009), it seems that he was applying another wrong lesson when reviewing financial happenings in Europe. Of course the excuse is obvious that he could not be expected to have an intimate knowledge of what was happening on the ground.

But what about ECB officials who were meant to have such knowledge?

Consider a speech by Board Member Gertrude Tumpel-Gugerell, *'in honour of Mr Alessandro, Chief Executive Officer of Unicredito Italiano S.P.A., European Banker of the Year'* on 30 June 2003:

> It is my privilege today to honour Mr Allessandro Profumo, chief executive officer of UniCredito Italiano, as European Banker of the Year 2002 (a prize proffered by the 'Group of 20+1'). [...] With the euro, monetary stability has been achieved in Europe.
>
> [Can monetary stability really be judged over a three-year period?]
>
> Our attention should now be devoted to the efficiency in the usage of capital as well as in other fields. This, I believe, is an area where Europe still faces considerable challenges. [...] One of the reasons put forward by the Group of 20+1 for awarding the title of European Banker of the Year to Alessandro Profumo is his success in forging a 'strong, lean and very profitable bank'. I welcome in this decision the wish to reward success in achieving efficiency. Indeed, UniCredito ranks highly among European banks in terms of its return on equity (no mention of leverage!). [...] The vocation of the euro is to serve, in due course, all the citizens of the European Union. In consequence there is the overriding need to further and complete the ongoing process of European financial integration. – This cannot be achieved by the authorities alone. It must also be achieved by market partici- pants themselves. In this context it must be possible for market par- ticipants to exploit the potential economies of scale generated by the broader dimension of the euro area relative to the national markets. A market for corporate control within the euro-area's financial sys- tem needs to emerge to allow the creation of pan-European players in all areas of finance. And the perimeter for integration needs to be thought of increasingly as the future Member States of an enlarged European Union. [...] The considerable investments of UniCredito in Poland, in the Czech Republic and in Slovakia (in 2000 Mr. Profumo had spent US\$2billion on acquisition of 4 banks in Eastern Europe) in particular testify to the creation of a banking group on a scale commensurate with that of the enlarged union.

Tumpel-Gugerell's enthusiasm about financial integration is under- standable but was she at all focused on the possibility that what was passing as exemplary in carrying out that aim was in reality evidence of inefficiency in European financial markets? In particular, were the equity markets, under the influence of much irrational exuberance stoked up by US and European monetary disequilibrium, over-rewarding bold expansion by various European banking groups – providing the means for this to take place – without taking due sober-rationalist note of other possible interpretations? For example were the banking groups in Spain and Italy that were spearheading the euro-banking industry expansion being rewarded with high equity prices due to rapid earnings growth within their home territory which were related to some mixture or rising leverage and rising credit market temperature? Were these high equity prices in turn facilitating the takeover of banks in staid over-banked markets? Italy and Spain had been the two large high-interest rate currencies prior to monetary union and the collapse of rates coincident with their entry into union had set off domestic mortgage lending booms.

And in the case of UniCredito, was the arbitrage opportunity of issuing equity with the benefit of a high P/E to pay for the acquisition of a German bank with a low P/E in fact phoney – in the sense that the low P/E may have reflected justifiable angst on the part of investors about the earnings outlook especially with respect to its real estate loans in Germany and abroad? Moreover the high P/E of UniCredito could have been a reflection of market failure to correctly assess the role of leverage in its performance. To be fair to Tumpel-Gugerell the big merger was to come later in 2005, when UniCredito made its all-share offer for HVB and its Austrian and Polish subsidiaries (Bank Austria Creditanstalt and BPH in Poland) for a total price tag of $23bn. UniCredito was offering five new shares for every HVB share.

One of the real issues already alluded to by Tumpell-Gegerell was the accelerated expansion into Eastern Europe. Were the profits in what was growingly to be described as the 'Wild East' the fruits of pioneering a benign process of integration or of introducing a version of US subprime lending (in this case the teaser loans were denominated in Swiss francs) on a very thin (highly leveraged) equity capital base which one day would go terribly wrong?

Euro-banking empire-building

In most cases, the rapid expansion of the new mega banks in Europe went along in each case with a hero, who became a celebrity in the financial world for his or her acumen. As in the world of the hedge funds where a warm market or even bubble developed in the market for human talent the same was true in the banking industry. An article in *Economics and Finance* (19 February 2007) described Alessandro Profumo's objective as to build up a European Citibank and to grapple for the world's largest markets of India and China. *'The pushing, aggressive business style peculiar to Alessandra Profumo was like a cold shower for Italian bankers'.*

In the case of Banco Santander, the Spanish bank which rose to global stardom along with the euro, the hero was Emilio Botin. According to an article in Forbes (14 March 2005), the billionaire had now fulfilled his lifelong ambition to transform a small regional bank once run by his grandfather into an international player. Already the largest bank in Latin America by assets it made a series of large acquisitions during the first six years of EMU (1999–2005) culminating in the $15 billion purchase of Britain's Abbey National in 2004 (what could be more incestuous than a bank in one of the hottest credit markets in Europe – Spain – buying a bank in probably the hottest of all, the UK?). The equity market, to be fair, had judged that takeover harshly with Santander's share price tumbling by almost 10%, but that had not caused Botin to pull back – an interesting case where executive empire-building rather than a hot financial equity market was the driving force behind expansion or what was lauded as 'European financial integration' by the eurocrats!

The phenomenon of empire building and rapid expansion of European banking groups was not limited to the euro-area (where other examples included Joseph Ackerman at Deutsche Bank and Jean-Paul Votron at Fortis). UK and Swiss banking groups were all prominent in the process, and again in each case there was an individual who was personalizing the process – Fred Goodwin for the Royal Bank of Scotland, Marc Ospel for Union Bank of Switzerland.

Is it possible to pinpoint the launch of the euro as a key factor in explaining how such empire-building took place on the edge of (just outside) the euro-area? Perhaps the strongest argument in that direction can be made for the UK in that RBS, thanks to EMU, had access to a rapidly growing interbank deposit market (where funds obtained were swapped from euros into pounds), with its operations there oiled by the ECB's discount facilities, and had become a major player in the booming Spanish real estate market, itself in part a product of the euro.

Empire-building whether inside the euro-area or on its edges would not have raised in itself a red flag within the ECB even if top officials there had been on the look out for credit warming. It had long been conventional wisdom, even before the launch of EMU, that monetary integration would be a stimulus to the formation of larger banking groups which would be no bad thing (so the wisdom went) given that

European banking had become backward in comparison with the bold new era of efficiency, high profit (and hidden leverage!) which characterized US banking (including investment banking scene).

At the Bank for International Settlements, William White, who later became renowned as a lone voice in official supranational institutions warning against the dangers of inflation targeting, had written in 1998 about the forces (including the euro) which would bring consolidation in European banking over the coming decade. Definitely, though, he did not welcome this unreservedly, warning that the development would pose challenges for national regulators and other policymakers concerned with the maintenance of financial stability (see White, William, 1998).

Euro financial integration camouflages credit bubble

More generally there was such a general condition of optimism about how the launch of the euro and the evolution of monetary union would speed the benign process of European financial integration that it would have been hard even for the shrewdest policymaker or indeed market participant to realize that much of what was passing for integration on the ground was in reality an emerging credit bubble. Some analysts, though, were perceptive even at an early stage.

For example Gabriele Galati and Kostas Tsatsaronis (July 2001) were already drawing attention to some features in the rapidly growing euro inter-bank markets which were symptomatic of temperature rise (greater degree of irrational exuberance), albeit not pressing the alarm bell, undoubtedly because of the overriding difficulty in disentangling the success of euro-led integration from bubble danger.

In that paper the authors drew attention to the boom in issuance of corporate bonds denominated in euros and related this to the global wave of merger and acquisition activity in 1999–2000. Bonds offered a flexible and attractive means of financing transaction. More specific to the European scene was the financing of capital investments and corporate transactions related to the telecommunications sector. The single currency's contribution to these developments was in the form of widening the range of investor portfolios that could be tapped with a single bond issue, thus reducing the costs of capital market financing (compared to the pre-euro alternative of several issues in one or more national monies with a complex of array of currency swap transactions alongside). The authors noted also that banks dominated bond issuance in euros – 60% of all euro-denominated bonds, a share almost double that of banks in the dollar segment of the market. Significantly the authors highlighted the booming issue of Pfandbriefe (securitized mortgages) by the German banks and the importance (to their success) of the ECB's decision to accept such paper as collateral in repo- transactions:

The success of German banks in marketing Pfandbriefe and thus increasing the range of financing tools has prompted a number of countries to introduce legislation in recent years that would support the creation of similar types of asset backed securities.

Like so many investors, the ECB failed to see through the misleading AAA labels being stuck on these asset-backed securities by the credit-rating agencies. In any chronology, though, of how Europe's credit markets heated up through the early and mid-years of the first decade in the twenty-first century, the demonstration that ECB officials had woefully insufficient understanding or appreciation of that phenomenon only goes so far.

Yes, it is disappointing that with all the avenues of information at their command – beyond what the ordinary investor in the equity market place could assemble – that the officials did no better at detecting possible danger in the form of credit market temperature rise below the wrapping of euro-driven financial integration which so flattered their whole endeavour. There can be no disappointment, though, without appointment, and the old lesson to distil from this experience is that a stable monetary order must be based on firm rules that do not interfere with free markets discovering the neutral level of interest rates and whose application does not depend on any above average intuition on the part of central bank officials. European Monetary Union, as contracted, has no such inner robustness.

ECB officials ignore explosive growth of euro-bank dollar loans

Even so the lack of any focus at the ECB of at that time on the possibly bad implications of so-called euro-driven financial integration for economic stability and prosperity over the long run is striking. And there is no evidence of any scenario analsysis at that time concerning the danger of a future existential crisis for the euro which a violent bubble-and-bust sequence in European credit markets might bring.

There is no evidence from any speech or publication that any senior official at the ECB through those years had pinpointed the reality or the risks of the explosive growth in European banks' international dollar lending funded to a large extent out of non-stable sources (for example,

US money market funds or currency swaps). In practice, and in fairness, it was only six years later, well after the event, that the BIS produced its two excellent analyses of what was happening then in its March 2009 quarterly review – *The US dollar shortage in global banking* (Patrick McGuire, Peter von Goetz) and *US dollar money market funds and non-US banks* (Baba, McCauley and Ramaswamy).

Yes, for years (from the early 2000s onwards) the balance of payments data for the US highlighted massive foreign inflows into US non-government bonds and European payments data which showed massive outflows of capital via the banking sector. To some extent, though, there was the always-ready excuse that information from balance of payments statistics is so notoriously unreliable. Though the ECB statisticians (and the co-respondents at Eurostat and in the national balance of payments offices) had made valiant attempts to assemble and publish euro-area wide balance-of-payments data, the swings in errors and omissions were so large relative to the totals reported that who could have any confidence in what tentative message they seemed to be conveying about risks in the present pattern of global capital flows.

Nonetheless it is idiosyncratic at best that the ECB growingly through 2003 and beyond (into 2006) banged the table so loud at international gatherings about the US balance of payment deficit and about low savings being a source of potential serious crisis without realizing that a key source of fuel to the US warming credit markets (of which low savings were a feature) came from the European credit markets (especially the off-balance sheet activities of many European banks).

And as regards the lending boom into Eastern Europe, the ECB view (as illustrated by the Tumpel-Gugerell quote above – see p. 80) was that this was wholly a benign development accompanying the extension of the EU and ultimately the euro-zone into the 'Wild East'. In effect, officials in Frankfurt's Eurotower were wearing strongly filtered euro-spectacles. These apparently blocked out the landscape of growing sub-prime type lending boom (effectively teaser loans denominated in Swiss francs or euros) in some parts of Central and Eastern Europe alongside a gigantesque construction and real estate bubble. Instead, the officials saw a benign furthering of economic union.

EMU flaws block emission of monetary warnings

Let us take one step back. Suppose we accept that the leading monetary bureaucrats in Frankfurt for one reason or another would remain poorly informed about any real-world developments in European or global credit markets. Were there nonetheless indicators just from within the normal range of prudent monetary control systems that should have been flashing yellow or red and to which the bureaucrats should have been responding by making monetary policy adjustments that in turn would have controlled the temperature in the credit markets? And was the ECB by its heavy-handed pegging of short-term interest rates, together with its efforts to influence expectations in the market-place about how this peg would be adjusted through time, stifling the free market forces which would tend to bring interest rates in the capital market in line with neutral? A large gap of actual market rates below neutral would fuel temperature rise.

We come back to the flaws in the monetary framework which was designed in such a hurry during late 1998 and then revised with so little 'lateral thinking' in early 2003. If the ECB had been operating in a wholly different frame of reference from the Federal Reserve, imbued in a system of sound money (price level stability as assessed over the very long run rather than striving to make sure that inflation as measured over any two-year period did not fall too low) where market-forces could freely determine medium- and long-term interest rates without continual interference from the central bank's hubris about its intentions regarding the peg for short-term interest rates, the outcome would surely have been better than otherwise.

Trichet pursues French foreign policy in attacking Asian dollar bloc

While all temperature alarm systems remained turned off in the Eurotower regarding European credit markets, it was quite different with respect to the currency markets. Official statements and speeches from the ECB revealed growing anxiety through the early months of 2004 when the euro started to rise against the dollar as was inevitable so long as the ECB fell behind the Bernanke/Greenspan Fed in its pace of breathing in inflation! ECB President Trichet had played a distinct (unintended) role in the dollar's general fall by allying himself (and his institution) with Washington in an assault on the Asian Dollar Bloc (at Dubai in autumn 2003 – see p. 43). Trichet (and his 'cabinet' of French advisers) had imagined that the assault would bring a stronger euro against the dollar matched by a weaker euro against the yen and the yuan. The direction of the forecast moves turned out to be correct, but the extent of the dollar depreciation was underestimated whilst the appreciation of the ex-Asian bloc currencies (including the yuan) was overestimated.

While the ECB president (and Paris economic diplomats long devoted to the cause of further multi-polarity in the currency world as part of the broader mission of reducing US hegemony as pursued by the French Foreign Office) were joining in this East Asian adventure, giving speeches on why currencies there were not appreciating sufficiently and on how the US should bolster the dollar by saving more (mechanism totally unclear, but probably running through a lower US current account deficit in some variant of partial equilibrium analysis), there was an eerie silence in the Eurotower on the subject of monetary conditions in the euro-area. Alarm bells should have been ringing there about the imminent dangers of catching a bad bout of monetary disequilibrium from the US! Germany's monetary guardian at the ECB, Professor Issing, should have been leading the chorus of concern and calling for a change in monetary course.

Let us revert to the ECB's own scripted chronology to check what officials were in fact doing during the critical period of the Federal Reserve breathing inflation into the US economy from mid-2003 to mid-2005. This is the period the ECB in its anniversary review (June 2008) described as *'phase 4 – no changes to key ECB interest rates'*.

Why no change to ECB rates from mid-2003 to end-2005

Without comment the chroniclers state the strange facts that no sooner had this prolonged phase of ultra-low rates got under way (in 2003H2) than economic recovery started. Real GDP grew, on average, by 0.5% quarter-on-quarter in the first half of 2004, the highest rate recorded since the first half of 2000. On the external side, the growth of the world economy remained strong. On the domestic side, very favourable financing conditions, robust corporate earnings and business restructuring provided a positive environment for investment.

After some slowing in the first half of 2005, the expansion of economic activity regained momentum in the second half. So why was the real equivalent (taking account of inflation expectations) of the risk-free interest rate as pegged by the ECB still in slightly negative territory during this period, especially as the monetary pillar of the ECB's analytical framework was flashing yellow if not red? Moreover, expectations that the ECB would continue pegging money rates at such low levels for a considerable time and then only allow a gradual climb were bearing down on medium-maturity interest rates as set in the capital market.

The authors state that though headline M3 growth 'moderated substantially' through the second half of 2003 and early 2004, the series corrected for the estimated impact of portfolio shifts continued to grow at a sustained and slightly increasing rate through this period. In addition the annual rate of growth of loans to the private sector increased in the second half of 2003. And anyhow from mid-2004 onwards, headline M3 growth accelerated. The robust credit and monetary expansion from mid-2004 reflected the stimulatory effect of the then prevailing very low level of interest rates in the euro-area.

Eventually in December 2005, the ECB resolved on a tentative 25 bp hike in the repo rate (to 2.25%) indicating that there was no presumption of further tightening and thereby continuing to bear down on medium-maturity capital market interest rates. But in the course of 2006, the ECB got more definitively into 'tightening mode' by little steps of 25 bp each time, culminating in a hike to 4% in mid-2007.

What was the ECB Chief Economist, Professor Issing, thinking during the period of ultra-low rates (to December 2005 and beyond)?

One clue comes from his speech at an ECB Workshop in October 2005 (*What Central Banks can learn from money and credit aggregates*):

[E]xtraordinary increases in asset prices in financial history have typically been accompanied by strong monetary and/or credit growth. This empirical relationship suggests that monetary and/or credit aggregates can be important indicators of the possible emergence of asset price 'bubbles' and thus are crucial to any central banks' approach to maintaining macroeconomic and price stability over the medium-term. [...] The acceleration of money supply growth from mid-2004 has been judged to be of a different quality to that observed between 2001 and 2003 (when portfolio shifts important). On the counterparts side, stronger monetary growth has been associated with increasing demand for loans to the private sector rather than capital flows from abroad. On the component side, higher M3 growth has been driven by its most liquid components, pointing to a significant impact of the low level of interest rates on monetary dynamics. Stronger monetary dynamics can no longer be interpreted as reflecting heightened financial and economic uncertainties, which have normalised since 2003. Since faster monetary growth appears to have been more fundamental in nature since mid-2004 than was the case between 2001 and 2003, the likelihood that strong monetary developments ultimately find their way through to higher prices must be seen as considerably higher. Moreover strong money and credit growth in a context of already ample liquidity in the euro-area implies that asset price developments, particularly in housing markets, need to be monitored more closely, given the potential for misalignments to emerge.

There is no doubt from this quote that Professor Issing was aware of the potential bad news for economic and financial stability contained in the monetary bulge. But there is some fuzziness (in the remarks) about whether house price or other asset price developments are in themselves cause for policy course correction or only in so far as a link can be made between these and the probable behaviour over the medium-term of the price level.

Moreover there is a total lack of urgency. It is only in autumn 2005 that Professor Issing is delivering this speech, and wait for the denouement, a micro-rate rise (25 bp) two months later amidst a verbal barrage (to the effect that any further rise in the official peg for money rates would occur at a glacially slow pace) aimed at holding down medium-term interest rates! On available indices, house prices in Spain and France (and a range of small countries) had been racing ahead (in similar if not greater momentum to the Case–Shiller indices for the US) for two years or more. Yet despite the note of disquiet there is no serious indication of this development making a big difference to the planned monetary course.

Very possibly, residential real estate market developments were a background factor in the decision to raise rates by 25 bp in December 2005. But surely a careful analysis of the present situation at that date would have suggested that the neutral rate of interest in the euro-area was already at 4–5% p.a.?

The signalled glacial pace of advance of the pegged repo rate from a super-easy level to a still well below neutral level over the next year just created much further financial and economic disequilibrium. And there is a big item not mentioned at all in Professor Issing's speeches or articles – the rising temperature in credit markets across the euro-area and even in Germany itself (not vis-à-vis German residents but as regards German bank aggressive expansion into non-German loans and other assets – including the amassing of government bonds in periphery and mid-periphery zones of the euor-area despite the relevant yield spreads being at only feeble levels relative to potential risks).

Would a 200 bp higher rate in 2005 have pre-empted credit bubble?

One potential response of Professor Issing or any other central bank practitioner to the charge that monetary policy was critically to blame for the subsequent euro or global bubble and bust is to question whether say 200 bp or even 300 bp extra on money market rates would have made a critical difference to the outcome. That is a question which we take up in much more detail in the trial chapter (Chapter 4). For now the provisional answer is 'yes, a great deal of difference'.

Why? If investors globally and in the euro-area in particular could have earned 4% p.a. plus (in nominal terms) rather than a feeble rate of 2% p.a. or slightly more they would surely have been less desperate to bolster yield (income) by falling into the traps sprung wittingly or unwittingly by the array of financial 'innovators' in New York, London, Frankfurt or elsewhere. Why buy illiquid non-transparent paper, albeit with an AAA stamp, to get a little more return, when a good return could already be made on liquid transparent paper? Or why buy the government debt of Greece or Portugal at such tiny yield spreads over Germany without even considering seriously some dark scenarios which might become reality in the future? Moreover, there would not have been such a queue of borrowers at the opposite end of the line, ready to issue all the paper being lapped up in many cases with varying amounts of hidden or partly hidden leverage, unless the going level of interest rates (with respect to low-risk and even more so high-risk credits) was well below equilibrium level.

The merchants of various types of credit paper would not have had this in the store to sell unless there was a vibrant real asset market along with strongly rising real economic activity – both stimulated by interest rates far below neutral level – going on outside! The risks of leverage could not have remained disguised (except from the blind) if there had been a continuing roll call of bankruptcies. And the market for equities in financial intermediaries peddling the high-risk paper and in some cases taking this on to their own books would not have been in such a high temperature range with rates closer to neutral.

In sum, the ECB in its programme of adjusting its peg for the risk-free rate upwards towards neutral only at a glacial pace (and of clearly signalling this programme to the market) repeated with a lag exactly the same mistake as the Federal Reserve was making. This was a time of madness for the rate-peggers on both sides of the Atlantic.

It would have been such a feat if the ECB had distinguished itself from the rate-pegging, (quasi-) inflation targeting and inflation breathing-in Federal Reserve. But that was not to be the case. The sales material for EMU which made much of how the new creation would bring protection against 'Anglo-Saxon' monetary shock turned out to be bogus.

The ECB official anniversary report on monetary policy during the first ten years makes absolutely no reference to this failure. It is plausible – and indeed likely – that the perpetrators of the failure were completely blind to it!

'Withdrawal of monetary accommodation, 2006–2007H1'

The chroniclers continue into their next subsection of history under the subtitle of *'Phase 5 – withdrawal of monetary policy accommodation (since end-2005)'*:

> Since the end of 2005, the Governing Council has raised the key ECB interest rates by a total of 200 basis points, bringing the minimum bid rate in the main refinancing operations of the Eurosystem to a level of 4% by the end of June 2007. This adjustment of the accommodative monetary policy stance was warranted in order to address risks to price stability, as identified by both the economic and the monetary analysis. [...] As regards prices, average annual inflation was 2.2% in 2006 and 2.1% in 2007, mainly driven by domestic demand. In both years, the headline inflation rate fluctuated significantly, largely on account of developments in oil prices. In 2006 it followed an increasing trend until August, mainly as a result of substantial increases in energy prices, while the annual inflation rate fell below 2% in the remaining months of the year, largely as a consequence of significantly declining oil prices and base effects. Until the third quarter of 2007, annual inflation rates developed in line with the ECB's definition of price stability, partly because of favourable base effects stemming from energy price developments a year earlier.

In sum, a credit bubble of once-in-a-century magnitude was forming in the global economy with the European banking system arguably at its centre, with the essential fuel coming from extreme monetary disequilibrium created in Frankfurt and Washington. The monetary critic of this period in reading the notes of the policymakers cannot help but feeling like K in Kafka's *The Trial* when he comes to examine the judges notepads – all he finds is scribbling (in that case, obscene!).

And just before the bubble burst, with the maximum initial impact of the Great Credit Market Quake (August 2007) felt in Europe (to the total surprise of the ECB!) rather than the US, there had been the biggest moment of madness in the financial equity market place, also in Europe. This was the takeover battle for ABN-AMRO.

Merger mania: The takeover battle for ABN-AMRO

The saga had started on 21 February 2007 when a British hedge fund, TCI, specialized in finding profitable opportunity from triggering changes in corporate control (or management), asked the chairman of the Supervisory Board (of ABN-AMRO) to actively investigate a merger, acquisition or break-up of the bank, stating that the current stock price did not reflect the true value of the underlying assets. TCI, with a small but significant shareholding in the bank (ABN-AMRO) asked its chairman to put their request on the agenda of the annual shareholders meeting (April). Four days later the President of the Dutch Central Bank (and thereby a member of the policymaking council of the ECB), Dr Wellink, was quoted in the Dutch newspaper NRC *Handlesblad* as saying that it was unprecedented that a hedge fund should call for a bank to be broken up. President Wellink warned that there could be repercussions beyond its borders:

> A bank is different from other listed companies. For us, that is a bridge too far.

Evidently President Wellink got no public show of support – albeit that there is no evidence that he requested this! – from his colleagues in the ECB. Meanwhile TCI went public with its case citing that excluding dividends ABN-AMRO had returned zero since May 2000 compared to a 44% return for its European banking peers! This stodgy bank had not been a full participant in the go-go profitable opportunities of investment banking, and TCI was determined to exploit the profit from acting as catalyst to a change in direction (towards full participation!). The CEO of Citigroup was famously to say (in early summer 2007) that when everyone else is dancing then you have to get up and join. ABN-AMRO management, according to TCI, were failing to join the dance. By getting ABN-AMRO into the dance (fully involved in the global credit bubble) TCI was to make its profit.

The rest is history – the bid from Barclays and finally a superior cash offer from a joint syndicate of three European banks all deeply steeped in the euro- and global-credit bubbles (Fortis, Santander and RBS) and all enjoying valuations in global equity markets which rested on a high degree of confidence in a never-ending rapidly growing profits stream from investment banking (albeit that in the case of RBS there had been periodic jitters about the aggressive expansion plans of its CEO on some previous occasions) and on an unawareness of actual leverage.

Among the big gainers were the shareholders of ABN-AMRO who collected the cash and were not tempted to join the dance by buying other financial equities! Among the big losers were the tax payers in the UK, Holland, Belgium and Luxembourg, who had eventually to foot the bill (around one year later) for rescuing two of the three consortium banks – RBS and Fortis – and of course the shareholders (and some categories of bondholders) in the consortium banks which had squandered their capital in the takeover.

The takeover could not have taken place if the financial equity markets had been operating efficiently – correctly discounting the huge risks which accompanied Europe's highly leveraged big banks (by and large the regulators ignored leverage concentrating instead on a flawed BIS bank-risk measurement system, widely described as 'Basel 2'). But the many years of serious monetary disequilibrium both in Europe and the US had sent temperatures so high across the credit and financial equity markets that the normal forces promoting efficiency were now weak.

Incredibly in hindsight, the vote of Fortis shareholders in favour of the takeover took place literally on the eve of the Great Credit Quake (August 8). Despite an ominous warning from ABN-AMRO's CEO, Rijkman Groenink (carried in *Het Financieele Dagblad*, the Dutch financial daily) to Fortis shareholders that a successful bid by the consortium would further weigh on Fortis's share price and that shareholders should vote against it, an overwhelming 90% majority voted in favour (August 6). The loud pre-quake rumblings already to be heard in the global financial market place apparently had no impact on the shareholders. Even more incredibly the following Friday (after the Great Credit Quake of August 8), RBS shareholders gave their approval.

A little more than a year later both groups of shareholders had lost almost everything. Well, we all know the saying that the Gods make mad who they want to destroy, albeit that in this case the catalyst of destruction TCI, was laughing all the way to the bank. The much bigger question relates to the policy issues raised by this madness.

First, there is the general point that the madness could only have developed in a climate of extreme monetary disequilibrium such as had been fostered by inflation-targeting central banks on both sides of the Atlantic.

Second, if the ECB had been assuming at all any role in monitoring and controlling possibly dangerous rises in credit market temperature and ready to use instruments including but also going beyond its pegging of the overnight rate in the euro-system, then it would have been doubly unlikely for such madness to occur.

And third, despite all the literature on efficient capital markets and empirical evidence supporting that hypothesis, huge irrationality had apparently become prevalent in a core component of the global equity market. (The hypothesis of irrationality or inefficiency could be rejected on the basis of huge failure in the market for information, including gross asymmetries and lack of big enough incentive for investigative journalists or analysts to make discovery and publish their findings.)

As regards that third issue, one plausible hypothesis was that not only ECB officials but also equity market investors had been so lulled by the music of financial integration and its potential efficiency (and profit gains) that they had become uncritical of the underlying business models and blind to the growing risks which lay behind the demonstrated bank profits. All three of the bidding banks had share prices which in their fullness at the peak reflected an uncritical appraisal of continuing the go-go profits from a European-made component of the global credit market (Spanish mortgage boom, East European lending, UK commercial and residential real estate mortgage boom, private equity boom) and of the risks (including those built on leverage) related to these.

Some (but not all) of this (in its full extent) might have happened even with the most sober of ECB monetary policies over the preceding years (and including 2007). After all there had been a Great Bubble and subsequent Panic in the US in 1905–7 without a central bank there yet in existence. Even in that early historical episode the proverbial monetary monkey wrench had not been absent – but it was de-personalized and de-institutionalized (instead gold discoveries and shifts in demand for high-powered money related to financial innovation, together with huge uncertainty concerning the natural interest rate level in the wake of the San Francisco earthquake, played key monetary roles). And in the days following the Great Credit Quake of August 2007, there was much speculation and hope about how the new central bank in Europe and its US counterpart could act to alleviate the consequences. Few could imagine at this early stage that the ECB, together with the Federal Reserve and Bank of England, all in their own ways, would make the consequences much worse.

3
The Bursting of the Bubble

The monetary policies on both sides of the Atlantic leading up to the global credit bubble (2003–7) and accompanying its burst (spring 2007 onwards) may not have fully satisfied the definition of catastrophic. But how far short they were of that benchmark and the definition itself will doubtless long remain a matter of heated historical debate.

The global turmoil and distress (whether economic, political or geopolitical) associated with global monetary disequilibrium, especially in the US, China and Europe, during the years 2004–15 in the twenty-first century may turn out to be of a lower order than for the years around the Great Crash and the Great Depression (say 1925–38). It is arguable that there has not been the same degree of monetary nationalism this time round which so heavily contributed to the devilish chain of European political and geopolitical events in the 1930s. That is still an open question, though, given the legitimization and use of currency war by the Bernanke Federal Reserve, euro-nationalism as practised by the Trichet ECB, President Sarkozy's 'Napoleon III' euro-policy (turning EMU into a 'transfer union' in large part via the ECB under M. Trichet expanding massively its bad bank operations in defiance of German remonstrance) which raised the danger of an eventual rupture between Paris and Berlin, and the aggressive currency policy of Beijing.

Even so, the financial crisis in Europe early in the twenty-first century has not featured as in the inter-war years the biggest economy (Germany) in the throes of the most severe credit and real estate bubble-bursting episode in modern history experiencing a savage tightening of monetary policy when already in deep slump (1929–31) with its own policymakers (and even well-meaning policymakers in leading foreign capitals) unwilling or unable to to contemplate the possibility of devaluing or floating the currency (Reichsmark).

There were considerable obstacles to such a step (devaluing or floating the Reichsmark) given the commitment of Germany under the Dawes Plan – a US-sponsored treaty in 1924 under which the Weimar Republic obtained an international loan and re-scheduling of reparations obligations towards stabilizing its money in the wake of hyperinflation – to maintain a fixed parity between the mark and the gold dollar (see Brown, 1986).

Simultaneous with that German predicament, another large European country (the UK) unleashed a beggar-your-neighbour devaluation (September 1931), triggering a deep crisis of confidence in much of the remaining world on the gold standard (with the important exception of France which had returned to gold at a very cheap exchange rate level in 1926–8), most particularly the US.

Yet there are echoes of the earlier catastrophe in the present-day monetary tumult (or catastrophe?) which are eerie and troubling for those who believe strongly in human progress. True there is now a renowned professor in monetary economics at the head of the Federal Reserve, who on the occasion of Milton Friedman's ninetieth birthday party said that the monetary mistakes which surrounded the Great Depression would never be made again. There are grounds to question, though, whether the professor had learnt the right lessons.

No monetary progress in US or Europe?

The professor (Ben Bernanke) had been the key proponent (back in 2003 already) of the expansionary policy (breathing in inflation) which had played such a critical role in generating the bubble in the first place (even if the buck ultimately stopped at Alan Greenspan's desk). Indeed, much of the 'neo-Austrian' critique (see Rothbard, 1972) of US monetary policy in the 1920s under the leadership of New York Federal Reserve Governor Benjamin Strong in the 1920s could be replicated against the Greenspan–Bernanke Federal Reserve.

At a time when real forces (productivity surge due to technological revolution and terms of trade improvement) were putting downward pressure on the equilibrium level of goods and services prices, the Federal Reserve was setting monetary conditions such as to produce a stable or gently rising price level. In doing so the Federal Reserve created grave monetary disequilibrium with its main symptom being a sharp rise of temperature in credit and asset markets. This had already happened in the second half of the 1990s, culminating in the severe recession of 2001–2. Then the Greenspan/Bernanke Federal Reserve (Professor Bernanke joined the Board in autumn 2002) had sought to force-feed the recovery from that recession by 'breathing inflation' back into the economy whilst exhibiting deflation phobia to an extreme degree.

Some critics, including in particular John Taylor (2009), highlighted how the ignoring of monetary rules (his own brand in particular – the so-called Taylor Rule!) – more complex than those of Milton Friedman and requiring (unlike Friedman's) considerable discretion on the part of policymakers – had sewn the seeds of crisis. And then, Milton Friedman's co-author of *A Monetary History of the US*, Anna Schwartz, argued that Professor Bernanke had misdiagnosed the crisis which erupted in summer 2007 as a liquidity crisis (the situation in autumn 1930) when in fact it was a solvency crisis (in the 1929–33 episode as examined by Friedman and Schwartz a real solvency issue erupted only much later on in the depths of depression) (see Schwartz, 2009). That misdiagnosis led on to that fateful weekend in mid-September 2008 when there was no contingency plan on the shelf for the threatened insolvency of Lehman. John Taylor provided additional important evidence to bear on that point (see Taylor, 2009).

Finally, the critics of cyclical fine-tuning accused Professor Bernanke of having made even bigger mistakes than the much criticized successor (George Harrison) of Benjamin Strong (see Meltzer, 2004), who after all had not stood in the way of risk-free rates generally (including T-bill and short-maturity government bonds) collapsing to virtually zero immediately following the October 1929 Wall Street Crash. The New York Federal Reserve had then supplied adequate extra reserves to the banking system (equivalently expanding the supply of monetary base) for that purpose.

In the later episode the Federal Reserve got in the way of the powerful move down to zero of risk-free rates, engaging in a novel type of sterilized lending to the weakest banks, while seeking to break the overall rate decline out of residual concerns about meeting the quasi-inflation target in the context of transitorily sky-high oil prices. Indeed in early October 2008, in the darkest days of the financial panic, the Bernanke Fed unbelievably announced the innovation of paying interest on reserves with the express purpose of strengthening control over risk-free rates (extending this to assets beyond the Federal Funds market) and preventing their collapse to below the implicit official target range for these!

However troubling the echoes on the western side of the Atlantic (of the mistakes in the mid and late 1920s/early 30s), those on the eastern side were even more so. As in the US, the policymakers in Frankfurt had pursued quasi-inflation targeting (no ECB official would admit to that!), blind to the real (non-monetary) forces (such as productivity growth or terms of trade improvement or business cycle dynamics) which might be lowering the price level, and sceptical of or unsympathetic towards monetary auto-piloting based on constitutional rules.

In Frankfurt's corridors of monetary power there was apparently a very low state of alert (if any) with respect to the financial and economic dangers emanating from the US, even though a key justification for European Monetary Union (EMU) in the first place had been to protect the member countries to a greater extent than before from US monetary shock! ECB officials had responded to the unwelcome strength of the euro against the dollar in 2003–4, triggered ultimately by US monetary disequilibrium, by disabling any putative alarm system (in the Eurotower) installed to detect imminent or present US monetary shock.

Frankfurt had the excuse (for poor overall monetary policy performance) of an unreliable indicator board (with money supply data hard to interpret because of the newness of monetary union) and the difficulties of steering one policy to suit all in a union with much greater regional divergences and far less flexibility (whether in terms of relative wages, prices or inter-regional labour movements) than the US. These, though, were a self-wrought problem for the participating members of the EMU. The consenting democracies which had signed up surely reckoned with such significant costs to range against the potential benefits (even though some of the smooth-talking euro sales persons may not have spelt this out!).

What the consenting electorates (in so far as they were asked for approval) could not have reckoned with (as a certainty as against a low-probability scenario) was the seriousness of monetary framework error and subsequently monetary policymaking error which lay ahead, both during the period when global credit market temperatures (including those in Europe) were rising and later when they started to descend precipitously. Yes, the errors continued to resemble those in the US, but eventually they rang out even louder. That is running ahead of our story.

Summer 2007 credit quake

The story of those serious monetary policy mistakes in the post-bubble period starts in summer 2007 with the seize-up of the inter-bank money markets on 9 August. John Taylor describes this seize-up as the 'Landing of a Black Swan in the Money Market' (see Taylor, 2009). (For two excellent chronologies of the crisis see Jordan, 2008 and. Brunnermeier, 2008.)

The immediate trigger to the seize-up was the announcement (9 August) by BNP Paribas, France's biggest bank, that it had halted withdrawals from three investment funds because it could not 'fairly' value their holdings now that US sub-prime mortgage losses were roiling credit markets. The funds had about 1.6 billion of euros (on 7 August), with about a third of that in sub-prime mortgage securities rated AA or higher. This followed announcements in the days before by Bear Stearns that it was stopping similar redemptions. And on 2 August the German bank, IKB Deutsche Industriebank, had revealed it was in trouble because of investment in US sub-prime loans where these had been in an off-balance sheet structured investment vehicle.

After US house prices had peaked in 2006, it became more and more obvious to some market participants that a rapidly growing number of sub-prime borrowers would soon be unable to service their debt with the amount of potential shortfall becoming ever more alarming. Prices of sub-prime-backed securities had started to ease in early 2007.

As 2007 progressed, the deteriorating sub-prime market began affecting the confidence in related structured finance products and during the course of July 2007 had triggered a sudden general re-pricing of credit risk beyond the confines of residential mortgage products. There was a ballooning of credit spreads in the credit-derivative markets, especially as related to higher-risk categories of credit (whether mortgages or leveraged loans to non-financial corporation). And in the US banking industry, the worsening plight (and slide in equity price) of Countrywide, the giant aggressive California-based mortgage lender, was making it into the daily financial headlines.

All of this formed the background to a sudden and general 'seizing up' in European inter-bank money markets on the morning of 9 August 2007. The catalysts were the events which demonstrated that many of the European banks had huge exposure (hitherto camouflaged) to the US sub-prime market and especially via off-balance sheet vehicles (so-called structured investment vehicles) which financed themselves in the so-called asset-backed commercial paper markets.

ECB's panic response to money seize-up, 9 August 2007

It seems (there is no hard evidence of discussions and unless a revolution takes place within EMU the practice of official secrecy means that no such evidence will become available in the future) that the ECB President, M. Trichet, alerted in his Brittany summer house to the seizing up of the European money markets, shared in the view of his colleagues assembled in teleconference that this was an epic crisis of liquidity stemming from the bubble-burst in US sub-prime mortgage markets.

Some hearsay evidence suggests that the Bundesbank played the lead role in initiating and coordinating the initial response to the seizing up.

This role in part may have been forced on the Bundesbank by circumstances – the lightness of the holiday staffing in the ECB and M. Trichet's absence on vacation. The hearsay evidence is consistent with the later revealed role of the Bundesbank as staunch defender of the Separation Principle according to which liquidity provision was to be distinguished from the chosen path for the policy interest rate (see p. 49). There is no evidence that any key Bundesbank official had a premonition that by starting down this road the ECB would lose its political independence. This realization came much later – in fact in spring 2010 (see Chapter 5) – when Bundesbank President Weber openly defied (unsuccessfully) ECB President Trichet.

The response of the ECB to the crisis was to make unlimited funds available through the secured lending markets to all applicant banks at around the official repo rate (4% p.a.), which remained unchanged. By such operations the ECB (on Thursday, 9 August) 'put' nearly €95bn into European financial institutions, followed by a somewhat smaller operation (€61bn) on Friday. On the same Thursday and Friday, the Federal Reserve's Open Market Trading Desk injected funds in similar fashion, 'putting' in a total of $38bn.

'Putting' here did not mean an expansion of the monetary base. Rather, at issue was a sterilized operation, in which ECB lending to banks experiencing a sudden shortage of funds was matched by ECB borrowing from banks in the reverse situation (unwilling to lend out surplus funds in the inter-bank market, except possibly to a limited extent at much greater margins over risk-free rates than normal). This borrowing (by the ECB) could take the form of those institutions piling up excess reserves in the deposit facility at the ECB earning interest rate at just one percentage point below the unchanged official repo rate (at 4%), or repo operations in which the ECB would borrow short-maturity funds and lend out government bonds or bills.

What exactly were the forces generating such huge intervention?

With the benefit of hindsight and much circumstantial evidence it has become clear that what happened on 9 August far transcended a crisis of liquidity. This was already a crisis of solvency. (And as AEI scholar Alex Pollock points out the two phenomena are inevitably linked in varying degrees – see Pollock, 2009).

The huge reported (sterilized) injections by the ECB involved much more than liquidity provision. They were in effect a combination of massive price-rigging operations (suppressing or containing any rise in risk premiums in the inter-bank deposit markets) and of emergency quasi-capital assistance (to the weakest banks) by the central banks.

(The term quasi is used as there was no matching change in the banks' legal capital structure). The capital could not have been available in the given circumstances from any other source.

The solvency issue stemmed in the immediate from the unknown amount of loss on so-far camouflaged holdings of sub-prime US assets by some European financial institutions. But there was also another dimension to the solvency issue – one about which ECB officials were totally mum and apparently ignorant. This was the extent of potential loss on holdings of European financial institutions in their own domestic (European) credit markets – whether related to hot residential real estate markets in Spain, UK, France and Holland, or to private equity lending in those same countries and including Germany, or to the booming loans into the Wild East (much of which was related to hot real estate markets and booming construction sectors there), or to massive investments in the government debts of periphery-zone EMU member countries (especially Greece, Portugal and Ireland) and mid-zone (Italy, Spain and Belgium).

Those banks with a chronic surplus of funds (more non-bank client deposits than non-bank client loans) – as was largely the case in Germany, corresponding to that country's massive savings surplus – which during recent years had simply lent the excess into the booming inter-bank (unsecured) loan market in Europe suddenly realized that they had become greatly overextended to credit risk there. What to one bank had seemed like a low-risk overnight inter-bank loan suddenly came into view, in terms of the bigger systemic picture which was emerging, as high risk.

As the less weak banks in surplus pulled their funds out of the inter-bank markets, they had a choice between deploying these in short-maturity government bond markets (of which the safest and most liquid in Europe is Bunds) or into the deposit facility at the ECB (on which interest accrued at a fixed small margin below the official repo rate). Arbitrage between these two (denominated in euro) meant that rates on both remained closely in line with and not far below the official repo rate.

Failure of the ECB (and Fed) to promptly diagnose insolvency

If the ECB (and Federal Reserve) had looked around hard in those late summer days (of 2007) they would have discovered plenty of evidence suggesting a solvency element to the crisis. (See Schwartz, 2009 and Taylor, 2009 for two strong critiques of the Federal Reserve under Professor Bernanke for its similar failure to make such a diagnosis with resulting huge cost for the US – and global – economy). For example, whereas rates on repo-transactions secured by top quality government bonds between banks remained steady, unsecured rates in the inter-bank market (in so far as funds were available to any particular bor-rower) rose sharply as did rates on secured borrowing (repos) where the security took the form of less than tip-top government bonds (for example, AAA-rated mortgage-backed paper).

In this situation of a sudden re-appraisal of risks (meaning solvency risks) across the whole spectrum of credit including especially bank (and inter-bank) credit, the emergency decision by the ECB on 9 August 2007 to supply all bank demands for secured funds (against any eligible collat-eral – not just top government bonds) at the fixed repo rate (a virtually risk-free rate of 4% p.a.) was bound to create huge round-tripping.

Banks with funds flowing back, courtesy of the ECB, from the repay-ment of asset-backed commercial paper or from maturing inter-bank loans or from repos secured on mortgage-backed paper took the money and ran. Where did they run – mainly to the ECB stupid (otherwise into short-maturity Bunds)! The ECB was keeping the rate on its so-called deposit facility at just one percentage point below the repo rate (mean-ing in effect around 3%) and banks with excess funds (due to reflow of funds described) could now simply deposit these with the ECB. Some banks with excess funds available continued to lend in the overnight markets within tightened limits (and only to banks deemed safe) at an interest rate very near to the official rate (4% p.a.) as set by the ECB.

If the ECB's view about this all being a liquidity crisis were correct, then within a few days or weeks there should have been a reflux. Inter-bank lending at the old rates would have resumed and the ECB could have withdrawn its support. Of course this did not occur!

The ECB had constructed, unintentionally it seems through lack of knowledge and appropriate analysis, a whole pyramid of secured lend-ing (most of which was against increasingly dodgy assets such as the so-called AAA residential mortgage-backed securities emanating from Spain or the UK and then the government debts of the periphery-zone member countries of EMU) to the banks under most stress at well below the rates which would have prevailed without the ECB's intervention and in several important cases (the weakest banks) well beyond what would be available at any market rates.

Meanwhile the ECB strove with total success to keep the overnight rates (for those banks able to obtain funds there within albeit shrunken inter-bank limits) very close to the official repo rate of around 4% (and of course there was arbitrage between the repo and overnight deposit markets to keep the two in line with each other). Arbitrage operations by the less weak banks in surplus meant that risk-free rates (as quoted on short maturity government bonds denominated in euros) remained close to the ECB's overnight deposit rate (at a small margin below the official repo rate).

A superior crisis response ignored by the ECB (and Fed)

The outcome brought about by the ECB's massive response of 9–10 August was very far from a market solution or from a solution consistent with overall economic equilibrium. It was also ultimately in contradiction of the ECB's own prized political independence, as the eventual run-down of its huge secured lending to weak banks would require entering into negotiations with member governments to replace its support. Some member government could be too financially weak to support their own banks in which case the ECB would have inadvertently become the agent of a transfer union – implicitly drawing on taxpayers in financially strong countries (as guarantors of the ECB's balance sheet) to aid banks in the financially weak.

The monetary framework constructed at the dawn of EMU – in particular the payment of interest on excess reserves at only a fine margin below the official rate and emphasis on micro-management of micro-changes in officially set money interest rates (signalling the trend ahead) – had much to answer for in any serious investigation as to why a better solution did not materialize. What form would this have taken? Here are the main elements.

First, with a high degree of uncertainty relating to the non-transparent risks which may be residing in various banks, and yet an immediate presumption that these were heterogeneous (some banks suspected of being in much weaker conditions than others), it no longer made sense as an operational strategy for the ECB to peg one uniform overnight rate. Even in the overnight unsecured markets the weaker banks (those where possible solvency risks were higher) should have been paying a substantially higher rate for funds than the less weak banks.

In effect the operational strategy of the ECB would have changed from rate pegging in the overnight inter-bank deposit market to setting a quantitative target for monetary base (now to be non-interest bearing, see p. 104), evidently not possible to implement with any precision in the midst of a panic but only in broad brush terms so as to make sure that risk free rates would fall to zero. Alternatively the ECB could have carried out rate-pegging in the very short-maturity repo market based exclusively on top-quality government bonds (with the peg at a level well below the pre-crisis official repo rate, possibly already as far down as zero).

Second, the ECB would not have stood in the way of a wide spread forming between risk-free and higher risk rates (depending on counterparty) whether at short or long maturities. Nor should the ECB have acted to prevent a wide spread developing between repo rates secured on top-quality government bonds and those secured on dodgy collateral (albeit AAA), such as UK or Spanish mortgages. Consistent with this 'laissez-faire' approach, allowing markets to set spreads (related to solvency or credit risks) the ECB would have removed various obstacles (to such market determination) – including in particular the now well-above equilibrium interest rate (then fixed at 3% p.a.) on its deposit facility (where banks could place excess funds) and the now in most cases generous Lombard rate (5% p.a., only one percentage point above the official repo rate) which it charged on unsecured lending.

Optimally the ECB would have reduced the overnight rate on deposits with itself (regarded at this point as 100% safe) to zero (meaning that risk-averse banks could not gain interest by parking funds at the ECB; they would have had to place these in short-maturity government bonds, driving the yields on these down towards zero, or else taking on some risk and lending at higher rates). And ECB lending at the Lombard rate would have been strictly limited for any one institution (according to normal prudential yardsticks), with the Lombard rate itself set on a sliding scale (each successive tranche borrowed at a higher margin above the official repo rate). The amount lent by the ECB against eligible collateral would also have been restricted according to normal practice, and following market developments a higher rate would have been charged on secured lending against non-government than against top government collateral.

Third, the ECB in its estimation of the market-clearing level of risk-free rates of interest, which would be the basis for any quasi-pegging operation in the very short-maturity prime government bond markets or in the market for short-maturity repos secured on prime government bonds, would have deduced that this was now surely much lower than on the eve of the crisis. The rise of a whole spectrum of rates (in absolute terms) on higher risk credits surely had to have as a corollary (from the viewpoint of overall balance in the economy – including an optimal path back from present panic conditions to full equilibrium) a lower level of risk-free rates.

Moreover, in the new reality of financial crisis surely the likelihood had increased of recessionary developments being under way, adding further justification to revising down estimates of the neutral or natural rate of interest, as specified districtly for short, medium and long maturities.

Over and above all this, surely it was justifiable to lower the alert on inflation and increase the alert on depression. Sure, the ECB had a predisposition towards econometric modelling. But in present circumstances of extreme discontinuity any forecast from such a process had to be treated with the utmost caution. And in any case were a recession or depression to get going that could set off a vicious circle of ever worse insolvency within the financial system.

Fourth, there would have been the pressing issue what to do with banks which could not raise sufficient funds in the markets, even at the widened spreads prevailing, and who came up against the normal prudential limits at the ECB's official windows for Lombard credit or secured credit. This was not a new issue – it can be traced back through the financial history books to the whole discussion around the lender of last resort role. There were some novel features though in the case of EMU. In particular, the Maastricht Treaty had not in fact determined that the ECB should act as lender of last resort. And this was for good reason. How could the ECB enter into the whole area of taking calculated gambles on bank insolvency without simultaneously becoming immersed ultimately in the politics of burden sharing between the member countries as to who should be responsible for bail-outs? If the ECB was zealously resolved to protect its independence then at any hint of a bank insolvency crisis it would have to turn the issue of support and emergency funding over to the member governments, rather than assuming itself a lender of last resort role. In this role, the central bank determines first, whether the institution which is cash starved is still solvent. If so, then it lends, albeit at a highly penal rate, while seeking a resolution (either new equity capital raising or merger). By contrast where the central bank (or regulatory authority) determines that the institution is insolvent but with a going concern or net asset value which likely exceeds deposits outstanding, then a controlled de-leverage plan (imposing haircuts on bond-holders and debt-for-equity swaps) takes place linked to a re-capitalization plan.

In the dour case of deep insolvency being suspected right at the start (not enough value to match deposits) then there may be no alternative to immediate closure (with the deposit insurance corporation taking a lead role in disposing of assets).

If the ECB (and Federal Reserve) had gone down this route (incorporating points one to four above) of recognizing an insolvency crisis as such rather than mis-diagnosing it or mis-treating it (with an unpubli-cized correct diagnosis) as a liquidity crisis there are grounds for imag-ining that the eventual economic and financial outcome would have been better than what actually occurred. And the independence of the central bank would not have become so flawed in the process.

Instead the ECB rolled over vast amounts of loans largely secured against dodgy assets (some packaged together so as to meet the eligi-bility requirements of the ECB) to the weakest institutions at subsi-dized spreads and far beyond 'normal' prudent levels without exerting any of the standard textbook pressure for prompt re-capitalization. Simultaneously the ECB steered policy rates – and together with these risk-free rates in general – higher, out of fear that sky-high oil prices would push up inflation.

Counterfactual monetary history of autumn 2007 to 2008

Let us look at the counterfactual case in more detail so as to draw out how this would have been better than what actually happened (from the viewpoint of the overall economy and financial system). Suppose in reaction to the trauma of 9 August (2007), the ECB had indeed lowered dramatically the floor to risk-free rates (for example yields on short-maturity top government bonds) by cutting its overnight deposit rate to zero allowing these in principle to fall sharply – indeed possibly all the way to zero as had occurred during some great previous world financial panics including October 1929). That step would have been the catalyst to a wide span of interest rates (according to the risk of the borrower) forming.

Then weak but still widely deemed as solvent banks might have been able to borrow say at 5–10% p.a. in the overnight markets and at some premium above that (to a limited extent) in the term money markets (unsecured). Repo rates fixed with respect to dodgy (non-government) collateral would have been well above the risk-free rate especially where the borrower was a weak bank. Less weak banks would have been able to fund themselves at rates much below those risky rates (with the exact rate depending on the category of collateral used if any). Repo rates based on top government bonds would have fallen towards zero in line with the downward pressure on risk-free rates.

The ECB would have injected additional high-powered money into the system so as to relieve any shortage due to banks seeking to build up excess reserves to protect themselves against deposit withdrawals. One guide to the adequacy of the injection would have been rates on risk-free near money assets (such as short-maturity government bonds) not re-bounding due to banks scrambling out of anything for cash.

Note that even if the ECB had not thought through this plan of action on day one, instead supplying unlimited funds as in fact occurred, it could have implemented it in the days that followed, by refusing to roll-over repos or other lending except according to the counter-factual framework as described here.

In this counter-factual world the less weak banks would have scrambled to demonstrate their financial soundness – revealing to the marketplace the full extent of their loan and asset portfolios and the extent of the cushion (to depositors) provided by their capital base. This scrambling process is evident in that great financial panic of 1907, the last great panic before the creation of the Federal Reserve and the advent of Keynesian policy prescriptions, in which the less weak trust banks demonstrated their soundness to the rescue committee instituted by J. P. Morgan in the wake of the failure of Knickerbocker Trust Company (with a lead role played by Benjamin Strong, then Bankers Trust vice-president and protégé of Morgan, later of Federal Reserve fame or infamy for his role in the 1920s credit bubble – see Bruner and Carr, 2007 and Rothbard, 1972).

The less weak banks would have had a big incentive to go out and raise more equity capital – as by doing so they would push down their overall cost of funding (in non-insured deposit markets) to nearer the risk-free level and capture market share from their weaker rivals. Their well-cushioned (by extra equity protection) deposits would appeal to a widened base of (non-insured) retail and wholesale clients, meaning they could make a new pitch for deposit business and the long-term profits (for example, through the sale of other products) that might be associated with this. (These equity-bolstered banks would have been able to carry on charging the same elevated rates reflecting client credit risk across a broad spectrum of their floating rate loan book).

It is true that the issuance of more equity capital could have diluted present equity outstanding if indeed (as would be probable) there were no mechanism for the original shareholders to claw back windfall gains bestowed by the re-capitalization on the holders of bank debt. But that dilution would be less, most likely, than the extra present value to be gained from business profit enhancement derived from being able to market deposits with a deepened equity cushion. (Note that the mechanisms leading to this outcome are weakened in the situation of government, or its agencies, issuing blanket insurance on deposits across all banking institutions, weak or strong).

What would have happened to the weakest banks which could survive only with lender of last resort assistance?

Autumn 2008 would have been brought forward to autumn 2007 in terms of the individual European member governments having to provide explicit injections of capital towards an emergency stabilization of the weakest elements within their own political jurisdictions. But that task would surely have been less daunting (and damaging) in 2007 than in 2008 or indeed later given the lack of intervening recession and fear of depression which emerged.

If the US authorities had been similarly pre-emptive then the train of financial history may well not have made it all the way to the Great Financial Panic of autumn 2008. And a sharp fall of the risk-free rates of interest in Europe and the US, perhaps all the way to zero already in Autumn 2007 would surely have reduced the severity of the looming downturn. Instead the ECB steered policy during the year from the First Big Quake of August 2007 on the basis of three disastrous premises.

Three disastrous premises of ECB's reaction to credit quake

The first premise was that the euro-area (and especially Germany) would be on the edge of any economic storm sweeping through the global economy in the aftermath of the First Big Quake.

The second premise was that there continued to be a serious danger of inflation in the euro-area economy and indeed that this had increased in consequence of the surge in oil and commodity prices (from late 2007 into mid-2008). Buttressing ECB explanations of this danger was a reference to the 'monetary pillar' (in reality never constructed) and in particular to a continuing rapid growth of bank lending as reflected in contemporaneous banking sector statistics.

The third premise was that the central bank monetary pilots, in steering the rate of interest in the overnight money market (a dubious concept at a time of extreme heterogeneity of credit risk among the banks), should focus unswervingly on achieving the aim for the price level over the medium-term (2% p.a. inflation or just below over say a two-year period) while blocking their ears to the financial storms raging around them. It should be left to the liquidity crisis management team (which included the monetary pilots wearing different hats) to use an entirely independent tool (subsidized and sterilized credit operations) to alleviate the funding stress in the banking system. This last premise in effect amounted to the pernicious 'separation principle'.

The basis of the economic optimism (as indeed inflation concern) was German-centric. Germany continued to enjoy booming business with Russia, Eastern Europe and the Middle East oil exporters in particular through the first few months of 2008. It seemed as if the strength of the euro (reaching a crescendo in the first half of 2008 as the ECB allowed monetary conditions to tighten sharply while the Federal Reserve was in more temperate mode though far from aggressive ease) was having no serious negative influence on German export industry. Had the Deutsche Bundesbank not long sung the tune (as far back as the late 1960s!) about how well German exports withstood a strong currency?

Blinded by econometrics and statistics

The Deutsche Bundesbank, now (since 2004) under the presidency of a renowned economics professor (Axel Weber), seemed to be putting more emphasis than ever before on the output of the economic forecasting models which continued at this stage (the first half of 2008) to be upbeat. Otmar Issing, the *eminence grise* in the ECB at the start, and to a moderate degree sceptical of econometrics according to his autobiographic account (see Issing, 2008), had retired in autumn 2006. To his term's end, Professor Issing showed not the slightest regret nor regard for the fact that the ECB had been unable to reconstruct a monetary pillar founded in monetarism such as had supported the Deutsche mark and Bundesbank during their heyday of performance and popularity.

The warnings of Professor von Mises (1971) carried no weight in the ECB Council:

> There is not, and there cannot be, such a thing as quantitative economics. The usual method employed in business forecasts is statistical and thereby retrospective. They depict trends that prevailed in the past and are familiar to everybody. They in no way answer the questions that all people, and especially businessmen, are asking. People know that trends can change; they are afraid they will change; and they would like to know when the change will occur. But the statistician knows only what everybody knows, namely, that they have not changed!

The data which was being fed into the econometrics model on which the ECB prided itself, supplemented by the ECB's analysis of the 'second pillar' of its monetary framework, did not produce any hint of serious recession risk ahead. Instead it was the amber or even red inflation light which was blinking! Money supply data was still growing strongly, reflecting in part strong increases in lending to the business sector. Could this lending surge represent a crisis-led re-intermediation, with corporations no longer able to tap the euro-denominated bond market (in that one main investor there, the credit-hedge funds, were in crisis) tapping already negotiated credit lines?

ECB and Bundesbank officials shook their heads in doubt. Figures are figures they said! On the subject of figures, though, should monetary data and the monetary pillar not to be interpreted in a long-run sense which transcended the econometric focus? So why was such a big point being made of the most recent money supply and lending behaviour in the midst of a financial panic? No answer!

As for the Jeremiahs who came to Frankfurt or Paris and started to talk about potential asset price declines in France (where according to OECD indices the real estate market had been as bubbly as in UK) and more urgently in Spain or bursting real estate and credit bubbles in Eastern Europe they were politely ridiculed. French banks had been so conservative, unlike their US counterparts. And there was absolutely no sign of weakness ahead in the French real estate market. In any case there had been no over-hang of construction in the key Paris metropolitan area. And in Spain, had analysts not been warning about this for years? Moreover Spain could gain offsetting benefits from its strong Latin American connections. To suggest that the East European miracle might be largely a speculative bubble was to ignore all the solid evidence of remarkable economic progress built on solid integration with the advanced economies to the West. Perhaps the Jeremiahs were early in their dire warnings about French real estate but not about anything else. (Indeed temperatures were to rise even further in the Paris real estate market during 2010–11 following some small fall in late 2008 and into 2009.) And in general the Jeremiahs were not pessimistic enough about the credit bubble which had emerged in periphery euro-zone government debt; in fact, most did not yet mention this topic.

The broadly optimistic attitudes about the economic outlook which could be gained first hand in interviews with monetary officials in Frankfurt at this time (spring and early summer 2008) also percolated through the official reports and autobiographical accounts of the period. Thus in mid-2008 (in the tenth anniversary report), the ECB editorialists wrote:

A cross-check with the monetary analysis confirmed that upside risks to price stability prevailed at medium to longer term horizons. Money and credit expansion remained very vigorous throughout this phase (end-2005 onwards including 2007/8), supported by a persist-ently strong growth of bank loans to the private sector. Viewed from a medium-term perspective, the marked dynamism of monetary and credit growth reflected a continuation of the persistent upward trend in the underlying rate of monetary expansion observed since mid-2004. As such, it added further to the accumulation of liquidity which, in an environment of continued strong money and credit growth, pointed to upside risks to price stability over the medium to longer term. [...] Thus far there has been little evidence that the financial market turmoil has strongly influenced the overall dynam-ics of money and credit expansion.

Further evidence of the ECB's state of mind comes from the press con-ference on 3 July 2008, of which the main task was to explain a surprise 25 bp rate hike (taking the official repo rate up to 4.25%; market rates were well above 5%). M. Trichet explained:

This decision was taken to prevent broadly based second-round effects of the oil price rise (then near its peak level of around $150 per barrel) and to counteract the increasing upside risks to price stability over the medium-term. (Second round effects were euro-speak for fear that powerful German union, most of all IG Metall, would set off a process of wage-price inflation by seeking compensation for rising oil prices). HICP inflation rates have continued to rise significantly since the autumn of last year. They are expected to remain well above the level consistent with price stability for a more protracted period than previously thought.

Moreover continued very vigorous money and credit growth and the absence thus far of significant constraints on bank loan supply in a context of ongoing financial market tensions confirm our assess-ment of upside risks to price stability over the medium-term.

Whilst the latest data confirm the expected weakening of real GDP growth in mid-2008 after exceptionally strong growth in the first quarter (arithmetically this stemmed entirely from Germany then at the peak of its export boom), the economic fundamentals of the euro-area are sound. [...] On the basis of our current assessment, the monetary policy stance following today's decision will contrib-ute to achieving our objective. [...] Whilst moderating, growth in the world economy is expected to remain resilient, benefiting in particular from continued robust growth in emerging economies. This should support euro-area external demand. The fundamentals of the euro-area economy remain sound and the euro-area does not suffer from major imbalances. In this context, investment growth in the euro area should continue to support economic activity, as rates of capacity utilization remain elevated and profitability in the non-financial corporate sector has been sustained.

In the question-and-answer session which followed, M. Trichet admonished *those (i.e. the German trade unions or French public sector workers!) who think they can embark on second-round exercises, because they want to deny that there is a transfer of resources from consumers to suppliers, are paving the way for a long period of a high level of inflation, slow growth, stagnation and unemployment at a higher and higher level. There was full employment in Europe before the first oil shock, and at the end of the 1970s we had dramatic mass unemployment which we are only starting to get out of. So that is a similarity and that is why in particular we are so attached to our message on 'no second-round effects.*

ECB in 2008 believes it is the reincarnated Bundesbank of 2003!

In his usual show of verbal eloquence (some critics would say this was practised so as to stifle the opportunity for criticism!) M. Trichet had let the cat out of the bag.

The ECB saw itself as repeating the success of the Bundesbank in 1973–4, which by contrast to other central banks at the time had single-mindedly attacked virulent monetary inflation notwithstanding widespread gloom about the near-term recessionary or even depressionary economic outlook. In consequence, Germany could balm in the sun of price stability for the following decade while other countries delayed coming to grips with the disease.

Within weeks this reading from the laboratory of history was shown to have been completely misapplied in the contemporary circumstances as Europe joined the rest of the world in a sharp deep recession and the price level in the euro-area started to decline (albeit that this did not signify monetary deflation).

M. Trichet's aim to emulate the success of the Bundesbank back in the mid-1970s by pioneering a distinct monetary response which turned out to be right where everyone else was wrong and so bringing long-run fame to itself and its currency turned out to be total pie in the sky! He evidently had not learnt one key fact about the 1973 Bundesbank success. That had not been based on economic forecasting prowess, with the crystal ball gazers in the Bundesbank having greater skill or luck than their counterparts in foreign central banks. Rather the success was due to the Bundesbank pioneering (coincidentally with the Swiss National Bank) a new framework of monetary control sharply at odds with the consensus wisdom of central bankers elsewhere at that time (including prominently the US).

The Bundesbank in 1973–4 had been the first central bank to switch to monetary base targeting and jettison Keynesian type fine-tuning. Its pioneers, influenced by the monetarist revolution which had erupted in parts of the academic economic world, staked out an adventurous course, the achievement of monetary stability after the cumulative policy flaws of the recent past. In summer 2007, M. Trichet and his colleagues had designed no new monetary framework (to replace in this case quasi-inflation targeting implemented by micro-pegging of money rates of interest) and they were certainly not monetary pioneers.

In the crude language of US presidential election campaigning, one could say, 'No, M. Trichet, no Professor Stark, you are not Dr Emminger and Dr Schlesinger!' That may well be an unfair comment to make but it would be the stuff of a more democratic and transparent monetary policymaking process.

The heightened concern about inflation which M. Trichet voiced in his (now) notorious July 2008 press conference is puzzling in several respects. Just a month later, after the first violent move down of the oil price as the commodity bubble burst, M. Trichet told the subsequent (regular monthly) press conference (7 August 2008):

> I consider that the peak in the price of oil and commodities was abnormal and did not correspond to what would be an equilibrium price. But we will see what happens. We have to be, again, totally humble in the presence of facts and figures, and we will see what happens. I think 'high and volatile' is a good description, a good way to capture things in the present situation.

But where was that humility (as regards price-level forecasts) to be found the month before (July) when he was admonishing labour unions not to seek wage awards which compensated for oil price movements. Indeed the unions (and wage negotiators) appeared to have greater understanding of the volatility of the oil price than the European central bankers in that there is no evidence in retrospect for the first half of 2008 of any wage-price spiral getting under way. And it is on the question of how to respond to CPI jumps related to the oil bubble where a significant (but not wrenching!) difference can be found between the ECB and Federal Reserve at that time in their steering of monetary policy (otherwise so similar).

The Federal Reserve did not respond to the oil price bubble by raising its peg for short-term money rates though it did in spring and early summer hint at the possibility that this may have to rise, thereby having a perverse influence in driving market interest rates for say medium maturities further above neutral level (see below). The particular concern around the ECB policymaking table, by contrast, appears to have been that the $150 oil price might immediately dislodge the anchor to stable and low inflation expectations formation in the euro-area (particularly in the heavily unionized German auto industry).

The reality was totally different from the perception of the monetary policymakers – not least in that the US and Japan had already entered recession the previous November (2007), although that date was not fixed until a year later by the statisticians. Recessionary forces with their source in the bursting of the global credit bubble had already become very strong (albeit not registered in the backward-looking real economic data and puzzling monetary data) in the euro-area. (Indeed one research group – the Centre for Economic Policy Research – was to claim much later in March 2009 that the euro-area had in fact entered recession in January 2008 if applying the same metrics to that determination as the National Bureau in the US). The spike in the oil price turned out to be a seriously lagging indicator of the business cycle.

Though the Federal Reserve in spring and summer 2008 did not join the ECB in the mistake of an alarmist response to the so-called oil price-induced 'inflation' scare, critics fault it for treading still a deeply sub-optimal path. In particular, as Leo Hetzel (2009), a senior adviser to the Richmond Federal Reserve Bank, points out the Federal Reserve's repeated references to a possible looming rise in its peg for the Federal Funds rate drove term money market rates higher through spring 2008. The growing gap between these term rates (together with short- and medium-maturity bond yields influenced by expectations regarding Federal Reserve rate pegging) and the falling neutral level contributed materially to the severity of the recession already in the summer quarter of 2008 (Q3) before the Lehman collapse. Hetzel writes:

> What caused the appearance of a deep recession? The explanation here highlights a monetary policy shock in the form of a failure by the Fed to follow a decline in the natural interest rate with reductions in the funds rate. Specifically, the absence of a funds rate reduction

between April 30, 2008 and October 8, 2008, despite deterioration in economic activity, represented a contractionary departure. Moreover the FOMC effectively tightened monetary policy in June by pushing up the expected path of the federal funds rate through hawkish commentary. By June 18, futures markets predicted a funds rate of 2.5% for November 2008.

Hetzel points out that it was not just the Federal Reserve encouraging expectations of higher rates at this time. There was also the example of the ECB and Bank of England. And then there was the BIS which in its annual report published in late June 2008 appeared to call for higher rates. The sadness here stems from the recognition that the BIS chief economist (William White) had been for many years a rare contrarian in the world of central banking, arguing against the follies of inflation-targeting. But in this case, White failed to recognize that the credit bubbles of which he had written were already bursting and with such force as to mean that lagging indicators of previous monetary excess (such as the spike in oil prices) should be ignored.

Again, as discussed earlier in this volume (Chapter 1), the issue is not so much one of whether the ECB was piloting monetary policy marginally worse or better than the Federal Reserve, but its complete failure in the mission of developing and following a superior monetary framework (and eventually monetary policy) to the highly disequilibrium-prone US one.

ECB's analysis of inflation danger from high oil was deeply flawed

The difference (modest not large!) in attitude between the Federal Reserve and ECB towards oil price developments was not a new feature of 2008. For several years back (since energy prices started to rise at the beginning of the decade), the Federal Reserve had focused on a core measure of price level rise (the private consumption deflator excluding food and energy) whereas the ECB had insisted that its focus should remain the overall measure (in the case of the euro-area including food and energy, but excluding almost totally any imputed rental equivalent of house prices – see p. 33). And no consensus existed among economists outside the central banks as to what measure of inflation should be adopted for the purpose of monetary policy steering.

There were two main arguments for focusing on the core measure.

First, oil (and food) price changes over short periods could be violent and self-reversing. Hence, if the central bank were trying to assess the underlying rate of inflation it was best to filter the short-term changes in oil prices out of the reckoning.

Second, in line with the Austrian School teachings, the objectives of price level stability in the very long-run and monetary equilibrium did not require (and might indeed be inconsistent with) price level stability over the short- or even medium-run. During periods of negative resource shock (such as would be symptomized by a jump in energy prices) not allowing money to become a source of disequilibrium would mean accepting a transitory rise in the price level and conversely during periods of positive resource shock (such as a big improvement in the terms of trade or a jump in productivity).

The Federal Reserve, in focusing on core inflation measures, was influenced mainly by the first argument. At no point in that institution's almost 100 years' history have Austrian ideas gained any traction or even any written mention in its policymaking.

The ECB in choosing to stress the overall inflation measure (without taking out the volatile food and energy component) bizarrely made implicit reference to Austrian school teaching but came to a policy conclusion at total odds with it. The authors of the ECB monthly reports on several occasions made comments to the effect that yes, there was a trend rise in energy prices – an inevitable consequence of China's rapid growth; but by the same token China's entry into the global economy was a source of significant downward pressure on the price of manufactured goods (a terms of trade gain). These two real source effects – according to the ECB – would broadly offset each other in trend terms. So yes, monetary equilibrium might imply price level stability over the medium-term notwithstanding real source upward pressure on prices from growing oil shortage.

The problem in this synthesis of real effects – including oil – on the price level (by the authors of the ECB report and apparently reflected in ECB policy discussions) was that the huge jump in the price of oil during the second half of 2007 and the first half of 2008 could hardly be described as in line with an underlying trend. Only the trend component of the oil price rise should have been netted against trend terms of trade improvement when calculating actual upward pressure on the price level from real sources during this period. Most of the actual oil price rise should have been treated as a real resource shock, even after netting out other real related forces on the price level.

The author can say on the basis of meetings with ECB officials that there was some sympathy for seeking to decipher the underlying rate of inflation without the white noise of oil price spikes. But there was a concern that any such doctoring up in public would be the beginning of a slippery slope away from the absolute respect by all 'social partners' for price level stability. It was best from this perspective to keep measurement simple. That would have been fine if actual decisions on policy interest rates took the core measurement (rather than the headline price level change) into account without this being publicly stated. There is no evidence of such 'sophistication'.

Rather, at a time of growing recession around the globe including the euro-area (a wide recession in the euro-area was not yet generally recognized albeit that there was no doubt already about a downturn in Italy), the ECB raised in July 2008 its policy rate and rates on virtually risk-free money market rates rose upwards in step (rates on unsecured inter-bank loans – to the limited extent that these could be arranged – rose by somewhat more, but the corresponding risk premiums were compressed well below where these would have been under the hypothetic alternative monetary policy described above). These term money market rates were the basis for many loan rates fixed under rollover contracts in commercial borrowing agreements.

Perhaps under a sane monetary policy some of the higher risk borrowing rates would have risen in absolute terms consistent with equilibrium tendencies. But the risk-free rates so heavily influenced by the present and prospective rate-pegging operations of the ECB (or Federal Reserve) should surely have plunged even during the oil bubble (if they had not already done so in autumn 2007). The response from Frankfurt monetary officials to any such suggestion was that lowering the official rate or reducing its visibility (by allowing a wider market determination of the interest rate structure) would interfere negatively with its supreme task of assuring price stability (according to the refined definition of 2003).

Bogus separation principle becomes ECB mantra

The separation principle had become a mantra – one policy tool (the pegging of the overnight money rate) for preserving price stability and one policy tool (a mass of subsidized sterilized lending collateralized against increasingly dodgy assets) for dealing with the 'liquidity problem in the banking sector' (in fact an insolvency problem, but not yet admitted as such).

It is the first time in monetary or financial history that the separation principle was applied. And that first time event was related to another first time event – the intensity with which central banks in Europe and the US were now seeking to fix short- and medium-maturity interest rates (rather than leaving these to market forces) and to target an exact level of inflation over a short period of time (say two years). In previous great financial panics, the central bank did not stand in the way of risk-free rates generally (including rates on near-money assets such as short-maturity government bonds) falling towards zero (under the pressure of a general flight into safety by investors) unless they were constrained to do so by a threat to the national currency's exchange rate or gold parity (under a fixed exchange rate system or international gold standard) (see Eichengreen, 1997). The euro is a freely floating currency not subject to such legal constraints on monetary action in crisis.

Two main obstacles now stood in the way of the fall of risk-free rates.

First, there was the payment of interest on reserves (until the start of EMU almost all major central banks paid no interest on reserves at any time) coupled with a total lack of flexibility in savagely cutting that interest (rate) in financial crisis.

Second, the ECB was applying the 'separation principle' in a way to veto swamping the system with extra reserves (high-powered money) as would be required to prevent a pre-cautionary surge in demand for reserves inducing a monetary squeeze (see p. 103).

No exit plan from crisis intervention following 2007 quake

Now it would certainly have been no surprise if in secret ECB officials throughout winter 2007/8, and spring/summer 2008, were in desperate communication about the exit problem (how to run down massive ECB lending to the financially weak institutions) with national finance ministries, including those in EU countries outside EMU whose banks via branches in the euro-areas had heavily availed themselves of ECB 'liquidity help' (the UK was the outstanding example of such a country).

How would the ECB one day shrink back its balance sheet to normal level and extricate itself from massive secured lending operations to the weakest banks? These operations now threatened to transform the ECB into the 'European Bad Bank', with its assets composed to a considerable degree of dubious loans and its liabilities implicitly guaranteed by taxpayers in the financially strong countries. All of this jarred with the contention, fundamental to the Maastricht Treaty, that sovereign countries could enter into monetary union without this becoming a 'transfer union' (citizens in one member country making aid payments to citizens in other member countries) which in principle would demand solidarity as found only in political unions. But the members of the EMU had not joined in a political union.

Yes, the ECB loans were secured. But if the ECB refused to renew those secured loans and grabbed the collateral it would trigger widespread insolvency from the viewpoint of the banking system as a whole. The weakest banks had no possibility of refinancing themselves from private sources. And given the dodgy nature of much of the collateral, what could the ECB realistically obtain for it in a fire sale? Yes, the ECB could enter into negotiations with member governments seeking their action to recapitalize banks with public funds, so allowing them to raise funds again in the private markets (which could be used to repay the ECB). But the weak periphery-zone governments might not be able themselves to raise finance on the scale required for such supportive action.

In fact the only exit (for the ECB from secured lending to the weakest banks during the crisis) was an EU-wide effort to re-capitalize the banking system (at least the weakest banks). And the solvency together with the related re-capitalization problem would be all the more difficult if meantime ECB policies contributed to a steep recession. Here was another big reason for caution in anti-inflationary zeal.

No evidence of such discussions at this early stage (spring and summer 2008) has filtered out into the public domain. The plunge in US and European bank stocks in summer 2008 (an obvious indicator of a deepening insolvency crisis) was not sufficient to provoke any change of monetary policy tune in Frankfurt.

The Separation Principle remained supreme.

Lehman bankruptcy causes rate-fixers in Frankfurt to dig in

Even when (in autumn 2008) the Lehman bankruptcy and threatened insolvency of AIG eventually triggered a rash of bank insolvency crises in Europe (the first crisis point being Fortis, followed in quick succession by middle-size banks in Germany and France and then one of the largest UK banks) the rate fixers in Frankfurt could not immediately let go.

In fact the rate-fixers tightened their grip! Simultaneous with an internationally coordinated 50 bp rate cut in early October 2008, the ECB announced that it was narrowing the bands either side of the official repo rate within which money rates could float as set by its marginal deposit rate and marginal lending rate. The narrowing was apparently prompted by the Bundesbank which was concerned about the ECB losing strict control of market rates (and thereby allowing a greater than optimal easing of monetary policy) under present turbulent conditions.

By narrowing the gap of the marginal deposit rate below the official repo rate to just 50 bp the ECB continued to set a high floor for the broad span of risk-free rates for short-maturity top euro-government bond markets and for government-bond secured repo rates. These continued at well above 3% into the period of intense crisis.

No wonder that record round-trips took place in the form of the less weak banks depositing excess funds at the ECB which in turn lent them out at subsidized rates (and beyond any normal prudential limit) to the weakest banks. This was such a far cry from what would have occurred under a classical monetary system in which high-powered money (deposits at the central bank and bank notes in circulation) was all non-interest bearing.

In the 'classical system' risk-free rates on near-money assets (for example, Treasury bills or their equivalent) would have been driven down by a flight into safety and the central bank would have been busy pumping in high-powered money to pre-empt any shortage of this developing amid the panic. The architects of the ECB's monetary framework had almost certainly overlooked that danger (the perverse overriding of automatic stabilizers during a financial crisis) in their ordaining that deposits at the central bank should pay interest.

Indeed, under the classical monetary system (with no interest paid on reserves) risk-free rates would come under downward pressure most likely before the full crisis erupts, as investors sought safety. The spread between the risk-free rate on, for example, short-maturity government bonds and money market rates is there a leading indicator of crisis. And in the thick of the crisis, the collapsed level of risk-free rates stimulates banks and others with surplus funds to lend into the now riskier or illiquid segments of the money market.

The action of the ECB shoring up the risk-free rate to above 3% p.a. in the depth of the financial crisis (October 2008) is evidence that the separation principle was still reigning intact and consistent with there being little sympathy around the policymaking table especially on the part of the Bundesbank President, Professor Weber and ex-Bundesbanker Professor Stark for the hypothesis that the profound shock had driven down the market-clearing risk-free rate to near zero or even negative levels at the same time that high-risk rates had risen.

The econometric modelling so highly valued in ECB policy deliberation could not provide any insights in the situation of financial panic. (It is plausible – but there is no evidence to support this – that the Bundesbank economics staff was somewhat behind real time in realizing the slump now occurring in the German economy in consequence of its special vulnerability to a precipitous fall in world trade induced in considerable part by a freezing up of many trade credit channels).

Indeed nothing suggests that the policymakers judged that a broad span of rates should emerge to reflect the present unusual degree of heterogeneity in credit quality and liquidity (in money markets).

The monetary officials in Frankfurt were still apparently in the mode of thinking that setting an adjustable peg for one interest rate, the overnight rate, was the only way to implement policy and that strict monetary control meant keeping all market rates as close as possible to that overnight rate whilst steering expectations as to where the peg would be moved further ahead. The proposal to target instead the monetary base under such unusual circumstances and allow money rates to be freely determined in the market just did not come on to the policymaking agenda.

The bogus separation principle was to re-emerge during the Italian debt crisis of summer 2011. As waves of capital flight buffeted Italian government bonds and (to a lesser extent) Italian banks, markets drove down the yields on risk-free assets – in this case short-maturity German government bonds. But so long as the ECB kept its overnight rate paid on reserves at just a small margin below the repo-rate (of 1.5% p.a.) this set a floor to the decline in the risk-free rate. Relatively strong banks in Germany or elsewhere chose to re-lend a growing surplus of deposits to the ECB and to reduce holdings of short-maturity German government bonds (on which yields were falling). If the ECB had cut its overnight rate on reserves promptly to zero that could have kick-started some on-lending of surplus funds to Italy and by allowing German short-maturity bond yields to fall to virtually zero taken some of the strain off the Italian government bond market. But the ECB had just raised its repo rate in June (2011) after many months of deliberation about rising risks of inflation related to sky-high energy prices. Any early reversal was out of the question! Instead the ECB initiated a vast new security purchase programme under which it now bought Italian government bonds to help restore normal monetary transmission within EMU.

Insolvency crisis in European banking deepens, late 2008

Let's return to the solvency crisis in Europe which continued to deepen through autumn 2008. The ECB persisted in applying the tools appropriate to a severe liquidity crisis. The ECB in any case could not arrange on its own remedial action for a deep solvency crisis. If this were to include public sector financing of a recapitalization process for the weak banks then governments had to become involved.

The most intense pressure was in the US dollar funding markets. European banking groups had huge short-term dollar borrowings outstanding in the repo markets where a chief lender had been the US money market funds.

The freezing up of those funds and massive demands for repayment in the aftermath of the Lehman bankruptcy (and other simultaneous credit events) had had a violent knock-on effect to Europe.

European banks scrambled to withdraw loans from the rest of the world (especially where repayment could be effected easily as from South Korea and Russia) in order to alleviate their immediate shortage of funds. In turn the ECB arranged vast swap lines with the Federal Reserve so as to provide dollar funds to cash-starved European banking groups (see Hördahl and King, 2008). The solvency crisis in European banking, however, transcended this issue of funding interruption. (And indeed if the banks now short of US money market provided funds were of undoubted tip-top quality they could readily have replaced these from other sources).

At the end of the line there was growing anxiety (among non-secured lenders) about the extent of possible loss not just on the now much publicized holdings of European banking groups in US credit markets (mortgages, levered loans, etc.) but also on loans against real estate (where some regional markets were already displayings signs of distress) and on loans to the emerging market economies in the Wild East (much of which was secured on once hot real estate markets and in euro or Swiss franc denomination). (The potential problem of huge investment by European banks in periphery-zone sovereign debts did not yet feature in financial commentaries.)

As national governments closed in to salvage banks from insolvency (starting with the Dutch and Belgian governments taking over Fortis at end-September 2008) an EU summit in October (2008) agreed that individual governments should introduce packages of re-capitalization or emergency loan guarantee operations to be determined in detail at a national level. In effect, the much-vaunted financial integration fostered by the launch of the euro had come to an end and gone into reverse – at least in respect of the banking systems.

Will a weak EMU member government default?

Bank salvage operations implemented at the national level were bound to put downward pressure on the credit-rating of governments in the euro-area where the public finances were already in weak condition or where the extent of aid to the banks was very large relative to economic size (or both!). In principle, the credit rating of governments in the euro-area was more immediately sensitive than that of governments (outside the euro-area) which still retained ultimate sovereign power over a national money printing press to the deterioration in the state of public finances – including the contingent liabilities taken on in guaranteeing the banking sector or the implicit losses incurred in paying well above market price for banking assets. In practice, though, that heightened sensitivity (of credit ratings to the state of public finances) should not apply to the sovereign debt of core EMU countries (let us say France, Germany and Holland) as in the ultimate the ECB would surely print money to avoid a default (within the core).

In principle, if sovereign credit risk is defined in economic terms to include deliberate partial default by the government (including the central bank) unleashing an inflation shock to write down the real value of government debt, then the distinction between the credit risk of governments with and without access to printing press becomes blurred. After all, the Weimar Republic did not default on its debt in 1921–3 according to a technical legal definition, in that the printing press was used to service all obligations punctiliously, but in reality there was a default. In practice though there are important differences.

In case of a sovereign government with its own money, or a government of a core EMU country, doubts about eventual deliberate real partial default via inflation do not translate fully into a present spike in long-term interest rates or equivalently a massive tumble in today's nominal price of government bonds. The means of generating monetary inflation involves keeping money rates of interest far below neutral for a prolonged period. Long-term interest rates are an average of short-term rates expected on a roll-over basis from the immediate present to far-out dates and thereby give those depressed money rates a substantial weight in the averaging process. Instead the pressure of default risk in the form of deliberate inflation is likely to be felt most of all through an immediate decline of the sovereign government's currency.

By contrast, in the case of a sovereign government with no effective access to a national printing press (as for a government of a periphery-zone EMU country) a rise in default risks translates directly into lower bond prices and even into a total funding crisis (in a market panic it may not be possible at all for the government to issue bonds) and wider financial crisis (in that banks and other financial institutions hold large amounts of government bonds, now slumping in value, to match fixed money liabilities).

A danger scenario began to be painted by a few market analysts around this time (late 2008) for EMU in which a New York City style crisis would erupt in one of the weak government bond markets and spread by contagion to other weak government bond markets. This scenario did not yet get a wide airing (and amazingly there was not as yet any spotlight on Greece). According to the scenario, depositors with the banks in those political jurisdictions subject to substantial default risk might flee out of fear that the debt crisis would bring down the banking system (in this political jurisdiction) or trigger an exit from EMU. The vulnerability of the banks would reflect their holdings of poor quality assets (including private loans and sovereign debt) together with the fact that the sovereign government might not be in a position to provide support.

Perhaps the financially fragile government involved could summon the needed political consensus (within its country) to effect a package of draconian budgetary cutbacks (tax increases and expenditure increases). Yet this may fail to build confidence if investors feared that this is the first step to Brüning-style depression economics with the budget deficit becoming ever wider (at least relative to the shrinking size of the economy) despite the best efforts because tax revenues plunge and unemployment benefits soar.

Brüning was the Chancellor of Germany during the depths of the depression from 1930 to 1932 who instituted savage budgetary cuts under emergency decrees, legally bypassing the need for Reichstag approval. Some critics have argued that he followed this path of driving Germany into the grave so as to prove that the reparations bill was unpayable. And indeed in 1932 the Treaty of Lausanne effectively brought reparations to an end – but at what a cost!

Under such re-incarnated circumstances the only alternative to a forced exit from EMU might be a mega financing loan from the stronger governments – either directly or via an agency created for that purpose. But would the political will exist in France, Germany, and say the Netherlands, to accomplish that? Again that question was in very embryonic form if it were heard at all during winter 2008/9.

We turn in a future chapter (Chapter 5) to a more detailed analysis of how the weak government could be forced to exit EMU and include a description of how a revised treaty could provide for this explicitly.

As a matter of historical record, though the possibility of forced exits from EMU had entered the range of scenarios viewed by some investors in spring 2009 and become a focus of media attention, it was still a long way from the mainstream (not to enter there until the Greek debt crisis erupted in early 2010). Greece's debt problems were still not being picked up by market radar.

ECB journeys into monetary irrelevance as recession deepens

The ECB had almost exhausted by spring 2009 the scope for conventional monetary easing. Risk-free rates in nominal terms were at last below 1% (near zero for some money market operations, somewhat higher in the illiquid one-year German government bond market).

In December (2008), a broad coalition of policymakers around the ECB table had unusually won the argument against the Bundesbank (there is no proof of this given the rules of secrecy under which the ECB operates, but the hypothesis rests on a collection of anecdotal and media reports) and been successful in bringing about a re-widening of the interest rate corridor such as to allow short-maturity risk-free rates to fall by as much as 100 bp (rather than 50 bp) below the belatedly declining official repo rate. (The overnight deposit rate was reduced to 100 bp below the repo rate; subsequently in early 2009 as the repo rate was cut further, the Bundesbank was successful in arguing against a cut of the overnight deposit rate to 0% and so the gap narrowed to 75 bp).

Most probably the willingness of the Bundesbank to concede at this point stemmed from the accumulation of evidence that the German economy was now in slump (of greater severity than in France). In fact the euro-area was now (December 2008) in a great recession and financial panic where the neutral interest rate level in real terms across short and medium maturities was surely negative.

There was no evidence that ECB policymakers realized how irrelevant they had become. And their continuing reference to implicit inflation-targeting as built into the framework of monetary policymaking 'perfected' in spring 2003 (even though by now the flaws in the framework should have become abundantly evident) was unhelpful to the economic recovery process. For example at the summer (August) 2009 monthly press conference, President Trichet told reporters that although year-on-year price level rises had turned negative, these would return towards the target of '2% or close to (from below) 2%' over the medium-term.

Presumably this reference to the expected re-emergence of low inflation was made to justify holding back from the final 25 bp cut in the overnight deposit rate. But there was surely a mainstream scenario under which the price level in the euro-area would be falling for several years, even though the German price level might be stable (reflecting the relative price adjustment downwards required in the ex-bubble economies). In so far as the ECB promoted an underestimation in the marketplace of the likelihood of that scenario of a falling price level, it contributed to nominal medium and long-term interest rates on euros remaining at higher-than-otherwise levels.

The recovery would depend most of all on self-corrective forces of non-monetary source. The best hope here was that the steep drop in international trade brought about by the post-Lehman freeze of the global financial system would reverse itself as freeze now gave way to thaw. Businesses would cease their emergency slashing of inventories (once back into line with sunken sales volumes) and capital spending programmes. And hopefully the equity markets might lead a recuperation process.

If investors there had confidence in a better future, companies would be able to justify investment projects with pay-offs over the long run (where this future income would be priced in present value terms by equity investors) even though present profit prospects were dismal. Justification would take the form of the simple answer to a simple question – does the adoption of this capital-spending programme bolster the value of my equity?

The policymakers continued through spring 2009 to debate the merits of a further 25 bp rate cut, with the Bundesbankers in particular expressing caution – as if the difference between a risk-free rate of 75 bp (the then level of yields on three-month German government bills) and 50 bp or even zero would make much difference to anything when the equilibrium level was transitorily far below that in deep negative territory! The big mistakes had already been made!

ECB refuses to admit any mistake in crisis

No one, though, would have heard the word mistake, in M. Trichet's keynote address in mid-march 2009 on '*What lessons can be learned from the economic and financial crisis?*' (speech at the '5eme Rencontres de l'Entreprise Europeenne' organized by La Tribune, Roland Berger and HEC, Paris). His introduction was promising:

> Tonight, I would like to examine the roots of the current crisis and the policy responses which are taken to address it and to inspire a new sense of direction.

Unfortunately, no illumination was to follow!

In the last ten years we saw a dramatic shift in influence away from entrepreneurship in the real economy to speculation and gambling in the financial sector. The assumption and the hedging of genuine economic risk gradually ceased to be the main concern of international finance. [...] At some point, the financial system seemed to be no longer there primarily to hedge existing economic risks, but more and more to create and propagate risks on its own.

The credit boom had three multipliers.

First, ill-designed compensation schemes for loan managers reinforced the shortening of lenders' horizons. In the eyes of many loan managers, the short-run gains from an expansion of credit obscured the need for any consideration of the potential losses that their institution could incur over the long-run.

Second, the complex structure of securitized products made it difficult for the ultimate holders to assess the quality of the underlying investment.

Third, international imbalances and their potential to encourage liquidity creation on a global scale acted as the macroeconomic – and perhaps most powerful – multiplier. A chronic shortage of savings in some of the world's advanced economies was funded by an excess of savings in other parts of the world. These global macro-economic imbalances contributed to the creation of international liquidity and therefore further fuelled credit and debt accumulation.

These three multipliers went into reverse – suddenly, although not unexpectedly – sometime in the middle of 2007. Liquidity dried up. [...] The ECB moved pre-emptively. It ensured the continued functioning of the money market at the very first signs of the turbulences in August 2007. We have not shied away from action at any time since then. Our actions have been early, resolute and broadly based!

Who could M. Trichet have been hoping to fool, unless the worst fears were true about the European central bankers now inhabiting an ivory tower totally removed from the real world?

There is absolutely no mention at all in M. Trichet's speech of the cardinal error of the ECB, together with the Federal Reserve, moving in spring 2003 towards a super-easy monetary policy out of misplaced fear of deflation; or of the ignoring or lack of alarm at growing evidence of credit and asset market warming through 2003–5; or of the glacial pace of tightening through late 2005 and 2006; or of the failure to distinguish between liquidity and solvency crisis in summer 2007 and the suppression of all private market forces which might have brought about an early re-capitalization of the healthier parts of the financial system; or the implicit rejection of stabilizing monetary action found in previous great financial panics (risk-free rates falling being allowed to plunge and huge injections of monetary base to meet raised demand for reserves and currency).

Instead there is the old pre-EMU French prejudice against Anglo-Saxon finance, the dogma about global imbalances (US savings deficits, East Asian savings surpluses) and financial casinos (in London and New York) being the source of a US-centred global credit bubble. The story defies all accounts of how the invisible hand of market forces if left unrestricted and if operating under conditions of monetary stability should cope with the transfer of capital from parts of the world where savings are plentiful relative to domestic investment opportunity into those parts where the reverse holds. The total silence is deafening on the tightening of euro-area monetary conditions through 2008H1, the ECB's driving the risk-free rate of interest to well above 4% p.a. when recession had already started in major parts of the world and the misplaced reading of history (imagining a phantom danger of wage-price inflation).

The ECB's chief economist and board member Professor Jürgen Stark (ex-Bundesbanker) did not provide any more clarification when he spoke in March 2009 to a German-Luxembourg economic conference. He thankfully kept away from any historical account as to how the crisis came about. But his analysis of how the ECB was now conducting monetary policy could only mystify.

In fairness Professor Stark started by making the reasonable point that though the price level may be falling (due to sharp declines in oil prices) this was not deflation (a persistent broad-based and self-sustaining decline in the overall price level reinforced by anticipation that prices will decline further in the future) but disinflation (linked to a transitory movement in relative prices). If he had had more time he might have added a cyclical drop in the price level to the disinflation list (suppliers in the most cyclical sectors of the economy cutting profit margins at the depths of the recession and re-building them during recovery). But then he started to tread the murky waters of the separation principle:

> To better understand the scale of our interventions in the interbank money market, one needs to appreciate its importance in the implementation and transmission of monetary policy. Money market interest rates, especially of short maturities, mark the starting point in the transmission of monetary policy. They determine the marginal costs of refinancing of the banking sector and thereby act through the bank lending channel. Money market interest rates are a key factor in determining the entire yield curve and thereby are crucial for the expectations channel of monetary transmission.

Professor Stark leaves no doubt about what his attitude would have been (and presumably was!) to any suggestion, if made (and there is absolutely no evidence or reason to believe the suggestion was ever put forward at the ECB's policy meetings), that in the wake of the August 07 quake, a wide span of rates should have been allowed to form, with the risk-free rate falling towards zero and risky rates (for example to the weaker banks) rising. Any such messy outcome would have blurred (in the viewpoint of Professor Stark) the signalling from firm rate control by the ECB.

We can also see that Professor Stark was a key opponent of any idea to widen the corridor between the overnight deposit rate and the marginal lending rate in late 2008 (and why M. Trichet had to stall questioners at the November and December press conferences as to why this was not happening despite massive round-tripping, saying that it was 'under review'!).

Professor Stark then ventured into the liquidity-solvency debate, by implication suggesting that the ECB's massive interventions from summer 2007 onwards had been for liquidity purposes. He quoted the maxim:

> Central banks can alleviate liquidity risks, but they cannot address the perceived solvency problems that impair the financial system.

So why had the ECB spent the year or more from the August 07 quake lending more and more on a secured subsidized sterilized basis to the weakest banks in Europe when it was apparent to almost all (except perhaps at the ECB) that there was a serious solvency issue?

The sterilization occurred via the ECB conducting reverse repo operations in the market – in effect lending securities and borrowing funds from non-banks and the stronger banks – so as to offset the loans to the weakest; and in a bazaar decision the ECB as late as June 2009 decided to amplify this sterilization operation by making the same overall amount of funds available now for one year (rather than as previously for six-months) at a below-market rate, at least with respect to the weakest banks, of 1% p.a.

There is no record in the ECB transcript of a question to Professor Stark on the futility and indeed deceptiveness (in terms of public accountability) of such lending to the insolvent!

Implicitly Professor Stark offered a defence of why the ECB had driven the risk-free rate of interest higher in spring and early summer 2008 – wait for it! If it had not been for the (avoidable) US shambles of allowing a big investment bank to blow up, the euro-area was not on course for a recession:

> The crisis started in Summer 2007, as losses in the US sub-prime mortgage market, a relatively small segment of the US housing market, triggered the ongoing financial turmoil. However, its impact on

the global economy remained relatively limited until the summer of 2008. However after the collapse of Lehman Brothers last September, the tensions in global financial markets escalated to a full-blown financial crisis and thereafter turned into a global economic crisis. The severe global economic downturn has now become much more synchronized. The collapse in global trade has amplified the adverse impact from the financial turmoil and caused emerging market prospects to deteriorate drastically.

Was the source of the problem really just a small section of the US housing market? Or was Professor Stark blind to the much bigger picture of a global credit bubble of which the US sub-prime mortgage market was just one component and for which the ultimate source was a monetary madness which embraced the ECB as much as the Federal Reserve?

As regards this gentle economic slowdown environment in the first half of 2008, were Spain and Italy not already in serious recession? Indeed from January 2008 the whole euro-area was subsequently identified as in recession. And yes, most analysts would undoubtedly agree with Professor Stark that the Great Panic following the Lehman bankruptcy was the immediate catalyst to a 08Q4 and 09Q1 slump in business activity around the world (driven by a near freeze-up of international trade credit and many other forms of credit, especially those where the now defunct 'shadow banking system' had been important). But how could Professor Stark still in March 2009 justify the only gradualist adjustment down (the previous autumn) of the peg for the overnight rate and all the efforts to prevent a sharper fall at that time in the risk-free rate (at first narrowing the corridor around the repo rate in September 2008, subsequently allowing it to return to the previous norm under the sheer weight of the round-tripping which the move triggered)?

And was the main justification for what rate declines did actually occur really the avoidance of a bigger decline of inflation over the medium-term (the next two years) below the target level of 2% p.a.? Or did the justification lie in the much more urgent objective to prevent severe monetary disequilibrium such as would arise from sustaining market rates for short and medium maturities at far above the almost certainly now lowered neutral or natural level?

That severe monetary disequilibrium may or may not have ended up with inflation in the euro-area undershooting the target as set by the ECB. Even without the appearance of such undershoot, would not all the other pain of monetary disequilibrium, including financial institutions failing and severe recession or slump together with precipitous asset deflation, justify bold action now? And did not the survival of the euro itself in present form not depend on alleviating monetary disequilibrium? Otherwise how could a forced exit from EMU of the periphery-zone countries (Portugal, Ireland, Greece and Spain) be prevented?

A French diplomatic coup to diffuse existential crisis, spring 2009

ECB officials remained effectively mum on the issue of existential crisis of the euro as recession deepened through early 2009. This is understandable to the extent that the same officials realized that survival of the euro-area in its present wide form (as against a narrow union of France, Germany and Holland) might depend ultimately on the willingness of electorates in France, Germany and Holland to make transfers to the foreign governments within EMU at high risk of defaulting.

Even so, there were some forms of support which might not require such willingness – either because they could be camouflaged from electoral view (such as the ECB providing cheap 'liquidity' to Spanish, Greek, or Irish banks – a non-exhaustive list!) or because they were forthcoming from other sources, as for example the IMF. This Washington institution, now under a French ex-Finance Minister, hit it lucky in spring 2009, obtaining huge new resources from China, Japan and the US. Only a few months before there had been widespread chatter in G-7 circles about whether there was any rationale for the IMF's continued existence, so incompetent had been its analysis and actions during the global credit bubble.

French economic diplomacy enjoyed crowning success at the G-20 summit in London (April 2009), where the main resolution was a recapitalization of the IMF. All participants in the G-20 summit realized that the main destination of re-vamped IMF lending would be European countries in distress. The most obvious distress stories were in the 'Wild East' (ex-communist countries of central/Eastern Europe). But the more perspicacious delegates at G-20 knew that not far behind in the queue for assistance would be the periphery-zone members of EMU.

The new Obama Administration promised to obtain the necessary approvals (for IMF funding) from the US Senate (no difficult questions asked as to why Germany was still the number one exporter to Iran, or conditions imposed such as EU promising to expedite Baltics' entry into EMU – see p. 55). Treasury Secretary Geithner had ascended the ladder of official stardom via the first rung of IMF apparatchik. He and the rest of the Obama economics team (including the Federal Reserve chief, Professor Bernanke) had been traumatized by the fallout from the

Lehman collapse and saw it now as self-evident that anything similar must be prevented in Europe; they were in no mood or mind to contemplate laissez-faire solutions. Moreover a deepening European banking crisis would most likely mean a sharp fall in the euro which would dash the Obama economics team's plan to use a weak dollar towards promoting US recovery. Japan and China signed up to massive loans to the IMF at least in part towards keeping the peace in currency relations with Washington.

Less understandable (than the traumatized state of the Obama economics team) is the glibness with which ECB officials repeated the mantras that exit from EMU was impossible or disastrous and that euro-membership had spared the weak countries from much greater pain. For example, when asked about exit pressures on weak governments at his press conference in mid-March (2009), M. Trichet answered as follows:

> As regards your question on the issue of members of the euro-area that could be in extreme difficulty, first of all the euro-area is an area where you have considerable automatic help through the very existence of the single currency itself. For instance the balance of payments deficit, if any, is financed automatically by virtue of belonging to the euro-area. Let us not forget that. I say regularly when I am asked more direct questions that I do not comment on absurd hypotheses (any mention of exit is absurd!). I have confidence in the capacity of the governments of the euro-area in line with their own pre-eminent responsibility to convince their own people and markets that they are going in the right direction and that they are credible as regards the medium- to long-term path for sound fiscal policies.

The critic could question the notion of automatic help being bolstered by the existence of EMU. If Spain were now in slump and its private sector savings deficit plunging (as construction spending collapsed, non–real estate companies also cut back outlays and households' propensity to consume fell), the net inflow of capital from the rest of the world (especially the euro-area) – which Trichet describes as 'balance of payments deficit' – would decline in line (adjusted for the simultaneous widening of the public sector deficit). Membership of the euro-area meant that the decline in the 'balance of payments deficit' would be less gradualist than otherwise. If Spain had its own currency, nominal interest rates there could fall below the level in the euro-area. Devaluation, if reflected in higher inflation expectations, could bring real rates speedily into negative territory. Hence the contraction of the private sector savings deficit would be slower than inside EMU.

The cheapness of the Spanish currency (together with expectations of a potential eventual re-bound) would act as a magnet for foreign financing allowing its savings deficit to stay larger for longer (despite negative real rates). And why was the notion of Spain leaving the euro absurd? After all during the era of the gold standard, countries left gold. The mechanics would be broadly similar for exit from the euro-area. When it came to the government of Spain or any other weak member convincing its own people about the need to tighten fiscal policy and follow the right path during a recession had M. Trichet not read in the history books how Chancellor Brüning inflicted that medicine on Germany during 1930–2 and with what results rather than pursuing the path of exit from the straightjacket of the dollar exchange standard?

At last ECB refuses to join the crowd: It rejects quantitative easing

Another big topic at press conferences during the two quarters of economic slump which followed the financial system freeze-up of early autumn 2008 was why the ECB abstained from following other central banks (first the Federal Reserve, then the Bank of England) in adopting a policy of 'quantitative easing'. This meant expanding the monetary base (excess reserves in particular) aggressively once the risk-free interest rate had fallen to the zero rate boundary with the aim of providing further stimulus to the economy.

There was a perfectly respectable intellectual case to be made for the central bank not venturing down this particular path. In particular, in the situation where equilibrium risk-free short and medium maturity interest rates had fallen to significantly negative levels in real terms and pre-existing inflation expectations were very subdued if present at all, it was highly dubious that the non-conventional toolbox contained any device at all – other than the highly powered tool of negative interest rates – capable of effective use. It would be better to allow good cyclical deflation to work its wonders – a fall in prices to a below-normal level during the recession matched by expectations of a rebound of prices into the recovery and expansion phases. (Hence low nominal medium-term interest rates during the recession would be negative in real terms taking account of the likely rebound in prices further ahead.)

Yes, the ECB could follow the Federal Reserve and buy massive amounts of government bonds in the secondary markets, though there would be the ticklish question of deciding which bonds of which governments would form part of this operation. Would this include the government debt of the periphery-zone members (of EMU) where prices were already reflecting some significant risk of default or EMU exit? But beyond that 'technical' problem, why would the banks respond to a flotsam of extra reserves by increasing their risky loans rather than just parking these at the ECB (in its overnight deposit facility) and levying increased charges on their deposit customers? If the banks lent out the money at rates which did not fully reflect raised risk premiums and increased risks (at a time of deep recession) and to an extent which went beyond the maximum leverage ratios appropriate in any case (where these are determined in particular by deadweight bankruptcy costs and moral hazard) they would find their equity prices plunging as investors in the bank took fright.

Yes, quantitative easing 'worked' in Communist China already during the first half of 2009 in producing a lending boom of fantastic proportions, with banks commanded to meet loan quotas by Beijing. But this was not a model to follow in a market economy and political democracy. The implicit shareholders of the banks in China, the public, had no effective voice. And a command-driven lending boom not based on market price signals would surely not bring about the efficient deployment of new capital so essential in the long run to steer the Chinese economy on to a path of economic prosperity and away from a path of bubble-and-busts with so much collateral damage.

After a financial panic and deep recession in a market economy such as those in Europe, Japan or the US, it is likely to be the financially fit firms which lead the process of recovery, drawing on funds from the equity and bond markets. The more fragile firms who are particularly important as borrowers in the bank credit markets emerge as effective demand there at a later stage in the recovery. By that point the optimal path of market-clearing risk-free interest rates may well have entered again positive territory. Bank lending growth would be consistent then with rising bank equity values – in that risk premiums and the risk level of many borrowers have decreased since the panic and its aftermath.

Quantitative easing in itself might well cause expectations regarding the price level over the medium-term (say 3–5 years into the future) to shift upwards even before strong recovery becomes evident, on the basis that the central bank by moving even further away from a conventional monetary system with its known rules would be likely to make serious mistakes, most plausibly in the direction of inflation. That anxiety about potential inflation, inflamed perhaps by the central bank committing itself to holding rates down at abnormally low levels for an 'extended period' (with the likelihood that they will not be raised in line with inflation when it emerges) might frighten some financially fit households into spending now rather than run the serious risk of their monetary assets depreciating eventually (in real terms). But it is far from clear that these stimulus effects would be particularly powerful. The strongest effect might be downward pressure on the currency. That pressure could be increased by the central bank buying massive quantities of government bonds, raising thereby the spectre of long-time monetisation as the eventual 'solution' to a deepening crisis in public finances. The floating of such a policy strategy by ECB officials, even if in their hearts they had no stomach to carry it out, would conflict with their 'sworn' mission of price stability according to the Maastricht Treaty.

In fact ECB officials have shown no enthusiasm to proceed down the track of quantitative easing. But nor have they been enthusiastic promoters of laissez-faire solutions driven by some initial good cyclical deflation. The officials did not make the case that exit from recession should be powered to a considerable degree by natural forces of recovery (deep price discounts encouraging consumers and businesses to bring forward spending, bold speculators in the equity market supporting prices there at levels which priced expectations of returns in periods beyond the present recession from new capital expenditure at a reasonable level, so allowing projects to be adopted now, recuperation of international trade and business confidence led by thawing of the financial system freeze).

Speeches of ECB officials during this time did describe the likely problems of quantitative easing (for example, see Bini-Smaghi, 2009), albeit tending to put great focus on possible losses for the ECB in holding the assets bought rather than on inherent flaws in theory! And if so concerned about losses, how could some of the same officials already in spring 2010 be advocating huge buying (by the ECB) of Greek sovereign debt now transformed into junk or lending through the ECB's back door on the collateral of increasingly dubious periphery-zone government debt? The less in-depth speeches emphasized the point that the central bank should ignore all cyclical fine-tuning and just concentrate on the long run, without analysing the particular issues related to quantitative easing (see Stark, 2009). But there was no coherent shift evident anywhere in Frankfurt away from the collection of hypotheses which lay behind the monetary framework designed in 1998 and refined further in 2003. A shift in particular away from the misconceptions of quasi-inflation targeting would have differentiated policymakers in Frankfurt from those in Washington or London.

In designing a new framework – a distinct European alternative – the ECB would have stood to win (if vindicated by history!) the sort of esteem which the Bundesbank won in 1973 from not following the 'global central bankers' pack'. Instead, there was a buzz which just sounded like excess caution, intellectual laziness or both – and of course the policymakers had still not exhausted conventional policy tools by allowing risk-free rates to fall to zero. A question-and-answer session at the early March 2009 press conference (of the ECB) is revealing:

Q: With the main refinancing rate at 1.5% do you think you are getting close to the limit? Last time you said you considered 0% rates inappropriate? Do you still think so?

Trichet: I confirm what I have already said. We see a number of drawbacks associated with a zero late level. [...] As regards non-standard measures, there is no pre-commitment for any kind of non-standard measure. I exclude nothing, it would be the decision of the Governing Council and we are looking at it.

Q: You have just said you are studying the implementation of non-standard measures. Does that mean you are studying the process by which you might implement them or you are studying the need for them?

Trichet: We are discussing of course both the need and the process. And any decision would suppose that we see the need and that we agree on the process.

The reader can judge for him or herself what the ECB was up to, but none of this interchange would encourage confidence among investors in the monetary policymakers at a particularly dark hour in European financial history. Perhaps the ECB was at last refusing to follow the latest US monetary fashion (this time quantitative easing, previously quasi-inflation targeting). But did the officials in the Euro-tower realise the challenges that would lie ahead were the Federal Reserve to use its non-conventional policy tool as a weapon of undeclared currency war? It was too bad that the Frankfurt policymakers by their previous mistaken policies had left the euro-area in such a weakened economic condition. How much better it would have been if the ECB had forged its own and better-designed way right from the start of monetary union!

4
The Trial

It is time to 'give the floor' to what the leading officials in the project of European Monetary Union (EMU) have said and continue to say in its defence (or more aptly, in trumpeting its success). A ready-made brief on their behalf comes from Stephen Cecchetti and Kermit Schoenholtz (2008). These authors (the first is Economic Adviser and Head of the Monetary and Economics Department at the Bank for International Settlements, the second is professor at Stern School of Business, New York University) conducted a series of 17 extended interviews between June 2007 and February 2008 with a range of current and former high officials at the ECB, and with other policymakers and scholars who viewed the evolution of the ECB from privileged vantage points outside the institution.

The authors of the brief conclude:

> We share the assessment of our interviewees that the ECB has enjoyed many more successes than disappointments. These successes reflect both the ECB's design and implementation. Looking forward, we highlight the unique challenges posed by enlargement and, especially, by the euro area's complex arrangements for guarding financial stability.

Plan of the trial

The plan in this chapter is to first, extract the main features of the positive case made in the Cecchetti–Schoenholtz brief, raising some doubts along the way. Second, we look critically at alternative direct testimonial evidence available from leading ECB officials, including in particular speeches and press conferences. Third, we seek to weigh up the evidence and consider in particular one key issue. How far, even given the policies of monetary disequilibrium pursued by the Federal Reserve, could the ECB have steered its own monetary policy in a way so as to lessen the extent of the global credit bubble and in particular the savaging of the euro-area economy by wild temperature swings in credit and real estate markets?

Leading central bankers and ex-central bankers in Europe and the US continue to press their claim either explicitly or implicitly that monetary policy played little or virtually no role in the debacle of credit bubble and burst for which the overall economic costs are already so awesome. (In private conversation, there is some remarkable capacity for self-criticism below the top in both the Federal Reserve and Bundesbank. And within the Federal Reserve System such self-criticism has found its way into print in regional research output – see for example, Hetzel, 2009.)

Does that official claim of central bank innocence stand up to scrutiny? Or is this continuing official denial of responsibility in the economic debacle one aspect of a further troubling concern – that the central bankers have abused their independence?

This concern, particularly with reference to EMU where central bank independence is constitutionally rooted in accordance with the German ordo-liberal school's concept that institutions critical for the benign functioning of the market economy should be insulated from the turmoil of political democracy, if found to be justified, calls for remedies as to be explored in our next chapter.

First entry in the defence of EMU – It survived!

Let's revert, however, to the first entry in the positive case (as summarized in the Cecchetti–Schoenholtz brief) for EMU.

EMU made it successfully past the starting line! Otmar Issing (one of those interviewed) stressed this particular point (in his comments to Cecchetti–Schoenholtz):

> There was a clear view from a number of outside observers that we would fail and that it would be a disaster in any respect.

The authors (of the report) continue with this same point:

> As late as 1997 there was widespread scepticism about whether EMU would begin on schedule as a broad union and in some quarters whether it would happen at all. Yet, here we are a full decade later and there are 15 countries where the euro is legal tender.

The 21 members of the Governing Council of the ECP make monetary policy for a region of 320 million people with a GDP of roughly €9 trillion. And it is hard to find major fault with what they have done over the past decade.

Evidently the authors of the brief were not thinking of the indictments and the commentary found in the first three chapters of this book! But let us look at the narrow claim that EMU had a successful birth.

Was a successful birth an accomplishment?

Without doubt a lot of able organizers took part in the process of launching the euro. There was no equivalent to a monetary blackout due to a mega-technical hitch. That is undoubtedly a cause for pride or at least a sense of relief among those making or fitting the nuts and bolts. The monetary version of the Titanic did not fall apart on its first voyage. The vans arrived on time with the new banknotes, there was no robbery, and the distribution occurred ahead of schedule! (The authors of the brief relate an interviewee's comment that 'this enormous logistical process went more quickly and smoothly than many had expected. Most of the legacy currency was replaced within a matter of weeks, rather than months'.) The clearing system for inter-bank transfers worked efficiently. The ECB could peg an overnight rate immediately. Its operational framework for implementing monetary policy (strict control of a very short-term money market rate) did not encounter any serious technical glitch.

This pat on the back for the monetary union engineering corps and its supervisors is to lose sight of the big picture. The absence of glitch or hitch in no way demonstrates that creation of the new monetary system was an act of progress. Such demonstration would require matching, as a first step, the record to date of monetary union with the heterogeneous intentions of its advocates. Then there would be an assessment of how it performed relative to the alternatives – whether contemporary regimes in other parts of the world, or counter-factual regimes in Europe – and in absolute terms.

Yes, despite some reservations most of all in Frankfurt, the train to EMU made it all the way through to a broad union (including in particular Spain and Italy) rather than stopping at the earlier destination of narrow monetary union including France, Germany, Holland, Belgium and Luxembourg. But as subsequent events turned out, including especially the extent of the credit and real estate bubble in Spain, would it not have been better if the train had stopped one station short of that final destination?

Defence claim no. 2 – Euro as good a store of value as its predecessors

A second claim of success comes from a comment by Jean-Claude Trichet, quoted by the authors of the report:

> The main challenge we saw was to transfer to the new currency what had been promised: namely, that it would be as confidence inspiring, as credible, and as good a store of value as the previous national currencies had been.

The authors of the brief (Cecchetti et al.) buttress M. Trichet's claim:

> The policy tests facing the ECB at its inception were numerous and daunting. It is evident that the ECB faced an extraordinary challenge as it sought to inherit from the start the credibility of its most successful predecessor central banks. There also were great risks, as there would be no honeymoon or grace period. Any significant rise of inflation expectations or of inflation risk premiums in the run-up to EMU might have branded policy a failure even before the ECB began to exercise monetary control. [...] There was concern whether the powerful NCB Governors – and their large staffs – would overwhelm the ECB, and potentially undermine the euro-area focus of the new central bank. [...] And the ECB was to begin operations in an environment of overt scepticism. [...] The broad membership of EMU, which included several formerly high-inflation countries, raised doubts about credibility.

The authors quote Alexandre Lamfalussy (a key figure in the creation of the euro, first as President of the BIS during the period when the Delors Committee was meeting regularly there to draw up its blueprint for monetary union and later as the head of the European Monetary Institute, the predecessor of the ECB) as saying:

> I feared that they would have technical problems of all kinds. Ultimately I was wrong. The implementation went extraordinarily smoothly.

They also relate a comment from Otmar Issing:

> What really shocked me (when I arrived) was the lack of any reasonable information (data, etc). We were preparing monetary policy for totally unchartered waters.

A problem with the claims of survival and no technical hitch

There is a problem with all of these self-congratulations just recited. The claim that the ECB or EMU was successful because the new money is as good as the old and because really bad scenarios (of considerable likelihood) were avoided under which most citizens in the euro-area would have been much worse off than under the old monetary regime borders on the impudent! Indeed if there was really such a large probability of those bad scenarios becoming reality (and the best that could be said about the new money is that it is as good as the old) then why were those advocating the project of EMU doing so in such unequivocal terms?

Did M. Lamfalussy for example act in accordance with the highest democratic principles in deciding not to go public with his forebodings of chaos? It was not a time of war when secrecy concerning all disaster scenarios might be justified.

Was there a flaw in the European democratic processes that the leading officials and ex-officials were not quizzed under oath about the risks which were being run? If the democratic processes had been alive, and the truth about risks revealed (including the key fact the launch may well turn into a glitch-laden disaster), would the citizens-to-be of the euro-area have continued to support the train going forward towards monetary union, even where they had originally voted for the Treaty of Maastricht (referendums were held in only a few countries)?

The inclusion of the previous high-inflation countries in EMU (Spain, Italy, Portugal, Greece, Ireland) did prove an initial success in terms of citizens in those countries having a domestic medium-of-exchange which was superior to the old in some respects (in particular as regards the extent of long-run inflation danger). Citizens of all member countries (with the possible exception of Germany) now enjoyed a wider range of highly liquid instruments to choose from without incurring exchange risk or exchange transaction costs. In any overall appraisal, however, we should consider the costs of that success.

A prominent cost was the economic damage wrought by the bubbles and subsequent bursts in credit and real estate markets (the bubbles, bursts and damage being spread unevenly across the new monetary union) in so far as such turbulence could indeed be traced to flaws in monetary union and serious mistakes in ECB policymaking.

Claim no. 3 – ECB developed a state-of-the-art forecasting apparatus

The authors do not consider the cost of monetary disequilibrium attributable to EMU, most ostensibly because they wrote their report before the most devastating phase of the bubble-bursting process. They continue instead with their claims of technical prowess, focussing next on the forecasting tools which the ECB assembled from a zero starting point:

> The ECB has developed a forecasting apparatus that is at the state-of-the-art in the central banking world – and as previously mentioned – routinely publishes its staff projections. In addition the broad research program of the ECB has reached a status that puts it at the frontier of applied policy analysis alongside the best research efforts of other leading central banks and academic institutions.

It was too bad that with all that it had at its command, the ECB made in its first decade three big monetary errors (first, easing in late-98/early-99 because price level rises during a period of economic slack were running at 'only 1% p.a.', ushering in a sharp decline of the euro and significant monetary inflation; second, fuelling a credit and asset bubble through 2003–6 out of concern that the newly refined inflation 'target' might be undershot; and third, pushing risk-free rates up to almost 5% half a year into the global recession – including Europe – which started in winter 2007/8 out of anxiety about the 'inflationary potential' of oil price rises and contributing thereby to the intensity of the economic downturn and the extent of financial system distress).

Claim 4: ECB has been a good European, ignoring national interests

The authors of the brief go on to reveal that in their discussions (with present and former senior 'euro-officials'):

> There was unanimity amongst ECB insiders that country-specific factors were irrelevant in the policy rate-setting process even at the start of EMU. Having feared a greater role for national interests, some interviewees reported reacting with surprise and satisfaction at that time. Others suggested that the long process of preparing for EMU – including joint preparatory work at the EMI – had fostered a

broad consensus among euro-area central bankers about the objectives and implementation of monetary policy that underpinned the ECB's behaviour.

We have all heard the quote from Shakespeare's *Hamlet*: 'the lady doth protest too much!'

Of course, the policymakers were all good Europeans! Yet how come at critical junctures Germany's situation seemed to get a dominating weight in policymaking (more than just due to that country accounting for around 30% of euro-area GDP and thereby influencing significantly overall euro-area aggregates)?

In winter 1998/9, the fact that the German economy was one of the most affected by the passing slowdown in world trade following the autumn-1998 mini-financial crisis (related to Russia's default, the troubles of LTCM, and continuing retrenchment in East Asia in the aftermath of the debt crisis which erupted there in 1997) had at least some relation to the Bundesbank taking the lead in the policy easing at that time (see p. 60).

It is also plausible that the unfavourable relative cost and price level at which Germany became locked into EMU (with so many of the other member currencies having obtained big real devaluations vis-à-vis the mark in the years before) and the business malaise which accompanied that situation played a role in making German policymakers on the ECB Board over-complacent about the big decline of the euro in 1999–2000.

And the later fact that Germany was not experiencing any temperature rise in its real estate and credit markets and its price level was flat (or even slightly falling) surely contributed towards the middle one of the three large ECB errors (2003–5), when overall monetary conditions remained excessively easy.

The export boom in Germany which continued into the first quarter of 2008, together with a doomsday concern of German monetary policymakers about the power of unions (IG Metall in particular) to push up wages in response to oil-price hikes, help to explain the third error (2008 – see p. 122).

Claim 5 – EMU achieved price stability and economic stability!

The Cecchetti–Schoenholtz brief was published in November 2008 just around the tenth anniversary time for EMU and so it is no surprise that some of those interviewed were in reflective mood. Anniversaries are a time for looking back and forward. Bundesbank President Weber expressed the view (to the authors) that:

> I think the success is the high degree to which price stability has been achieved [...]. Long-term inflation expectations have been stable and low and anchored at the level defined as price stability.

Hans Tietmeyer, founder ECB policy-board member in 1998 and Bundesbank President (1993–9) states (to the authors of the brief) that

> From the beginning, the ECB was seen inside and outside the euro-area as independent and credible.

The then (in early 2008) New York Federal Reserve President Timothy Geithner (subsequently Treasury Secretary under President Obama) told the authors:

> Since the ECB has been setting monetary policy, it has not produced a sustained period of sub-par growth; the euro-area has not experienced greater volatility of economic growth; and there has certainly not been any erosion of inflation performance. All this suggests that the ECB is performing well.

A problem with the claim of stability

Um! The Bank of France and Bundesbank had both achieved inflation of 1% p.a. or less before the start of EMU. What did the creation of EMU and the ECB offer French and German citizens that they did not have already in terms of stability?

In fact as highlighted in earlier chapters the ECB was most probably more vulnerable than would have been a still sovereign Bundesbank to the monetary preachers warning that 'inflation might fall too low'. 'Vulnerable' here includes lack of resistance to a false IMF-alarm on German and indeed global deflation risks. And it is hard to believe that the German government would have been ever been an ally of the IMF in swaying the 'Old' Bundesbank (defined to exclude the 1990s, see below) against its better judgement. (By contrast in spring 2003, Berlin, Frankfurt – including the 'new Bundesbank' and Washington – had all been in step about the phoney danger of deflation.)

And at no point was the Bundesbank an inflation-targeter or quasi-inflation targeter, as the ECB became, with its consequences of deep monetary disequilibrium. As for the record, the Bundesbank over more than a decade (1975–87) pursued a target for the monetary base (central bank money stock), putting much less emphasis than the ECB on rigid pegging of the overnight money market rates (see Leaman, 2001) or on signalling to markets the likely future path of any pegging operations (thereby influencing market rates for longer maturities). That was consistent with a set of principles emphasizing monetary stability of which a stable price level over the very long run would be the accompaniment but with no hang-up about delivering stability of a consumer price index over a two-year period. The erosion of principles at the Bundesbank came largely in the run-up to EMU (and even previously during the consummation of German Monetary Union) when the leadership of that institution became increasingly subject to the overriding European (and German union) objectives of Chancellor Kohl, buttressed by his choice of a monetary chief likely to be compliant with those.

Counter-factual peril – The old Bundesbank would have done better!

It is always dangerous to undertake counter-factual history-making. Even so, it is hard to imagine that without monetary union the member countries either singly or together would have gone down the road of breathing inflation higher. If the monetary order had remained unchanged – with the Bundesbank enjoying hegemony – there might have been some one-off exchange realignments in the late 1990s so that the mark would have fallen in value vis-à-vis some of its main partners. The German price level would not have been under any downward pressure in that event. In any case there is no reason to believe that a staunchly independent and self-confident Bundesbank, not weakened by a train journey to GMU (German Monetary Union) and then EMU, would have been inclined to follow currently popular monetary practice as set by the Bernanke/Greenspan Federal Reserve and praised by the IMF.

The ECB, however, as a new institution, had no such self-assurance or indeed inclination to defy fashion as set by the Federal Reserve. There was no 'old guard' within the new central bank, steeped in alternative monetary doctrine, and ready to do battle with the latest version of monetary populism. The Schroeder Government was siding with Washington on deflation risk (and the need to counter it). ECB officials were enjoying their time in the sun as issuers of the new global money and as partakers in the brainstorming of the annual Federal Reserve research symposium (at Kansas) or like events where the ten Bernanke principles of inflation-targeting (a follow on from the Blinder doctrine whereby the central bank should ignore temperature upswings in asset and credit markets, concentrating instead on goods and services price changes) made up the popular gospel (amid some dissent, most notably from the BIS chief economist, William White). The old Bundesbankers, by contrast, may have decided to just stay at home! (See Brown, 2008, for a statement of the ten Bernanke principles.)

The Bundesbank at this time (2003) was at a low ebb in terms of leadership, direction and exercise of influence. The current president, Ernst Welteke (the successor in 1999 to Hans Tietmeyer, the Bundesbank president who had never raised interest rates and had remained loyal to Chancellor Kohl throughout the five years running up to the launch of EMU, see Marsh, 2009) had been a blatantly political appointment of Chancellor Schroeder. Welteke's rise to the top had run from head of the SPD faction in the Hesse Federal parliament, to regional board member of the Bundesbank (appointed there by Hesse Prime Minister Eichel), to head of the Bundesbank (appointed there by Chancellor Schroeder on the advice of his finance minister, Hans Eichel).

In a counter-factual world in 2003 with a sovereign DM and a 'non-corrupted' Bundesbank still calling the monetary shots for Europe, it is hard to believe that any of the other central banks on their own would have followed the lead of the IMF or Bernanke/Greenspan Fed in deciding to breathe inflation back into their individual economies. If deflation were to in fact materialize in any of these countries outside Germany, a quick effective answer could be a downward adjustment of their currency against the Deutsche mark. There would be no need to take pre-emptive action now to bolster the inflation rate!

So what did Messrs Weber and Tietmeyer actually believe that the ECB had brought to the party? (see p. 144). The authors of the brief do not tell us! As regards Tim Geithner's comment, presumably he would not have made it six months later into the European Slump of winter 2008–9!

It is also dubious whether Professor John Taylor would have made his flattering comment quoted in the brief if interviewed a few months later:

> The biggest success of EMU to date has been to set it up from scratch, to deal with the inherent difficulties of communication and different traditions, and to have a policy apparatus which is basically working well in terms of interest rate decisions. That has to be viewed as a major achievement. It's the first time anything like that has been done.

Surely Professor Taylor as assistant secretary of the Treasury in charge of international affairs under the first Bush Administration (2001–5) was aware of the ECB's decision in spring 2003 to follow its own version of breathing inflation back into the economy (just as the Bernanke/ Greenspan Federal Reserve was doing at the time)? And indeed in his critique published in 2009 of the Federal Reserve's role in the bubble-and-burst he makes explicit reference to the monetary errors in the euro-area at the same time. (These are cast, however, simplistically in terms of whether interest rates were above or below the level specified by the 'Taylor rule' as calculated for the individual member countries, most notably those 'enjoying' warm temperatures in their credit and real estate markets, rather than in terms of faulty monetary principles.)

It is far less clear whether Paul Volcker (not interviewed by the authors of the brief) was so familiar with euro-history when he praised EMU in late 2008 (Volcker, 2008). He told the assembled dignitaries at a conference held in honour of Helmut Schmidt (the German chancellor under which the train to EMU started with the launch in 1978 of the European Monetary System) that

> Today, on the 30th anniversary of the EMS, the world economy faces a new and severe challenge reflected in the volatility of the US dollar and extraordinary pressure on the international financial system. In the midst of the great uncertainties, there is no doubt in my mind that Europe and therefore the world is better able to cope with that crisis by virtue of having achieved a common European currency.

Perhaps this was the type of glib praise which Paul Volcker might have re-considered later if in full possession of present and subsequent facts just as Milton Friedman might have revised subsequently his praise in 2006 (at age 94!) of Alan Greenspan (congratulating him as the Federal Reserve president whose record had refuted his long-run view of that institution as a perennial source of monetary instability).

Claim 6: A bogus comparison of inflation before and after EMU start

The authors of the brief (Cecchetti and Schoenholz) completed their work before the full financial panic developed which formed the back-drop to Paul Volker's favourable comments about EMU. They quote the fact that over the period from 2001 (assuming that ECB policy typically affects prices with a lag of about two years) until the latest data-point available at the time of writing (early 2008), HICP inflation averaged 2.3%. For comparison, in the pre-EMU period of 1991–8, headline inflation averaged 2.6% (but why do they exclude 1999, a year of very low inflation, from the pre-EMU performance measurement, on the same two year principal?):

> Even in Germany, which boasts the pre-eminent pre-EMU inflation track record, inflation has been lower and far more stable in EMU: under the Bundesbank, German inflation averaged 3.4% from 1965 to 1998 (with a standard deviation of 3.4%), while German inflation since 2001 has averaged 1.8% (with a standard deviation of only 0.6%).

Thank you for nothing!

What is the relevance of citing inflation in Germany during the period of the Great Global Inflation of the late 1960s and 1970s, from which Germany made an early exit but only after the final crash of the Bretton Woods system and its brief Smithsonian sequel (in March 1973) allowed the Bundesbank to follow an independent monetary policy?

As to the stability of the inflation rate, that should be a source of suspicion (like the stable returns provided by the Ponzi-schemer!). Central banks which find they are piloting under 'ideal weather con-ditions' of a stable price level for goods and services (or a stable low rate of price level rise) without interruptions should be on raised alert about inducing severe monetary disequilibrium into the system. The avoidance of throwing a monkey wrench of money into the machinery of the economy – by not creating gaps between neutral and market rates – requires some instability in the price level or in the rate of price level change over the short- and medium-run!

Claim 7: ECB did well in the context of 'trying circumstances'

The authors of the report go further in their dubious praise of the ECB's 'inflation record':

> In light of the trying economic circumstances of the past decade, the achievement of low and stable inflation in the euro area most likely reflects good monetary policy, not good fortune. Since its inception, the euro-area experienced large price shocks from developments in energy, commodity and currency markets – not unlike in the Great Inflation episode.

Well, yes, inflation over a very long period – high or low – is deter-mined to a large extent by the monetary regime and how monetary policy is conducted under that regime. But where were the 'trying circumstances'? On two big occasions (1999 and 2003) the ECB deliberately followed a policy of breathing inflation higher. The catalytic role of large price shocks (which may well subsequently reverse), better described as real resource supply shocks, in setting off a long-run process of monetary inflation or deflation is highly questionable. And in the short-run, the various types of real shocks (including sudden resource shortage, or big improvement in terms of trade) affecting an important price (such as energy) should be reflected in overall price level swings if indeed severe monetary disequilibrium is to be avoided.

The Austrian School pointed out long ago that central bank policy action to combat price level swings due to real changes in the economy (for example, terms of trade swings, an acceleration or deceleration of the productivity growth trend, real resource shock or cyclical fluctuations) is a recipe for monetary disequilibrium of which the chief symptom (after a potentially long and variable lag) might well be asset and credit markets overheating or cooling down excessively (see p. 9).

Take the ideal situation where money rates might fluctuate considerably with much white noise but where this (and more generally money) does not get in the way of the market estimating efficiently the neutral rates of interest and of setting rates for medium or long maturities at a level close to the respective neutral level. Then there would be significant upward and downward shifts in the rate of price level change (positive or negative) over the short- and medium-run, but no serious and prolonged monetary inflation or deflation. (Note that if very long run expectations of the price level are anchored at an average rate of increase of around 1% p.a. and that is indeed the aim as specified by the central bank, then that outcome is not technically 'monetary inflation' in the sense of stemming from monetary disequilibrium – see p. 68.)

Claim 8: EMU promotes regional and financial efficiency

The authors of the brief make no mention of Austrian School concepts (which descend from the monetary analysis of J. S. Mill). It is not surprising therefore that they make no connection between the credit bubble bursting process already evident in Europe from summer 2007 and earlier mistakes in euro-monetary policy. Nor do the authors relate the dynamics of the bubble to euphoria (about profits in the financial sector) bred by the euro's creation (and all the talk about the benefits of financial integration). Instead they comment:

> By securing price stability, ECB policy contributed indirectly to many other advances in euro-area welfare.
>
> One example is the progress in capital markets and the financial system. Government bond markets appear to have been largely integrated at a very early stage in EMU. The rapid expansion of markets for corporate bonds and for many derivative instruments over the past decade partly reflected the stable euro-area economic environment.
>
> The breadth and depth of these markets facilitate the efficient allocation of savings in the region. The gradual evolution toward banking integration also contributes to regional efficiency.

It is not clear what regional efficiency is being referred to here – surely not the facilitation of lending from the savings surplus countries in Europe (principally Germany) towards the countries 'enjoying' bubbles in credit (including the government sector) and real estate market (big examples include Spain and the UK). This transfer assumed such massive proportions due to a fundamental lack of recognition (whether by the institutions involved or their shareholders) of the credit risks involved, not least in the inter-bank markets (see p. 38).

Claim 9: ECB deserves praise for its response to August 2007 quake!

The authors of the brief move on to discuss the issue of the ECB's role in financial stability and regulation and generally absolve it of responsibility so far. Indeed they even shower some praise on the ECB:

> In the area of liquidity provision as a lender of last resort, recent experience has highlighted important ECB successes. In August 2007, the ECB boosted liquidity supply early and aggressively to counter sharp increases in funding rates as banks turned cautious and alternative private sources of funding shut down. The ECB's Bagehot-style marginal lending facility (MLF, designed to cap overnight rates in normal times) can be viewed as an automatic mechanism for calming liquidity fears in a crisis. [...] It seems fair to conclude that the ECB's toolkit for liquidity supply has been crisis-tested and satisfies current 'best practice' standards among central banks.

Well, that is light-years away from the conclusion reached in our last chapter that the ECB's application of the bogus separation principle, meaning the injection of massive amounts of sterilized liquidity at subsidized rates while fostering simultaneously a rise in risk-free rates (rather than allowing a sharp fall), was utterly counter-productive, both from the viewpoint of monetary stability and financial system stabilization.

The alternative course would have been to clear the way for an immediate fall of risk-free rate to zero, which would have made possible a sharp widening of margins on profitable loan business (where margins are measured relative to the rate banks able to offer well-equity cushioned deposits would have paid on these) and inducing thereby an early re-capitalization of still solvent banks (see Chapter 3). In the same spirit, the involvement of the ECB in providing US dollar funding to European banks who found the supply of repo-financing largely from US money market funds suddenly drying up should have been on an emergency basis only.

These (European) banks should have been forced at the earliest date feasible to replace these sources from a non-bubble source. Money market funds were a bubble source because they turned on investors in these funds believing irrationally that they could never fall below $1 in the dollar, and on the fund managers themselves mis-appraising the risk of repo-business with European banks – seeing these as risk-free when in aggregate they could not be repaid on demand. Forcing viable banks back into the markets beyond an immediate emergency period would have been close to the Bagehot principle. It was not the course which the ECB actually followed.

Claim 10: Passing the buck

One point which has been made in the ECB's defence against the charge that it promoted financial instability is that it lost the battle (due to no fault of its own) early in the decade for any strengthening of its supervisory authority.

Under the Eichel–Brown initiative of July 2002, EU governments and finance ministers, given their greater democratic accountability, were ultimately to be responsible for 'policing' financial institutions and financial markets. The Bundesbank in particular and also the ECB lost out at that time in the political competition as to who was to be responsible for the supposedly growing pan-European regulatory system. None of this means that the ECB or Bundesbank would have done a better job than what actually happened, but at least they have an excuse when it comes to the 'what went wrong with the regulators' discussion!

And on the subject of excuses, the authors have a few of these up their sleeves! They quote for example Otmar Issing:

> What is unique for the ECB is the complex environment. [...] The ECB still is a young institution, and the euro area is very complex, not least due to the language and communication problem.

Few would argue with that assertion. But were these problems sufficiently highlighted by the advocates of EMU before its creation and have they shown us the offsetting benefits which have accrued?

The authors also raise the hypothesis (which could in part exonerate the ECB but not EMU) that the euro-area might be a sub-optimal currency area, complicating thereby the conducting of a one-fit-all monetary policy:

> Risks remain because potential growth is low, labour markets are relatively rigid, and there is little scope for fiscal burden sharing. Moreover as Vice-president Papademos describes, some countries – including Greece, Italy and Portugal – exhibit divergent trends in the growth of unit labour costs that appear to diminish their competitiveness. [...] The ECB cannot alter its policy rate for the purpose of limiting economic divergence or to boost growth sustainably above potential.

The possibility – or indeed likelihood – that the euro-area is not an optimal currency area may indeed alleviate the blame for sub-optimal outcomes which should be borne by the ECB policymakers, but not by the creators of EMU. And there had been no shortage of warnings ahead of EMU that it might not be an optimal currency area. The authors do not pursue any line of defence against that charge (of EMU being a non-optimal currency area).

Claim 11: Pride and satisfaction in hard effort

The brief concludes with a summary which is highly favourable towards the EMU and ECB:

> Our ECB interviewees rightly express pride and satisfaction in their accomplishment. Literally thousands of people worked diligently for years to make monetary union not only a reality, but a success. It is difficult to find major fault with the operational framework or the monetary policy decisions of the first decade of EMU.

[...] The Maastricht Treaty ventured where no vessel had gone before, but it has worked well. That success presumably owes to the design and the crew, not to the lack of turbulence.

The readers of the first three chapters of this book know already the main planks of the counter-case to this glowing summary of the defence arguments.

An additional element (in the counter-case) has to be the sheer smugness of the leading officials in EMU, and their blindness (at least in anything public) to the charges against them. That lack of self-criticism – or of real (as against staged) exposure to vibrant and powerful criticism from outside (some of which might filter emanate from a well-function liberal political system able to seek retribution for mistakes and meaningful remedies, including the occasional 'killing of the admiral to encourage the others') – has been a salient feature of the first decade of EMU, especially as the flaws appeared crevasse-deep once the credit bubble burst.

ECB officials are not unique in smugness or in making serious errors of judgement (just take a look at the history of the Federal Reserve!). Much the same criticism can be justifiably levelled at other major central banks as regards the emergence of the financial crisis and their subsequent reactions. But as a new union with lofty ideals, could more not have been expected from Europe? There lies a main disappointment.

Towards buttressing the negative case against EMU as outlined in previous chapters and refuting the positive case put together in the Cecchetti brief, we now turn to direct evidence of what the leading actors had to say. Let us start with President Jean-Claude Trichet.

Introduction to testimony of Jean-Claude Trichet

In an anniversary (tenth) interview with Börsen Zeitung on 16 December 2008, President Trichet had the following favourable comments to make:

> As a symbol of European unity, the euro is already extremely successful. Since the outbreak of the financial crisis, the euro and the ECB have become, even more visibly, a central anchor for confidence. In this sense, I believe the emotional relationship of citizens to the euro has become stronger.
>
> [...] For me, the greatest success of the euro is that after having promised the citizens that the euro would be equal in terms of

stability and the maintenance of value to the previously most solid currencies we have fulfilled this promise effectively.

Unfortunately the interviewer does not pick up any of the broad indictments against the ECB and EMU made here or elsewhere but does pluck up courage to ask:

Q: Knowing what we do now, was the interest rate increase in July this year (2008) a mistake? And why is it generally so difficult for central bankers to admit to mistakes?

A: Long-term inflation expectations threatened to become unanchored. In addition, wage and salary demands in some euro area countries caused us serious concern that there could be broadbased second-round effects. The interest rate decision enabled us to bring medium to long-term inflation expectations back under control in line with our definition of price stability. And this regained control of expectations was, by the way, the precondition which allowed us to cut rates strongly from October when the crisis worsened. Do not forget: our definition of price stability in the medium term is 'less than, but close to, 2%'. The interest rate increase in July must be related to the 'less than 2%' part. Our recent decrease of rates after the intensification of the crisis in September must be related to 'close to 2%'.

We can realize immediately that M. Trichet gave no answer to the second part of the question and the interviewer did not follow it up!

Let us consider the answer to the first part of the question, which was in any case tame (why ask about an almost meaningless 25 bp hike in rates when the big question should have been why the risk-free rate was then being pegged at 4.5% or higher, rather than zero!).

The straight reply (albeit to the tame question) would have been – yes, if we the ECB had made the correct diagnoses in spring and summer 2008 that the oil market was in a bubble and the euro-area already in recession (from January) with a significant risk ahead of financial panic, there could have been no question of a rate hike in July. And our concerns about wage-pressures were misplaced, still influenced by events in a bygone age when labour markets had been extremely tight and anchor to low inflation expectations set loose well before any oil shock.

Instead M. Trichet provides justifications for the severe monetary tightness of spring and summer 2008 which could not convince even the most credulous! Who, other than a professor of philology, could really be interested in the exposition about the difference between less than 2% and close to 2%? This is inflation-targeting gone mad, in the worst senses possible as ever imagined by Milton Friedman or the Austrian School! And yet ECB officials continued to repeat the mantra about a monetary pillar to its operating framework which distinguished the ECB from the inflation-targeting central banks.

The most outrageous claim of M. Trichet

Could anyone really believe a subsequent claim made by M. Trichet in Strasbourg on 13 January (2009) at a ceremony of the European Parliament to mark the tenth anniversary of the euro?

M. Trichet:

> In recent months we have seen another benefit of the euro: the financial crisis is demonstrating that in turbulent financial waters it is better to be on a large, solid and steady ship rather than on a small vessel.
>
> Would Europe have been able to act as swiftly, decisively and coherently if we did not have the single currency uniting us?
>
> Would we have been able to protect many separate national currencies from the fallout of the financial crisis?
>
> I believe that we can be proud of the reaction of the European authorities, parliaments, government and central banks, Together we have shown that Europe is capable of taking decisions, even in the most difficult circumstances!

It is difficult, in fact impossible, to make sense of this claim.

What was solid about the euro-ship as its members plunged into deep recession and its financial system froze in the aftermath of the Lehman bankruptcy shock? And without the shackles of EMU, some countries could have bailed out into smaller boats (cutting their interest rates and devaluing).

Instead they were all being driven into the storm centre by ECB pilots among whom the most powerful included a president renowned for inflexible toughness in France's long run-in to EMU and Bundesbankers (one ex-Bundesbanker) still convinced in early 2008 that Germany was in boom (a conviction based on the reality that indeed Germany's export bonanza was lagging the world business cycle). Even in summer 2008, these pilots were worried stiff about wage-led inflation.

As a matter of fact, a small non-EU non-euro European country was faring better (in terms of avoiding severity of the downturn) than any euro-area member – Switzerland (whose central bank had to a moderate extent eased policy while the ECB and BoE were still allowing monetary conditions to tighten in 2008H1 and then in late 2008 had moved to a zero rate policy).

And to what swift decisive and coherent action could M. Trichet possibly be referring? The only candidate was the action authorized from (but probably not initiated from – see p. 95) his holiday home in early August 2007 to lend unlimited amounts (collateralized) in the midst of the 'seizing up' of inter-bank markets. It has been argued here (see Chapter 3) that that was totally the wrong decision. (And a similar point has been made in the US context by Taylor, 2009.)

As for the national currencies to which the ECB would have been unable to offer protection, M. Trichet is most probably referring here to the counter-factual world of say Italy and Spain having their own currencies. If these had still existed and they had dropped sharply as the economic and financial climate worsened especially with respect to their own circumstances that (devaluation) would have given a fillip to their economic recovery prospects compared to the alternative prospect which now loomed of Brüning-type policy (cutting back spending within a recession so as to maintain solvency of the state).

M. Trichet's warnings and the warning which he ignored

Indeed in reviewing other evidence in the form of President Trichet's spoken comments, a 'patting on the back' or self-congratulatory aspect is often there. He told the Fifth ECB Central Banking Conference in mid-November 2008 that he was one of the policymakers to realize early that credit markets had warmed to a dangerous level. He dated his own warnings to 2006 when he was chairman of the Global Economy Meetings of Central Bank Governors:

> We knew that a storm was brewing but, admittedly, we did not know exactly where. Neither did we know what would trigger it, or when it would come.

This is an amazing statement.

If M. Trichet and his other central bank colleagues were so aware of the looming dangers why were there no contingency plans to fit different possible scenarios? And why did the ECB make no effort to identify practices within the European banking field which might be the source of danger (for example, the off-balance sheet vehicles used for getting round the BIS capital requirements, lack of prudence in the inter-bank markets as regards credit exposure, European banks' dependence on overnight funding in the dollar repo markets where the source was primarily US money market funds etc.)? Once identified, these practices should have been the subject of discussions, as initiated by the ECB within the constitutional remits of the Maastricht Treaty, with the relevant authorities in Brussels or with member governments.

Should there not have been more urgent consideration given to a more assertive monetary policy, putting a higher probability on evidence of rapid money and credit growth being symptomatic of serious monetary disequilibrium and less fixation on inflation-targeting (by any other name)? Perhaps 2006 was already too late.

M. Trichet could not deny that he had been warned early on about the possible consequences of the US residential real estate market bubble. Back in November 2005 at his regular monthly press conference a reporter had posed the following question:

Q: May I put a question in French? I am from Canada. In the communiqué you said that you were looking at the situation and there's a lot of uncertainty at the moment. In this case, I would like to know whether you are worried about the real estate bubble in the US and whether you think that the situation could get even worse and if it were to get worse would you change your position?

Trichet: On this precise point I would only say that I signed the last statement of the G7. We had a consensus [...] that each continent and each major industrialised economy had its own homework to do. As far as Europe is concerned for us the homework is structural reforms. Structural reforms which we all think are absolutely essential. Looking at the US, it is quite clear that their main problem is the fact that savings in the US economy are far too low. So we agree as far as the diagnoses are concerned and we agree that these defects have to be corrected. We also agree that we have to correct them in the most resolute way possible. That is all what I would like to say on that point, but it is quite clear that there are defects that have to be rectified in all the major international economies.

Note that M. Trichet does not answer the question about real estate market bubble at all!

What he does provide is the well-trodden mantras about each country doing its homework, without any mention of the serious monetary errors which were in fact occurring in both Europe and the US and for which central banks were responsible (but they are not responsible for savings behaviour and structural reform!).

At the time of this question the ECB had just made its first tiny rate rise from the absurdly low level of 2%. The official rate (and related market rates) had been stuck since 2003 in spite of accumulating evidence of rising temperature in European credit and real estate markets and other symptoms of monetary disequilibrium (see Chapter 3). And why was M. Trichet so sure that 'low savings' were the real big problem for the US economy rather just one symptom of a growing and huge monetary disequilibrium created by the Bernanke/Greenspan strategy of breathing inflation back in?

In fact in his pride about having spotted credit market heating at an early stage, M. Trichet told a specially convened meeting of the EU's economic and monetary commission on 11 September 2007 (where he was to explain the massive ECB lending operations undertaken in August 2007) that already in the first issue of the *ECB Financial Stability Review*, published in December 2004:

> We had said that a high level of risk appetite was encouraging a search for yield amongst investors across a wide range of markets and asset classes.

The rest of that particular address (of 11 September 2007) was the customary pat on the back for action taken – action which we have argued here was highly damaging both in terms of economic and financial outcome (see p. 110). Suffice it to say that in retrospect at least M. Trichet made the following self-damning comment (with respect to ECB policymaking):

> We have considered that our monetary policy stance is still on the accommodative side.

That was just four months before the onset (January 2008) of euro-area recession, in the wake of a giant quake in the credit markets amid all the signs of a credit bubble now bursting (except for the ECB's data on bank lending which continued to grow for some months as bank intermediation grew in partial offset to rapid shrinkage of shadow banking system) and with money market rates up at 5%!

M. Trichet defends the indefensible separation principle

More of similar misdiagnosis can be found in President Trichet's press conference of September 2007. In particular Trichet introduced to his listeners (or viewers) the erroneous separation principle – whereby the ECB had one set of policies for dealing with illiquidity in the money market and another for price level stability:

> Let us not confuse the appropriate functioning of the money market and the monetary policy stance. [...] It is very important to make a clear separation between these two factors. [...] In what is observed today, there are elements of correction that were diagnosed before the correction took place (I could find first pages of financial papers in which I had expressed that opinion) and, as is very often the case in such circumstances there are hectic episodes in this correction, there is a level of volatility that can be quite high and there is also a large deal of overshooting. Again, we have to play a very important role in the central bank constituency, in both having the preoccupation of the medium and long-term solid anchoring of inflation expectations, and having a good understanding of what the pertinent trends are in the medium and long-term, of the global economy and of each particular economy; and on the other hand having to care for the appropriate functioning of the money market.

A journalist did in fact take up the separation principle, albeit only in a fleeting way (this is no criticism of the journalist, given the time and other constraints):

> Q: The ECB makes a clear-cut distinction between liquidity help for the money market and monetary policy in the medium term. Some economists argue that it is not really possible to make this distinction and that you have to use monetary policy, let's say the interest rate instrument, to rebuild confidence in the financial markets. What would you say to these people? What is your argument on that?
>
> A: As I said, we have our responsibilities. If we were to tell the market that the short-term consideration are now such that we are hampering our medium-term responsibility, then we would not

improve the situation, but make it worse. The dis-anchoring of inflation expectations would probably be the worst thing that we could do in the present circumstances.

There were two key issues not confronted by M. Trichet (or evidently by his fellow policymakers).

First, the bursting of the credit bubble had surely gone along with a substantial lowering of level of the risk-free interest rate in the euro-area which was consistent with overall equilibrium (even though it was possible that simultaneously the equilibrium cost of risky capital would have risen and it was a matter of debate how far the average interest rate across all risk-categories had fallen).

Second, the choice of the overnight money market and one interest rate there as the appropriate operating target of monetary policy was particularly destabilizing. The heterogeneity of credit-risks between banks even with respect to overnight borrowing meant that rates there were now summarized by a fan (if not artificially restricted) rather than by one rate applicable to all.

M. Trichet on the startling misdiagnosis of September 2007

In this September 2007 press conference, M. Trichet assured his audience that sharp US slowdown (or recession) would not have big impact on the euro-area. In his initial briefing he stated that:

Global economic activity is expected to remain robust, as the likely slowdown in the US is expected to be largely offset by the continued strong growth in emerging markets. This will continue to provide support to euro-area exports and investment. In addition, consumption growth in the euro-area should strengthen further over time, in line with developments in real disposable income, as employment conditions improve further.

It seemed like an occupational hazard for the ECB to expect on the eve of recession (whether in late 2000/early 2001 or late 2007) that the euro-area would be on the edge of the storm. Perhaps the hazard stretches back to the run-up to EMU when one main plank of the advocates (of EMU) was that Europe would be more sheltered from US shock (in consequence of monetary union). Already there were grounds in summer 2007 for doubting this hypothesis given the revelation of the extent to which the European banks had become caught up in the global credit bubble including its key US component.

M. Trichet's ignoring of US monetary danger

The fact that the ECB had turned off all alarm bells that might ring in response to US monetary events had already become clear as far back as July 2004 in the course of a press conference given by M. Trichet. Here was revealing question-and-answer for those listening carefully:

> Q: Mr. Trichet, does the move of the Federal Reserve yesterday (July 1. 2004, the first rate rise – in effect by a trivial amount – since the 'breathing in inflation policy' had been adopted by the Greenspan/Bernanke Fed) to raise interest rates influence or effect the ECB's decision in any way?
>
> A: We all have responsibility, all over the world. Certainly across the Atlantic the Federal Reserve has a very important responsibility, and it is not my responsibility to elaborate on that. We have our own responsibility: the US is the US and the euro area is the euro area! We are in different universes with different fundamentals and different episodes in the business cycle. Furthermore, we are both responsible for price stability in these different universes. So we are not influenced in any way by what has been decided across the Atlantic or what has been decided across the Channel, or what has been decided elsewhere in the world. Because of our own analysis of the present situation in the euro area, we have not changed our monetary policy stance. Again, on the basis of European judgement and diagnosis, we have no bias and we remain vigilant.

Of course we must be careful about over-interpreting statements in question-and-answer sessions at press conferences.

Perhaps if M. Trichet had had time to reflect and edit he would not have agreed with everything he said on the spur of the moment! Even so one obvious critique of this interchange is that M. Trichet and his ECB colleagues were deluding themselves about their independence or the independence of the euro-area from strong US influence.

Yes, in principle, the ECB could have composed an entirely different framework of monetary policy from the US, but it chose not to do so, and in fact in spring 2003 had mimicked the strategy of seeking to prevent inflation from falling too low. So what could M. Trichet possibly mean by saying 'we are not influenced by decisions across the

Atlantic'. This could be true only in the trivial sense of whether there would be a 25 bp rise in policy rates this month! Given the similarity of monetary framework on both sides of the Atlantic, and the considerable interdependence of credit market conditions, M. Trichet should have been taking more notice of US monetary actions or non-actions! The likelihood was that if one key segment of the credit market universe was overheating – in this case the US – something similar was happening in the European segment also!

The criticism follows from all of this that EMU had itself bred a complacency of insularity within the ECB, while in fact both the ECB itself and European financial markets had become more intertwined with US developments and fashions than in the pre-EMU decade. And one key factor which had increased the interdependence of US and European credit and monetary developments was the ECB's concern during 2004–5 about the strength of the euro against the dollar.

M. Trichet wears old hat of French currency diplomat

A rise of the euro towards 1.30 against the dollar triggered crisis activity at the head of the ECB, with M. Trichet (appointed president in autumn 2003) revelling in his old role of G7 diplomat, this time seeking to negotiate a fall back of the euro and rise of the East Asian currencies – see p. 46. That alarmist response to the euro's climb against the dollar is perplexing from the perspective of early 2008 when the ECB seemed totally calm about the euro heading for 1.60 despite the euro-area economy already being in recession!

The alarm ringing out loud at the Eurotower (in 2004), triggered by the rise of the euro against the dollar, neutralized any better inclinations policymakers there may have had towards charting an independent course (from the Federal Reserve) amid the evidence of credit and real estate market temperature rising.

M. Trichet had told a questioner at the February 2005 press conference that:

> In the euro-area – and it is the euro area as a whole that we have to look at – we have signs that credit dynamism might foster increases in the real estate sector. And this calls for vigilance.

There was, however, no rise in rates – and then only by a trivial 25 bp – until near the end of the year.

At the December 2004 news conference just two months earlier, M. Trichet had told his audience that he considered recent rises of the euro as 'unwelcome' and 'brutal'.

The message – also confirmed in individual discussions by the author with ECB officials – was that the ECB was holding back from tightening monetary policy because of the strength of the euro. The rationalization was that the strong euro would mean first, lower than otherwise inflation and second, weaker than otherwise aggregate demand (taking account of pressure downwards on profits in some key industrial sectors, perhaps most of all in Germany). Both shifts should translate into a downward adjustment of so-called neutral and natural rate levels for the euro-area as a whole.

The hazard in such a line of analysis was to exaggerate the significance of a likely transitory swing in exchange rates on inflation expectations and equilibrium real interest rates in the euro area. The ECB in responding to the near-term good news on inflation by delaying rate rises could destroy the potential insulation created by monetary independence against European credit markets heating up in response to the fire lit by the Federal Reserve.

ECB officials – at least those who spoke about such matters on the record – just did not see it that way. They diagnosed the euro's rise and the dollar's weakness as symptomatic of 'global imbalances' which had to be corrected.

Testimony of Professor Jürgen Stark

Monetary historians could imagine that Bundesbank officials would be least sympathetic to the concern about global imbalances given the long tradition within that institution during its heydays (1960–86?) of emphasizing potential clashes between external and internal stability (and the importance of keeping the focus on the latter). And indeed the German successor in June 2006 to Otmar Issing on the ECB Board (with more restricted power in that President Trichet used the transition to divide Issing's research and economics empire into two), ex-Bundesbank Vice-Chairman Professor Jürgen Stark, put it like this (10 December 2008, speech):

> The mandate of the ECB is to maintain price stability over the medium term. The mandate must be adhered to both in normal times and in times of crisis. The monetary policy stance appropriate to fulfil the ECB's mandate depends exclusively on its assessment of the balance of risks to price stability and nothing else.

In so far as this oblique statement meant not being diverted by stabilizing the exchange rate at the cost of internal stability that was strictly according to long-established Bundesbank principle and practice.

The disturbing element was the implication that Professor Stark, even at this late date, was unready to countenance the possibility that the framework of inflation-targeting or quasi-inflation targeting as designed by the ECB (never adopted by the Bundesbank when sovereign) had been basically flawed, as the Austrian economists had long maintained, and as BIS Chief Economist Bill White had argued during the period of the global credit warming.

Instead Professor Stark came out with the same paper-thin mantra as President Trichet:

> We should not forget how Europe would look today without the euro. The euro-area countries would be significantly worse off. Multiple crises would arise simultaneously; currency crises would go hand in hand with banking crises and real economy disruptions at country level, potentially ending up in political tensions between countries. [...] By eliminating the exchange rate channel, the euro has mitigated the risk of contagion stemming from national economic or financial crises. In this sense, the euro has been a very important stabilizing element in difficult times.

Saying something over and over again though is no proof!

As an ex-Bundesbanker, Professor Stark seemed to be surprisingly unaware of the counter-argument which could be put forward by the euro-sceptics, some of which had occupied the highest positions of authority in the Old Bundesbank, about how the euro might well have made the crisis worse (see p. 113).

And Professor Stark was certainly not above repeating the mantra about global imbalances being a scourge in the international economic environment and how this had been an important factor in the generation of the US 'central component' of the global credit bubble. He had done so in comments made a month earlier (18 November to the 11th Euro finance week, 2008) about the role of global imbalances in the crisis. His speech had started with an introductory quote from Goethe:

> Error repeats itself endlessly in deeds. Therefore we must repeat the truth tirelessly in words.

To be fair, this quote seemed to be attached to the section of his speech on macro-economic matters rather than the repetition of the mantra about global imbalances.

In the speech, Professor Stark dwelt on the contribution of macro-economic policy to the crisis in Europe, not just in the US, but ostensibly avoided pointing the finger at monetary policy:

> Expansionary macroeconomic policies around the globe have contributed to the build-up of macroeconomic imbalances. These policies have facilitated the strong credit expansion, excessive house price increases and the build-up of large current account imbalances, in particular in the US but also in other regions including some euro-area countries.

Testimony of Christian Noyer

Banque de France Governor and ex-vice chair of the ECB, Christian Noyer, displayed no such inner pangs of conscience when he added his voice to the anniversary chorus of self-acclamation in a speech in early autumn 2008 (10 October) under the title of *A Founder's Perspective on the Euro as a Global Currency* (before the Peterson Institute for International Economics in Washington). Here are snippets of his self-congratulatory remarks:

> Actually, one of the main gratifications of the job during the crisis has been the quality of our collective interaction and deliberation in the Governing Council, based on our willingness, in very challenging circumstances, to share judgements and exchange views in a spirit of friendship and mutual respect. (Author's comment: if so proud, why the obsessive secrecy which blocks all record of the discussions from ever seeing the light of day!). I am very proud to be part of such a group. [...] Overall, it is fair to say that the euro has passed the test and comes strengthened out of the current difficulties. The Eurosystem will keep fulfilling its priority mandate of price stability while also contributing to the broader objective of financial stability. [...] So the eurozone has shown it is well-equipped to live up to its responsibilities as a truly global player in the international monetary system of the 21st century.

Did ECB and Fed throw a monkey wrench?

Let us step back from these self-congratulatory exclamations to one of the biggest underlying issues in appraising central bank performance in the euro-area through the middle years of its first decade.

Was the global credit bubble which formed at this time stimulated in large part by policies of monetary disequilibrium in the US and Europe?

Or are the apologists for the US and European central banks correct in claiming that the fundamental source of disequilibrium lay outside the monetary arena and in fact stemmed from 'unsustainable global imbalances' (code word for excess saving in East Asia and in some accounts undersaving in the US)?

In assessing the role of the ECB in creating monetary disequilibrium and the contribution of that to bubbles in credit markets and real estate markets there is no realistic alternative to constructing a joint test for the ECB and Federal Reserve.

Did both central banks, together following similar policies, play a key role in global credit market warm-up? If yes, then we can consider the follow-up counter-factual question of whether the ECB, following a quite different policy stance from the Federal Reserve, could have exerted a cooling influence on global credit markets, most of all within Europe.

Alan Greenspan denies Fed (or ECB) to blame

The most eloquent defender of the view that central banks do not share responsibility (via their monetary stance) for the global credit bubble comes from ex–Federal Reserve Chairman Alan Greenspan. That is surprising in one respect.

If Greenspan could bring himself to concede that central bank monetary error played a large role – that to use J. S. Mill's metaphor they (the central bankers) threw a giant money wrench into the machinery of the economy – then that would remove the floor from below those critics who argue that a more fundamental flaw of free market economics was to blame (such as essential inefficiencies in global capital markets or the impossibility of the market 'matching' high savings propensities in East Asia with investment opportunity in the wider world).

Yet to provide that rescue for liberalism such as would be consistent with the Ayn Rand idealism which he long ago espoused, Greenspan would have to admit his policy was at fault – or at very least that he had unwisely allowed his better judgement to be swayed in 2003 by the bad advice from Professor Ben Bernanke, then the new Governor just arrived from Princeton University. There is absolutely no evidence on public record that Greenspan has made such admission even to himself.

Greenspan rejects the view that over-easy money policy was to blame by pointing to the fact that long-term interest rates remained at a modest level even once the Federal Reserve started to raise its key overnight rate from late-mid 2004 onwards. He attributes this (lack of long-term rate response) to the huge surplus of savings in East Asia. To quote from his *Wall Street Journal* article of 11 March 2009 ('The Fed Didn't Cause the Housing Bubble'):

There are at least two broad and competing explanations of the origins of the crisis. The first is that 'easy money' policies of the Federal Reserve produced the US housing bubble. The second, and far more credible, explanation agrees that it was indeed lower interest rates that spawned the speculative euphoria. However, the interest rate that mattered was not the federal-funds rate, but the rate on long-term, fixed-rate mortgages. Between 2002 and 2005, home mortgage rates led US home price change by 11 months. This correlation between home prices and mortgage rates was highly significant and a far better indicator of rising home prices than the fed-funds rate. This should not come as a surprise. After all, the prices of long-lived assets have always been determined by discounting the flow of income by interest rates of the same maturities as the assets. No-one to my knowledge employs overnight interest rates to determine the capitalization rate of real estate.

The Federal Reserve became acutely aware of the disconnect between monetary policy and mortgage rates when the latter failed to respond as expected to the Fed tightening in mid-2004. Moreover, the data show that home mortgage rates had become gradually decoupled from monetary policy even earlier – in the wake of the emergence around the turn of this century of a well arbitraged global market for long-term debt instruments. [...] Between 1971 and 2002 the fed funds rate and the mortgage rate moved in lockstep. The correlation between them was a tight 0.85. Between 2002 and 2005, however, the correlation diminished to insignificance.

The presumptive cause of the world-wide decline in long-term rates was the tectonic shift in the early 1990s by much of the developing world from heavy emphasis on central planning to increasingly dynamic, export-led market competition. The result was a surge in growth in China and a large number of other emerging market economies that led to an excess of global intended savings related to intended capital investment. That ex ante excess of savings propelled global long-term interest rates progressively lower between early

2000 and 2005. That decline in long-term interest rates across a wide spectrum of countries statistically explains and is the most likely major cause of real estate capitalization rates that declined and converged across the globe resulting in the global housing price bubble.

Before taking issue with this defence claim by Alan Greenspan, let's join it with the claims of his successor to the chair of the Federal Reserve.

Ben Bernanke adamant that central banks did not create bubble

Greenspan's successor at the top of the Federal Reserve, Professor Ben Bernanke, expanded on the same line of explanation, notably in a speech in spring 2009 (Morehouse College, Atlanta, Georgia). Modelling his enquiry on the 'four questions' of the Passover Haggadah, he asked the key opening question:

How did we get here? What caused our financial and economic system to break down to the extent it has?

Then simplicity gives way to complexity, always a dangerous sign! Bernanke continues:

The answer to this question is complex. Experts disagree on how much weight to give various explanations. In my view, we need to consider how global patterns of saving and investment have evolved over the past decade or more, and how those changes affected credit markets in the US and some other countries. [...] In the past 10 to 15 years, the US and some other industrial countries have been the recipients of a great deal of foreign saving. Much of this foreign saving came from fast-growing emerging market countries in Asia and other places where consumption has lagged behind rising incomes, as well as from oil exporting countries that could not profitably invest all their revenue at home. The net inflow of foreign saving to the US, which was about 1.5% of GDP in 1995 reached about 6% of national output in 2006, an amount equal to about $825bn in today's dollars. Saving inflows from abroad can be beneficial if the country that receives those inflows invests them well. Unfortunately that was not always the case in the United States and some other countries. Financial institutions reacted to the surplus of available funds by competing aggressively for borrowers and in the years leading up to the crisis credit to both households and businesses became relatively cheap and easy to obtain.

Refuting the evidence of Messrs Greenspan and Bernanke

Let us step back to Greenspan's alleged disconnect between long-term and short-term interest rates before returning on the further elaboration by Bernanke. A first general point is that the lack of close correlation between long-term and short-term rates in the years 2002–5 is not quite a conundrum.

Long-term rates already discounted some scepticism or even rejection by late 2003 of the deflation risk story put out by the IMF and central bankers. (The discounting was evident in the steep yield curve, illustrated by long-maturity yields being far above short. Long maturity yields had jumped through the second half of 2003 on growing evidence of a growth cycle upturn in the US economy and a fading of deflation concerns in the marketplace if not in the Federal Reserve.) The historically unique policy of deliberately breathing inflation back into the US economy (especially in the context of such scepticism as to its appropriateness) was likely to bring some perturbations of the normal relationship between short- and long-term rates. The fact that long-maturity yields did not climb further in 2004–5 as the Federal Reserve eventually proceeded with its long series of micro-adjustments upwards of the Federal Funds rate is consistent with the simple hypothesis that this policy had already been discounted. In this episode the Federal Reserve had laid out more precisely its projected path over the short- and medium-term for its official short-term rate peg than at any previous time in its history. (Indeed in earlier episodes there had still been the idea that money rates were to a considerable degree unpredictable, even by the central bankets, and dependent on supply and demand conditions in the money market so as to be consistent with a given stipulated path for money supply growth.)

Moreover, central bank policy explanations can themselves influence the expectations formation process that determines far out interest rates in the term structure of rates. The broadcasting of the 'Asian savings glut' and its hypothesized downward influence on equilibrium interest rates – emphasized by the central bankers themselves in many of their speeches and commentaries, especially Governor Bernanke – surely played some role in containing any rise of long-term rates as the economic expansion built up through 2004–5 (even though the hypothesis, as we shall see, was highly dubious).

The thrust of Federal Reserve action at this time in driving market rates (for medium and even long maturities) well below neutral level may have contributed towards a general lowering of risk premiums (see below) including a gradual downward movement of the inflation risk premium implicit in long-maturity conventional government bond yields.

Finally, a brake on the rise of long-maturity US government bond yields, as the temperature continued to rise in real estate and credit markets and the economy boomed might have been a growing concern in some segments of market opinion that there would be an eventual serious recession and financial crisis when the bubbles eventually burst! If the long-maturity yields were compared with likely much lower rates of price level increase (or even decrease) into the post-bubble aftermath, they were already remarkably high in real terms.

In sum, it is totally implausible that the lack of close correlation between long- and short-maturity interest rates proves that Federal Reserve actions had little or nothing to do with the level of long-term interest rates during 2003–5. The links between the two were as vibrant as ever, but in combination they produced the statistical appearance of non-correlation for some extended period of time as mentioned by Alan Greenspan. Also implausible is the view that East Asian savings surpluses in any case could have shifted the global equilibrium level of interest rates (neutral or natural) down by a large margin.

Numerical proofs are full of holes here. The estimates put together by the balance of payments statisticians on the Asian surpluses relate to observed magnitudes and these might (in a situation of economic disequilibrium) be quite different from the underlying surpluses. And there are giant measurement problems even with respect to the estimation process.

In particular, it is quite possible that though China's recorded savings and current account surpluses at their peak were running at \$400–500 bn p.a., the underlying surplus was less than half of this.

Over 50% of China's savings surplus was in its business sector, where largely state-controlled corporations were building up mountains of retained profits (with no distribution of dividends to shareholders) out of an export bonanza to the US fuelled by (among other things) excessive monetary ease there. Indeed there was some rationality to this behaviour. The Communist Party-appointed managers realized earlier than many US managers (in Detroit especially!) that the bonanza could not last, and that they should behave like the ant rather than the grasshopper. And into the subsequent recession, the ability of the ants to spend exerted a stabilizing influence on the global economy!

There is a purely statistical point to note in the downplaying of the mega-Chinese trade surplus in the mid-2000s. The officially recorded trade and savings surpluses of China were an overstatement of reality due to the widespread use of trade invoicing techniques (under-recording imports, over-recording exports) by Chinese corporations to circumvent restrictions on borrowing funds abroad (mainly in US dollars) so as to speculate on continued appreciation of the yuan.

So as illustration let us assume that no more than a $200 bn increase in the underlying Chinese savings and current account surplus took place between 2001 and 2005. Can we really believe that this would have put significant downward pressure on the global equilibrium level of interest rates especially when we take account of opposing upward pressure from such factors as the Bush tax cuts of 2001 and subsequent loosening of the reins on public spending or of credit market innovations (not all of them bubble-like!) which allowed a wider span of households to tap the credit markets?

Moreover, the successful assault on the Asian Dollar Zone by an Unholy Alliance of Washington, Paris and Frankfurt in 2003 (Dubai Summit, see p. 44) would surely have as one consequence an emerging risk premium on the transfer of capital into the US from the once Asian dollar bloc countries. This new risk premium should have gone along with an upward revision of the neutral/natural level of the US interest rates (and downward revision of the East Asian level).

In sum, central bank policies considered in their widest sense were very much part of the explanation as to why medium and long-term rates were most likely well below equilibrium rates during 2003–6, both in the US and Europe. But that is not where the rebuttal of the central bank apologists ends. A key further part of the rebuttal is the denial of Greenspan's claim that long-term rates rather than money market rates (with the latter most under the control of the central bank) or any other measure of monetary conditions were critical for the heating up of the credit and real estate markets.

In fact it was arguably the very low level of short-term rates and the expectation that central banks would indeed keep those down for an extended period (as reflected in short-/medium-maturity fixed rates) that spurred the perception among investors of 'income famine'. Towards maintaining or sustaining income, they became willing to assume a greater degree of credit risk exposure in their portfolios and at a lowered level of risk premium. And by the same token they may have become more ready to search out for human talent that supposedly could bolster rates of return above the thin levels available in an otherwise efficient market.

With market rates of interest so far below the neutral or natural level and for such an extended period, the supply of apparently suitable assets (including human talent) to meet the income famine-induced demand became self-generating. The irrational exuberance which is generated under such a situation of monetary disequilibrium grew and grew.

Prices of risk-credit paper and real estate rose under the influence of interest rates across the maturity spectrum far below the path consistent with a stable (non-heated) return of the US economy to prosperity. In turn many market participants perhaps wearing rose-coloured spectacles came to interpret those rises as due to some real factor (or 'speculative displacement', see Aliber and Kindleberger, 2005) – for example, in the case of real estate the dawning of universal home-ownership or societal shifts powering demand for residential space – which in turn lead to expectations of further rises. A booming construction industry and finance industry drew in (directly or indirectly) savings from around the globe which otherwise would have eventually pressed down the cost of capital (and critically the equity cost of capital) to other sectors of the US economy, raising the level of investment there. (It would have taken time for this channelling of global savings into alternative investment opportunities in the US to become fully operative. The process of creative destruction including the emergence of sound investment opportunity does not occur quickly. In the interim, the Asian savings surpluses would have been constrained well below their equilibrium level due to the slow pace at first of US economic recovery).

The credit assets manufactured in the US residential real estate market were largely swapped into floating rate form in which they were absorbed by the rapidly growing credit hedge funds (themselves highly geared) or by the off-balance sheet vehicles of the banks (these in turn issued asset-backed paper). The depth of the market (for investors) for the mortgage credit bubble assets was hence a function of the investor demand for a higher yield on floating rate paper. This is a point which Greenspan's focus on the long-term mortgage rate pure and simple fails to pick up. The availability of mortgage finance at growing levels of risk was a function of below-equilibrium floating short-maturity rates (and the expectation that these floating rates would remain below neutral for a considerable time).

Implications of verdict on Federal Reserve for euro-trial

All of the above discussion can be cast also in terms of the euro-area. Below-equilibrium levels of interest rates in Europe in the context of growing income famine generated demand for and supply of a rapidly expanding array of credit paper.

In the European context, this included the new phenomenon of residential mortgage asset-backed paper, much of which was based on real estate bubble markets in Spain and the UK in particular. There was also the leveraged corporate loan market and high-risk European corporate bonds much of which was lapped up either by hedge funds or bank off-balance sheet vehicles. And there were the massive flows of capital from Northern European member countries (banks and non-bank investors) into the sovereign debts of the southern countries.

Given the full scope of financial engineering which utilizes currency swap markets, supply and demand of high-risk debts in Europe would have been bolstered to some extent by monetary disequilibrium confined just to the US. In fact, accompanying European monetary disequilibrium magnified the euro-area source supply of and global demand for euro-denominated credit paper while stimulating US source supply of and global demand for dollar credit paper.

The effect of monetary disequilibrium did not stop at the credit markets. In principle there are risk-arbitrage flows between the credit markets and equity markets. Risk premiums most probably fell generally. (There can be no precision when it comes to the measurement of risk premiums in the equity market – or indeed any other market – as the multi-period expectations of return are unobservable. Moreover risk premiums are in the eye of the beholder, and in some market situations, especially related to 'speculative displacements', vision is highly heterogeneous.)

It is plausible that the biggest fall in risk premiums came in respect of any sober measurement of returns and risk in the growingly leveraged (off-balance sheet) banking sectors in Europe and the US. In principle and in practice, risk-arbitrage between credit markets and equity markets is quite inelastic at times. Such inelasticity would have been an important barrier to equalisation of risk-adjusted rates of return across asset categories (for example, corporate debt and equity) in the climate of the mid-2000s so soon after the bursting of the NASDAQ bubble and given the shift of many investors away from equity risk (at the margins of their portfolios).

Suppose in all of this, the ECB had stood out by not succumbing to deflation phobia and then to fear of the weak US dollar. Correspondingly it would not have engaged in the manipulation of market interest rates (especially for medium maturities) by holding money rates at exceptionally low levels and trumpeting its intentions to do so for a considerable period of time. How different would have been the rise of temperature in credit and real estate markets around the world?

A first point to consider is the interdependency between euro and US rates. If the ECB had indeed resisted the siren-calls of the inflation breathers-in, then the US dollar might well have fallen precipitously in 2003–4 (most of all against the euro), in reaction to which even the Bernanke/Greenspan Fed would have had to accelerate their glacial pace of rate rises. And so the monetary disequilibrium in the US might well have been curtailed by exchange rate shock – a slump of the US dollar (and its knock-on implications for inflation expectations in the US).

Secondly, in the universe of floating rate assets across all currencies a substantial sector, that in euro-denomination, would have been generating a good income, relieving any potential income famine generally and making investors globally less ready to take on extra risk at below normal levels of return. Even so, the euro would have been bidden up to such a high level that the real rate of return on euros from the viewpoint of investors whose shopping basket was concentrated on items outside the euro-area would have been partially eroded by the prospect of subsequent decline (once US rates rose back to neutral level). But similarly the real rate of return on dollars from the perspective of investors who intended to spend much of their wealth in non-dollar countries would have been boosted from ultra-feeble levels by the prospect of exchange rate gain once the ultra-easy US monetary policy came to an end.

The ECB could not single-handedly have totally relieved the income famine resulting from the Federal Reserve's breathing in inflation policy but there would have been some partial offset for many international-minded investors. In effect some of the higher income in the euro-sector would have been funnelled into the dollar sector as seen by international investors there (not US domestic investors).

Thirdly, in the euro-area there would have been less heating up of domestic credit markets. With the ECB steering rates at a faster pace towards neutral, the mortgage and real estate markets would have remained cooler throughout. And the banks in the once-high-interest rate countries (Spain, Italy) for example would have enjoyed less of a sudden bonanza of profit which set the market for their equity on fire, meaning their management teams would have been less inclined to continue along aggressive expansion courses.

Nonetheless, European banks could not have escaped the influence of US monetary led credit warming, even though that (US warming) would have been less than otherwise (due to knock-on effect of exchange rate to US monetary policy). The warm market in US banking shares would have had a contagious influence on the European banking industry.

European banks which had expanded their businesses into the US bubbly credit markets might well have found their share prices outperforming those that did not (join the dance), especially if the implicit leverage was camouflaged from view via off-balance sheet vehicles. Those 'aggressive' European banks would have been thereby in a position to take over European banks which remained more conservative. And similarly European banks which sought to match the rapidly growing earnings of their US peers by gearing up in the overnight dollar repo markets (using the proceeds to lend into the emerging market economies or to buy US credit paper) or in the Swiss franc inter-bank markets for lending into Eastern Europe (or into the Spanish mortgage market) might have been rewarded accordingly.

There may still have been some degree of imprudent lending from banks in savings surplus areas via the new overnight inter-bank euro market into banks in savings deficit areas (within the euro-zone), without due concern for the total risk of the inter-bank exposures created. But looking at the total picture, the temperature rise in European credit markets would have been less under a distinct and harder European monetary policy, the risks built up less, albeit that the overall performance of European banking shares would have been less gratifying than otherwise during the years 2003–2007H1.

Could there still have been a Panic of 2008 unleashed by the post-Lehman freeze-up which would have sent the euro-area into deep recession?

Panics are not pre-determined. They are a risk along the path of credit and asset market temperature decline from hot levels. The risk would have been less if the temperature had reached less hot peaks (as would have been the case if the ECB had not mimicked Federal Reserve policies throughout the first decade of the twenty-first century).

The extent to which European banks were caught up in the Panic (themselves coming under deep suspicion) would have been that much less, with calming implications both within Europe and for knock-on-effects to the rest of the world. European asset markets themselves would have been less vulnerable to the panic (if indeed starting from a less heated position). Beyond these measured counter-factual statements, the compass becomes totally unreliable!

Why does the ECB continue to escape indictment?

As we journey further into the second decade of the twenty-first century and the observed costs of the 2008 Global Panic accumulate, European central bankers have escaped virtually all reproach at the level of mainstream political debate. Indeed many US-centric economists, including those who have walked the corridors of power, remain blithely unaware of the European dimension to the monetary disequilibrium behind the global credit bubble and burst.

For example, Professor Taylor in his attack on the Federal Reserve for its role in the credit bubble and burst makes no international connection with events in Europe (see Taylor, 2009) And San Francisco Fed President Janet Yellen, who was bold enough in a speech in March 2009 to express soft criticism of the role of the Federal Reserve in promoting the credit bubble via ultra-easy monetary policy, qualified her remarks by an erroneous observation:

> Fed monetary policy may also have contributed to the US credit boom and the associated house price bubble by maintaining a highly accommodative stance from 2002 to 2004. [...] But it clearly was not the only factor, since such bubble appeared in many countries that did not have highly accommodative monetary policies.

But was Professor Yellen really unaware of the simultaneous disequilibrium nature of European monetary policy during those years or, for that matter, of the disequilibrium policy in Japan (where the BoJ was keeping rates below equilibrium level and thereby contributing to the bubble in the yen carry trade – see p. 45)?

In the following chapter we look at the possible remedies which might well lead to a better monetary outcome in Europe, but these will remain only remedies in principle until there is a recasting of the political debate. And essential to a constructive political debate is historical analysis rather than mythology. That applies as much as to the recent past – especially the conduct of monetary policy during the Great Credit Bubble of 2003–7 – as to the more distant past especially the Great Credit Bubble of the 1920s and its sequel in the Great Depression. The difference is that the mythology of the latest great bubble has not yet formed in any fullness and one challenge for economic analysts especially with a focus on Europe is to prevent the negative role of EMU and its central bank being omitted from the emerging mainstream account.

5
EMU is Dead: Long Live EMU!

When the first edition of this book was published in early 2010 it was still far from evident that a jury (made up of citizens from across the euro-zone, appropriately chosen so as to be representative of diversity) would sustain any of the prosecutor's indictments against EMU and the ECB. And a final catch-all indictment in the form 'it would have been better if EMU had never existed' stood hardly any chance of being upheld. Now, two years on, there is a much greater likelihood that a jury would deliver a guilty verdict, though much would still depend on the power of advocacy used by both sides. There are many floating half-credible hypotheses and prejudices out there which the defence lawyers (for EMU and the ECB) could use to sway the jury.

As illustration, in Germany the view circulates (and is promoted by officials in the government of Chancellor Merkel) that if it had not been for the euro, industrial activity would have been crippled by a super-strong Deutsche mark. Instead, under the cover of the euro, German industry gained huge competitive advantages. The flimsiness of this view can be seen in its blindness to the world of the counterfactual. Why would the Deutsche mark have been so strong in the context of lively currency competition in Europe where each country, or at least many countries, sought to build and maintain highly attractive monetary brands? Then global investors would have sought to diversify their portfolios into the French franc and Dutch guilder whilst also retaining considerable enthusiasm for the high coupon alternative monies outside the core (for example, Spanish pesetas and Italian liras).

If German citizens had been spared the eventual tax burdens of bailing out German banks busted by the euro-credit bubble and of making much broader repairs to the broken euro-system (including the re-capitalization of an insolvent ECB), and if their savings had flowed to a much greater extent into a rational assortment of foreign assets (with risk and return considered in sober fashion not in the glow of vast monetary disequilibrium) rather than financing bank lending to Europe's 'hot spots', they would have become the most prosperous of any large country on Earth.

Citizens in the periphery zone countries now suffering under EU-IMF drawn-up austerity programmes (for example, Spain, Portugal, Greece and Ireland) would be in many cases resistant to defence advocacy. But there could be many exceptions (and some of these might find their way into the hypothetical jury!). Indeed some citizens of those countries could still in 2012 look back and reflect that they had done very well out of EMU, taking account of the highly prosperous early years. These fortunates would include investors who had got into and out of the bubble real estate markets with good timing, workers who had enjoyed boom-time income without suffering subsequent economic distress and beneficiaries of public services which were swollen by bubble tax revenues and hot flows of capital into the respective government bond markets. And even the unfortunates could be swayed by non-economic advocacy particularly relevant to the periphery zone countries given their history. This would include EMU as a vital step in the long-run European integration process culminating in political union and how this would be a bulwark against meanwhile dormant fascist forces in the periphery zone countries re-emerging.

Plausibly French citizens in the jury could be most swayed by the defence case for EMU and the ECB, if indeed the advocates for the defence had a chance to speak to the jurors from France directly without risking the downside of annoying the non-French. Yes, French taxpayers will surely be picking up large bills for their share of the various bailouts related to the credit bubble bursting process in EMU. But the wider objectives of French foreign policy – and these resonate with many voters – have been at least superficially furthered in ways that few could have imagined at EMU's start (at end 1998). Back then it seemed that the ECB, in Frankfurt, would be a Germanic ordo-liberal (outside politics) institution run as a re-incarnation of the Bundesbank. Yes, there was soon to be a French president of the ECB (as agreed in a spring 1998 deal between President Chirac and Chancellor Kohl), but the passport office to which he reported would surely have little relevance to any policy outcome. The reality, though, is that President Trichet during his eight-year tenure (starting in autumn 2003) harnessed the ECB and EMU to French objectives.

The strong influence of Paris on the evolution of EMU and the conduct of the ECB did not start, of course, with President Trichet. Noteworthy in the earlier years was the role of Paris in ushering Greece (a long-time especially close ally and armaments client of France) into EMU. In spring 2000 the French Board Member in the ECB, Christian Noyer, presented a convergence report (both at a specially convened press conference and to the EU Parliament) which put no obstacle in the way of Greek entry. True the report was bland. But according to the Treaty of Maastricht the ECB could have drafted a strongly negative convergence report. This history is consistent with the hypothesis that Paris was intent on its Hellenic ally (a few years later to be invited into the Francophone Union) coming into monetary union at an early date even if that meant some statistical slight of hand. And Bundesbankers or others within the ECB Council who might have had their doubts chose to do the bidding of their respective foreign ministries who had entered into various trade-offs with Paris over Greece (for example, Germany would obtain further expansion of the EU into central and Eastern Europe).

French power within EMU has not ended with the retirement of Trichet. His successor, Mario Draghi, a consummate financial diplomat dedicated to the status quo (a monetary Metternich) was supported by Paris throughout the drawn out selection process, whilst President Sarkozy made no secret of his opposition to Bundesbank Chief Axel Weber, who eventually bowed out of the succession. Professor Weber voiced concern in particular about the transformation of the ECB into Europe's Bad Bank and the difficulties which he could have in announcing consensus decisions regarding Bad Bank expansion or indeed monetary policy when he might very likely find himself in a minority of dissidents. The Bad Bank expansion had occured largely in pursuance of France's ambition, as implemented by Trichet, to hold the present broad EMU together, rather than beating a strategic retreat to a group of core countries in which Germany would be the hegemon.

It is not self-evident how many French jurors in a hypothetical trial of the euro would be swayed sufficiently by proof of gains for the aims of French foreign policy as drawn up by the policy elite to dissent from an unfavourable verdict. Election results in France and political polling there tell us that many French citizens resent their political elite and the costly projects (including Greek membership of EMU) to which they become committed whether in the European or global stage. It is implausible that in 2012 a unified French bloc of jurors together with 'politically correct' (distrustful of any motion which might smack of nationalism) jurors from other countries would be successful in preventing a negative verdict emerging on EMU. The reality, though, is that this verdict would not lead on to a set of remedies handed out by the presiding judge. Only public opinion, as filtered through the political process, together with the responsiveness of the most powerful political actors to public opinion, can determine the shape and form of remedies, if any, against EMU and the ECB.

Of course there will be no trial! No European institution exists which would set up a 'Truth Commission' to get to the bottom of how European monetary integration was so badly conceived and then mismanaged. It is also implausible that the German Parliament would set up a Truth Commission to find out how past and present German statesmen failed to put effective obstacles in the way of France moulding EMU in ways which violated fundamental principles that the Kohl government had assured Germans were inviolable. The German Commission would also investigate how Professor Issing, as German monetary guardian at the ECB, totally failed to institute a monetary framework sufficiently resilient to prevent the descent of EMU into a giant credit bubble and burst, which in turn was to have such dire consequences for German taxpayers as the largest con- tributor to rescue missions largely driven by the French government and its close ally, Trichet, at the head of the ECB. There will be no panel in Brussels or Frankfurt seeking answers to a list of questions including how the writ- ers of the Maastricht Treaty failed to set up a constitution of monetary stability and instead handed over absolute power to central bankers who in turn instituted monetary authoritarianism; how the Maastricht Treaty failed to put any effective brake on the ECB's capacity to spawn within its balance sheet Europe's Bad Bank and thereby effectively becoming an agent of a European Transfer Union; how the Maastricht Treaty, by failing to provide for a full legal path and process whereby any member could exit EMU, increased greatly the dangers of monetary union transforming itself into a fiscal union; and how beyond those flaws in the Maastricht Treaty ECB policymakers made a series of such bad decisions.

Bold Remedy: Paris and Berlin launch a new monetary union (EMU-2)

The boldest remedy for all the revealed flaws of European Monetary Union is to end the present union and start all over again. No group of European central bankers or finance ministers, however, acting together would ever come up with such a programme. And even if they were collectively leaning in that direction, it would be impossible to prevent leaks of information about proposals setting off a tidal wave of specula- tive capital which would roll through financial markets.

The most plausible scenario under which the boldest remedy could emerge would be one laden with crisis. In this scenario massive capital flight might be taking place out of weak member states (included in capital flight would be residents there making withdrawals of cash, reckoning that euro banknotes were safer than deposits in the banks in that the latter would be devalued sharply if an exit from EMU were to occur) bringing an explosion in the ECB's Bad Bank operations and threatening to culminate in an almighty financial crisis involving waves of defaults by governments and banks throughout the euro-zone. Default here would mean most likely, a forced exit from EMU for the countries suffering a haemorrhage of funds (especially out of their banking systems) and re-incarnation of sovereign currencies in these at a steeply devalued rate.

Under these circumstances the future of European monetary union – in fact the question of whether there is to be a continuing union at all – would be up to the leaders of France and Germany to determine. If they took no action, by contagion capital flight might spread like fire. After the first one or two member countries had been forced to exit from the EMU (given that the ECB is not prepared to make an unlimited expansion of its Bad Bank operations and that a new intergovernmental bail-out does not become available), a torrent of capital flight could form from the next weakest countries, with investors trying to save their funds from devaluation or default in the probably short time before the gates slammed shut – what Kindleberger and Aliber describes as Torschlusspanik (see Kindleberger, 1973).

This would be the 'De Gaulle-Adenauer moment' (the term is taken from the historic signing by those two statesmen of the Franco-German friendship treaty – see p. 1). The President of France and Chancellor of Germany would meet in secret at an undisclosed military airbase and draw up an emergency strategy for the 'survival' of monetary union. Some European federalists might argue that the only survival strategy should be a joint guarantee of all weak member government debts by the strong and the instituting of political union. As a matter of practical and legal fact the Franco-German summit would be powerless to produce such an outcome. The French president would be there only because he or she had concluded that the grand vision so long entertained by the Paris elite of a wide EMU with German hegemony totally destroyed was no longer sustainable. Instead, the aim of the summit would be to save monetary union in Europe but not European Monetary Union as constructed by the Treaty of Maastricht with all its design flaws. And monetary union in Europe would not mean a union of 15 or more countries as in the present EMU. The essential core of monetary union in Europe is just France and Germany.

Indeed under the circumstances described the flawed union of the Maastricht Treaty would be non-salvageable. Survival of monetary union in Europe would depend on the French and German leaders realizing that fact (the realization would be particularly painful and difficult for the French leaders, but the alternative would be the total liquidation of the euro project so prized by the Paris elite over many decades) and moving promptly forward. They would start by formally agreeing (the French leaders under duress!) that the main flaws of EMU as constructed at Maastricht (let's call this EMU-1) are first, the lack of any constitution for monetary stability based on strict application of monetary rules; second, the virtually unrestricted scope for the ECB to turn itself into a bad bank by making huge back door loans to weak sovereigns and banks; and third, the absence of any legal provision and protocol for member countries to exit EMU. The leaders would then agree on a contingency plan whereby France and Germany would leave EMU-1 and form a new monetary union EMU-2. This new union would be constructed without the identified flaws. And the intention would be to send out immediate invitations to all members of EMU-1 to join the new union, EMU-2.

A new monetary union cannot be constructed in one summit meeting. An emergency structure, though, for managing an immediate makeshift union between France and Germany and possibly those few countries that signed up for immediate membership could be put in place. A Monetary Council would be formed from the participating countries (at the start plausibly just France and Germany). France and Germany would technically leave EMU-1 by declaring that euro deposits (reserves) which German and French banks hold with their respective central banks (and thereby indirectly in the euro-clearing system) could be used for clearing payments only within France and Germany but not outside. There would be a commitment to negotiate a full and comprehensive monetary treaty for the new union, albeit with no going back on the summit agreement to correct the three mentioned flaws of EMU-1. And the members of the new union (EMU-2) would have to agree with the ex-members of the now defunct EMU-1 who did not accept the invitation to join EMU-2 (their non-acceptance would be due to EMU-2, without a Bad Bank, being unable to offer them life support without which they could not survive inside) how to divide up the negative wealth of the ECB once it is liquidated (its liabilities would far exceed the market value of its assets including the now devalued or defaulted loans to the periphery-zone countries and holdings of periphery-zone government debt).

Hence the French central bank would continue to clear euro payments with the German central bank but not outside. Instructions in accordance with this would be sent to the Target System (which clears interbank funds) operated within the European Central Bank. During an interim period, banks in France and Germany might have to suspend or impose limits on 1:1 conversion of euro banknotes into bank deposits, as otherwise they would be faced with a flood of banknotes from all the old union coming into accounts on speculation that the currency of EMU-2 would float to a much higher value than 1:1 against the new sovereign currencies of previous member countries which were not strong enough financially to join (the new union). The old euro banknotes (as had cir-culated in EMU-1) might well sell at a discount to (less than full principal equivalent of) deposits in the EMU-2 member countries and also at a discount to the new banknotes in EMU-2 when eventually printed.

From the date on which emergency decrees set up the new Franco-German drafted monetary union (EMU-2), the ECB would cease to have any monetary policy-making function with respect to the new union, though the new monetary council might on application make use of its money market operational capabilities as far as required and under strict instruction. There would be the big issue to consider of currency losses (or gains) which banks in France and Germany would make as a result of loans and deposits to ex-member countries (who did not choose to join the new union) being now denominated in old euros or new national currencies, which would presumably be at a steep discount to the new French–German euro. Some type of bank compensation fund might well have to be set up (backed by French and German taxpayers) to facilitate re-capitalization for those banks most seriously impaired.

It is possible that all present member countries of EMU-1 except for the weakest at the periphery would reply positively to the French–German invitation to join EMU-2, in which case immediate potential losses on translation would be much smaller than if EMU had totally disintegrated. The in-between countries (not as financially weak as at the periphery of the old euro-area but not as strong as at the core) would face a difficult decision as to whether to accept the invitation to join EMU-2. Their gov-ernments would realize that a period of distrust in the market-place about whether their banks could remain afloat without European Bad Bank support and without access to money printing facilities or EU bail-out funds would go along with interest rates inside their country being much higher than in the core of EMU-2. That could impose heavy economic costs (which would have to be weighed against the alternative option of not joining EMU-2 and re-incarnating sovereign money). Perhaps in view of the close economic and financial links between Germany and Italy, Berlin would enter into a bilateral deal with Rome involving direct

German support to promptly re-capitalize the Italian banking system and so reduce the extent of interest rate premium there.

Some financially strong small members of EMU-1 might decide that rather than accepting an invitation to join EMU-2 they would rather have a national sovereign money, but peg this within narrow bands against the euro (or whatever the currency of EMU-2 would be called). One advantage of staying outside on this basis would be to retain some scope for independent fluctuation of short-term interest rates within the limits consistent with the national currency not straying outside its bands. This scope could be helpful in terms of reducing the severity of a business cycle fluctuation which was specific to that economy. More important though than such an at best modest plus (so long as bands of permitted fluctuation are narrow) would be the greater ease of a unilateral separation from EMU if only tied to it by a fixed exchange rate system.

EMU-2 closer to Latin Monetary Union than to EMU-1

The monetary union drafted in the 'De Gaulle-Adenauer moment' would be much closer to the grand-parent than the grand-child from the perspective of European monetary evolution. The grand-parent here is Latin Monetary Union (LMU), the grand-child EMU-1. LMU for most of its life (1865–1927) operated under the gold standard (with some relics subsisting from the bimetallic gold/silver standard). There was no committee of central bankers in LMU making monetary policy. Rather the growth of the monetary base, whether considered for each member country separately or in aggregate for the union as a whole, was determined in accordance with automatic mechanisms (these set the global production of gold and silver and also how monetary stocks of these precious metals were distributed amongst countries). The fact that gold (and silver) coins – all of standard size and content across the union – from any member's mint could be exchanged freely at par meant that the scope for exchange rate fluctuations between member currencies in the exchange markets was considerably smaller than for gold standard currencies outside the union. But national monies were retained, and any member country could exit LMU at any time.

EMU-2 would not be created under gold standard conditions. But it would share some resemblance in certain aspects to the gold monetary system.

A monetary authority separate from government (but tightly subject to constitutional rules as explained here) would strictly limit the growth of high powered money supply (monetary base) for the union as a whole, setting this according to a formula which would be consistent with price level stability over the very long run (whilst leaving considerable scope for price level fluctuations over the short and medium run). The simplest formula would be an annual rate of expansion (of monetary base) of $x\%$ p.a., where $x\%$ is the long-run estimated trend growth in demand for high-powered money in real terms. Sometimes there would have to be overruns or undershoots of the formula (say $x\%$ p.a. expansion of the monetary base) but this would be according to a set of principles which mimicked the gold standard system. For example, a big dip in prices of goods and services on average below a long-run flat path would bring some overshoot of $x\%$, as indeed occurred when a fall in mining costs relative to a fixed nominal gold price brought an increase in production. Or a sudden surge in demand for monetary base as might happen during a financial crisis would be met by a temporary increase in supply.

High reserve requirements would be restored on the deposit liabilities of EMU-2 member banks – meaning a return to the high reserves which were typical during the gold standard era. High reserves are essential to monetary base having a stable and powerful position at the pivot of the monetary system (see Brown, 2011). It is also essential that interest is not paid on reserves (or on excess reserves). Then demand for these is likely to be elastic with respect to money market rates, meaning that a fixed quantity rule for monetary base expansion would not produce wild money rate fluctuations. (And in any case long-term capital market rates would be largely unmoved by these). As this volume has highlighted already (see Chapter 1), the abandonment of high reserve requirements and of the zero interest paid on reserves as applied by the 'old Bundesbank' of monetarist fame was a big flaw in the design of EMU-1. Interest rates in the money markets would be set by demand and supply in the market for reserves (rather than by central bank rate-pegging operations) and other market interest rates would be totally free of the jawboning (concerning future rate pegging operations and more general considerations) that has typified European Monetary Union and indeed virtually all monetary systems around the modern world. Rates which are determined freely in the capital markets and which are not distorted by central banks trumpeting the likely path of their future money-rate pegging operations should come closer to the neutral level on average over time than is the case for jawboned rates, meaning that potential temperature fluctuations in asset markets should be smaller (less danger of credit bubbles and asset bubbles).

National monetary denominations would be restored within EMU-2 (these were abolished after the first two years of EMU-1, as pre-programmed from its start) as indeed were maintained in the Latin Monetary Union. These denominations would be standardized – specifically 1 French euro, 1 German euro, 1 Dutch euro – all convertible at 1:1 into each other. Banks in member countries of EMU-2 would clear balances between themselves in whatever member currency on a 1:1 basis (meaning that debts in say French euros would be cleared against credit of the same amount in German euros). And throughout EMU-2 banknotes in each national variety of euro would be exchangeable and acceptable (in retail payments) on a 1:1 basis. Inside each member country, governments would give preference to their own money in terms of requiring payment in this particular euro denomination. Similarly wages, rents, and other contractual payments would generally be settled in the national denomination of euro (in France, French euros; in Germany, German euros).

The provision as regards 1:1 clearing of payments throughout the EMU-2 area regardless of particular national denomination would mean that there would be no spot exchange market for the respective national currencies (unlike under LMU, where tiny fluctuations of spot rates, albeit within highly confined gold import and export points – very close as no substantial transport costs – were possible). There could be forward markets in the national currencies. These would function essentially as insurance markets – quoting premiums to cover loss by a particular date due to any suspension of the 1:1 relationship between two given member currencies. These forward or insurance markets would in normal circumstances be fairly narrow, if they existed at all, as the fixed costs of using them would far outweigh the minute risk of an exit taking place. Once, though, any tiny but significant risk of exit for any one member emerges, a discount on the suspect currency would form in the forward market (which optimistically, though not necessarily, would spring to life). Correspondingly interest rates on the suspect currency would rise to a premium above those in the safe areas of the monetary union (defined by no significant risk of an exit).

A monetary union in the style of LMU as described above is a rigorous regime, and more so than LMU was historically. There is no scope, however small, for the spot exchange rate to take some of the strain of distrust in the continuation of membership for a particular currency. Where the spot rate can fall slightly to the bottom of its band of permitted fluctuation or of possible fluctuation as set by the gold export and import points, then the emergence of distrust does not necessarily trigger immediate crisis. Investors who are not absolutely confident in the continuing membership of a given currency can trade off the possible exchange rate gain which they would make (from holding the currency) if such fears dissipated as against the possible loss should the fears intensify. There is no such trade-off in the case of monetary union in the style of LMU, as described here for EMU-2, as the member currencies are fully convertible into each other on a 1:1 basis. And so all suspicion has to become expressed in the current level of interest rate so that holders can see sufficient income advantage (with no possible supplement from exchange rate gain within the possible margins of fluctuation) to offset the risk of loss.

Of course as soon as any significant risk of exit from monetary union emerged, banks in particular would swing into action in managing their possible risk exposure. They would not leave big mismatches between their liabilities and assets in the given member currency, but seek to cover these either by adjusting denomination of particular sections of their balance sheet or taking out insurance in the forward market (if these indeed spring into activity). Interest rates could jump to fantastically high levels in the money markets and short maturity debt markets denominated in the suspect member currency if the risk of exit rose to even a modest level from zero. The toll of such interest severity on the economy of the suspect member country may become so great as to produce a self-fulfilling prophesy. Alternatively the potential toll might be a tremendously strong lever on the government of the suspect member effecting emergency measures capable of restoring confidence.

There would be no intergovernmental bail-outs or bad bank operations by a European central bank to sustain membership of any country. Indeed the European monetary institute piloting the monetary base (as defined in aggregate for all member countries of EMU) according to the set of constitutional rules discussed above would have no authority to lend to banking institutions beyond absolutely normal limits of every-day type operations which would be set in tight rigorous fashion. The institute would not have any authority to buy government paper either in new issue or secondary markets except as strictly set out towards achieving its overall target for monetary base growth.

A new European monetary treaty

Unlike the Treaty of Maastricht, the new treaty would not leave it up to the central bankers to design the key elements of the monetary union. And the central bankers would have much less overall power. Indeed, there should not be a European Central Bank at all. Instead, a European Monetary Institute (EMI) would be in charge of controlling the growth of monetary base for the union as a whole. The stipulated aim of the EMI would be monetary and long-run price level stability. This would be defined as the situation where first, monetary conditions do not become a persistent and serious source of economic disequilibrium and second the price level is stable when considered over the very long run.

The first part of that definition would correspond to J.S. Mill's prescription that 'most of the time the machinery of money is unimportant, but when it gets out of control, it becomes the monkey wrench in all the other machinery of the economy'. The Treaty would set rules so as to prevent money from becoming such a monkey wrench, at least in a big way. Monetary disorder would occur if the EMI by its actions seriously drove market interest rates across short, medium, and even long maturities, far away from the respective neutral level (for each maturity), and with much greater persistence than could occur if market forces were free to operate without interference. (This last term, 'without interference', means nonetheless within an overall framework of monetary stability. Monetary base would be at the pivot of the monetary system and the EMI would set the growth rate of monetary base according to constitutional rules.)

Where the monetary authority by its actions (either inadvertently or deliberately) pulls market rates seriously away from neutral persistently (in the same direction) over time it fuels two particular symptoms of disorder which may or not both be present at the same time. These symptoms may take some considerable time to appear and to be recognizable with a high degree of confidence by even the most trained observers. The first is a rise of temperature across a substantial spectrum of asset and credit markets (where heat is measured by the extent of irrational exuberance). The second is goods and services price inflation (where the focus is on evidence of underlying monetary inflation rather than price fluctuations which occur over time related to such factors as productivity swings, terms of trade changes, cyclical swings and which are consistent with no monetary disturbance).

Monetary stability (as defined above and to be the aim of the EMI as specified in the Treaty) and long-run price level stability are not in continuous harmony with each other. There are periods of friction between the two involving trade-offs, as indeed was the case under the gold standard. In particular, fulfilling the first aim (money not becoming the monkey wrench in the machinery of the economy) could mean that the price level strayed far from the long-run norm with no prospect of return. This would occur if there were a multi-year surge in productivity growth, followed by no period of sub-normal productivity growth. Under such circumstances the pursuance of price level stability could mean injecting a shot of extra monetary base growth, albeit done repeatedly by small amounts over a lengthy period, which could cause at least a small monkey wrench to get into the machinery of the economy (producing a moderate rise in asset and credit market temperatures).

Managing the trade-off between monetary stability and long-run price level stability would not be left to the discretionary judgement of officials. The monetary constitution would lay down strict guides and rules to be followed in any injection process (specifying for example how much the pace of monetary base growth should be boosted above the normal x% p.a. in relation to any persistent deviation of the price level from its long-run flat path).

The new Treaty would stipulate a monetary framework such that the aim of monetary stability and long-run price level stability would be pursued efficiently and with least risk possible of derailment by human error. The framework would be monetary base control (with high reserve requirements and no interest paid on reserves, an x% p.a. expansion rate, subject to various overrides) as described in the previous section. Any change in reserve requirements could take place only after an exhaustive process of justification and subject to a super-majority vote (67%) in every national parliament. This fence around high reserve requirements has been proved necessary by the failure of the first monetarist revolution which occurred in Germany and Switzerland in the early 1970s, where monetarism retained power for a decade or more. Ultimately banking lobbies in each country were able to whittle down the level of reserve requirements, so reducing the pivotal role of the monetary base and tarnishing the reputation of monetarism for stability.

What would be the enforcement mechanism for making sure that the EMI followed the monetary framework as set out? In that there is no political union, the EMI board would be answerable to either a council of ministers from the member countries or to the European courts or to national parliaments severally. Ministers or parliaments would not have the power to override the monetary framework or constitution except under highly restrictive conditions (super-majorities in every national parliament and subject to challenge in referendum and the courts). Parliaments could demand full access to the decision-making records (which must be comprehensive) of the EMI and require full explanations for actions (such as extent of overrides on the basis of various rules), and in the ultimate press for a rescinding or alteration of these if against the rules. Perhaps the construction of EMU-2 would include an independent panel of expert auditors which could judge on such matters, having received complaints from any national parliament. And the panel's decisions could be challenged in court.

Enforcement could also take place via private parties challenging the EMI's actions, whether through domestic political processes or directly to the European courts. And all of this would occur in the context of virtually complete freedom of information. Anyone could demand detailed transcripts of all meetings within the EMI leading up to any decision as regards the setting of monetary base expansion or any other monetary policy matter. Note though that the EMI would not play any direct role in the setting of money interest rates – these would be wholly market determined.

The treaty would include clauses to guard against a resurgent cult of the maestro central banker who could thwart the operation of monetary rules within a constitution designed to secure the aim of monetary and long-run price level stability. After all, in the world of the gold standard, no-one outside the money markets even knew the name of the central bank governor, and in the case of the Bank of England (pre-1914) the Governor served a two-year term with no possible extension. In similar fashion, officials appointed to the EMI would serve only fixed three- or four-year terms with no renewal possible. The head of the EMI would serve a two-year non-renewable term. Perhaps there could be some system of rotation based partly on nationality to determine the head at any time.

As outlined in the previous section, there would be clauses dealing with how any individual member could pull out of the monetary union, and its construction would be in a form so as to facilitate this. So national monetary denominations and banknotes would be maintained, even though these would all exchange against each other on a 1:1 basis. Amongst other matters the given clauses would stipulate the procedures for the exiting government to provide compensation for losses within the interbank clearing system (at the time of exit) and also for how the EMI should adjust its target path for monetary base (to take account of the shrinking of monetary union).

And there would be tightly scripted clauses to prevent the EMI turning itself into the European Bad Bank as the ill-fated European Central Bank did. Indeed there would be a positive prohibition against the EMI acting as lender of last resort. In any period of great financial tension where governments became convinced of the case for making highly speculative 'solvency loans' to stricken financial institutions, then it would be for their national agencies to lend, not for the EMI to act.

(If these agencies could not raise capital due to widespread investor scepticism about solvency of the financially weak government taking on such obligations, then a flight of funds might develop forcing the given government to pull out of EMU). Collateralized lending against government securities by the EMI would be limited to no more than what would be required to match the growth in monetary base as determined in accordance with the formula as detailed above (see p. 188). Government bonds held or lent against by the EMI would be strictly weighted by the relative economic size of each member country.

Total EMU dissolution and a return to free floating

Suppose there were no 'Adenauer-de Gaulle' moment in which the leaders of France and Germany, in the midst of an almighty flight of capital out of periphery zone countries, assured the future of monetary union in Europe at least between their two countries by bringing an end to the old flawed union and launching a new one in its place. (It would be a pre-condition of this moment that the present-day French leader could wear the Algerian cap of de Gaulle, explaining to his fellow citizens why the one-time grand aim of 'Europe in France' which had driven the euro project to date was no longer attainable and why a more prosaic aim was now 'on the table'.) Instead EMU blows apart.

First, the periphery zone countries would call banking holidays, as their insolvent banks could not pay the fleeing depositors without massive new loans from Europe's Bad Bank (the ECB) – and these would not be available, let us assume, beyond 'a certain point'. At the end of the banking holiday deposits and loans would have been redenominated according to the emergency decrees passed by the departing member government, whilst for an interim period (until new banknotes could be printed) euro banknotes would float freely against the new domestic euros.

Second, as the waves of capital outflow engulfed the middle-tier member countries (measured by financial strength), they also could be forced to exit EMU – though there could be a long interim during which deposit interest rates and bond yields here (in the middle-tier) towered well above those in the core, meaning that hot money could be drawn in to replace the capital fleeing. Beyond that interim, and with only an inner core still in EMU, a wave of capital flight out of France could sink the remaining union (of the core countries).

Let's leave to one side the gigantean process (in which there would be many losers and many gainers) of restoring financial order after the massive disruption of these successive waves of capital flight. What would be the shape of the new monetary universe which might evolve in Europe from the ruins of the old?

At one extreme, every country, small or large, which had been a member of the now defunct monetary union, could institute a regime of monetary base control (based on the same principles as already described above for EMU-2). Each independent national monetary institute would set a target for monetary base growth which was consistent with price level stability over the very long run. Each country would draw up a constitutionally enshrined set of rules which tightly constrained the actions of the national monetary institute (overrides of the $x\%$ expansion rule only allowed according to certain fixed criteria and challengeable by both parliaments and the courts; high reserve requirements proof against whittling down by banking industry lobbies). All the currencies would be freely floating against each other. Interest rates in money markets would be freely floating also throughout (no rate pegging by central banks) meaning that market rates elsewhere (especially in the capital markets) would be free of official suasion.

In practice and principle it is dubious whether the periphery zone countries which dropped out of EMU first in a crisis of insolvency, then succumbing to high inflation, could join anywhere near the start in the suggested world of freely floating European currencies each with their monetary base control. High inflation would be part of the bankruptcy proceeding in those periphery zone countries – in effect levying a windfall inflation tax on bank depositors and holders of government bonds. Only after some considerable period of time would the road to monetary purity become at all open to them.

The currencies of those European countries in the MBC (monetary base control) and freely floating universe would be far less volatile against each other than has been typical for the experience of the main traded currencies (say the yen versus the US dollar versus the euro or previously the Deutsche mark) over recent decades. Much of that volatility has derived from divergent monetary paths (central banks in their interest rate pegging programmes essentially sending their economies along different monetary trajectories with symptoms of monetary instability – whether in the form of goods and services inflation or asset price inflation – appearing in non-synchronous fashion). Moreover, a high degree of real economic interdependence between the European countries means that the real sources of potential intra-European exchange rate fluctuation (for example divergent business cycles, shifts in comparative advantage) should be fairly modest.

In no way should this European MBC and freely floating universe be presented as a first best system. The issue is whether it is a superior second best to others feasibly on offer, including EMU-1, EMU-2, or EMU-x.

One drawback of the European MBC and freely floating universe is the unstable relationship between demand for reserves (even where high reserve requirements and no payment of interest on reserves) and real incomes even over the long run in the very small and open economies. Households and businesses in these small economies are likely to hold diversified monetary portfolios; the shifts between the domestic and foreign monies may be considerable and yet not in accordance with any prediction, whether by rule of thumb or modelling process. Moreover, even where MBC were administered strictly in a given small country, this could be affected in a very bad way by monetary disequilibrium generated in the large country next door (or further afield). As illustration, if the German money machine got out of control, then symptoms of goods and services inflation or of asset price inflation could appear in Luxembourg or Holland, notwithstanding strict MBC in these latter two countries. And on the global scene, the US money machine getting out of control becomes a potential engine of asset price inflation or goods and services inflation elsewhere. Yes, incipient inflation in the small country appearing via traded goods prices could be reined back by local currency appreciation under the situation of strict MPC control. But local currency appreciation does not in itself prevent a tide of global irrational exuberance coming ashore in the small country and fuelling asset price inflation there in some markets.

These troublesome monetary overspills from large neighbours may be deliberate or accidental in nature. Perhaps the European big neighbours would indeed run MBC control with the best of intentions aiming for monetary stability (in its two dimensions of no asset price inflation and the price level oscillating around a stable path from the viewpoint of the very long run). But the monetary controllers might make mistakes. They might not apply the various overrides in a timely or efficient manner to the core rule of x% p.a. expansion in their monetary base. (These overrides would take account of evidence about shifts in the trend demand for monetary base in real terms, or a significant deviation of the present price level from the long-run norm, and other factors see p. 184). And so an episode of monetary instability in the large neighbour throws a monkey wrench into the rest of the European economy (as well as in the large country itself). If there is not complete trust, then the small neighbours might suspect that the accident was not an accident and that in fact the neighbour was following a policy of clandestine currency warfare. Sometimes these fears would be justified.

Of course there can never be complete trust between European countries each running their independent MBC systems, even if there are high standards of transparency and other important piecemeal confidence-building measures. And there is the problem already referred to of instability in demand for monetary base in the small countries. Lack of trust and the problem of small countries might stir at least some European governments to contemplate alternative monetary arrangements. These could include a limited monetary union, only between France and Germany, and other countries pegging their exchange rates tightly to the Franco-German currency. The small country under this arrangement has a greater ability to exit than under a grand monetary union where divorce has a higher cost. And the potential influence sacrificed by the small country on the MBC control authority when it decides to operating as a monetary satellite of a large country rather than continuing in union might be trivial.

Ideally monetary trust could be built within Europe by absolute transparency. If all decision-making by each national MBC authority (monetary institute) were wholly transparent with observers present from any country, this would help build trust. But there would still be the question of competence. If the monetary authority in say a small or medium-size European country (or the respective government) becomes fearful that the MBC authority in the biggest regional economy might be steering a disequilibrium path is there scope for any re-assuring dialogue on the subject to take place openly and with any result? That question should be asked in full recognition of the fact that the small country even in European monetary union would have little direct power over the actions of the EMI or ECB. Arguably, in fact, the small country which pegs its currency to a much larger country's currency has a bigger influence on the monetary outcome in the large country than if in monetary union or if treading the independent path of MBC. This would be the case if the authorities in the large country were concerned about the adverse effect on its national money 'brand' were a small country to break the link to it out of dissatisfaction with its MBC piloting skills.

Indeed in a Europe without any monetary union most likely some small countries would indeed opt to peg their exchange rates to the currencies of a large country. A pre-condition for that to happen is that one or more large countries are trusted to pursue monetary stability. There would be a choice – most likely whether to peg to a large European currency – the French franc or the Deutsche mark (both re-incarnated)

– or the US dollar. That choice would be the basis of monetary competition – in which the hypothetical MBC authorities of the large European countries would be aware that sloppy performance could mean a dwindling of their wider monetary zones of influence.

If indeed the total breakdown of monetary union in Europe led on to a system of floating currencies and MBC piloting under strict constitutional rules – albeit with some variations allowing for small currencies to be pegged to larger ones – and all within the context of full transparency and trust-building such that currency warfare in any form were impossible, that would be a big achievement to celebrate. Yes, it would be a pity that France and Germany had not managed to build EMU-2 as outlined at the start of this chapter. But the political liberal (in the classical sense) would find much to cheer in contrast to his or her despair at the monetary authoritarianism and instability which prevailed under EMU-1. After the era of mal-investment and squander which occurred under monetary union as constituted by the Maastricht Treaty a real likelihood of economic renaissance and growing prosperity would open up for all its one-time members.

There are also though ugly possible aftermaths to the breakdown of monetary union in Europe (though not necessarily uglier in a total sense than EMU-1). In particular one or more of the large countries might become subject to nationalist inflation-targeting regimes overseen by officials steeped in Bernanke-ism with its deeply disturbing features of deflation phobia and legitimization of currency warfare. Even in Germany, the joint cradle with Switzerland of the first monetarist revolution, it is far from certain that there would be a return to monetarism in any form. The modern Bundesbanker regards pure monetarism (built by putting monetary base firmly at the pivot of the monetary system) as impractical and in any case disputes that the old school Bundesbankers ever practised monetarism except in a highly modified form. Nowhere in Europe, unlike in the US, are there powerful political forces which could potentially lead to the success of a second monetarist revolution. If political forces in the US against Bernanke-ism prove too feeble to triumph, Europe would be vulnerable to the disruptions of US currency warfare irrespective of whether its monetary order was EMU-2 or MBC with freely floating exchange rates.

Twin menaces – US currency war and French monetary nationalism

US currency warfare from the 1960s onward has played a key role in determining Europe's monetary destiny. Another key factor has been

France's pursuit of monetary nationalism – broadly defined so as to include episodes when this showed up as aggressive currency devaluation (as occurred intermittently in the decades before EMU) or alternatively as the pursuit of 'France in Europe' meaning 'Europe in France'. In speculating about the future contours of the European monetary map, predictions about those two factors – US currency war and French nationalism – should be uppermost.

Historically the advocates of European monetary integration (and some of these advocates were French monetary nationalists!) made much of US monetary shock. They cited extreme US monetary turbulence as having caused great harm in Europe. First the monetary instability generated by the Martin Federal Reserve in the 1960s meant that the European countries, then effectively on a dollar standard, imported inflation. German resistance to imported inflation led to the Deutsche mark ultimately breaking free of the dollar in a process of revaluations and 'temporary' floats in the late 1960s. The arrival of Arthur Burns at the Federal Reserve in early 1970 brought the greatest US monetary disturbance yet (in the post-war world) culminating in the Deutsche mark's float of Spring 1971 – the precursor to the break-down of the Bretton Woods system. Paris, in particular, bemoaned the lack of common European response to US monetary turbulence and the related breakdown of fixed exchange rates in Europe. (If all countries in Europe were on the dollar standard, as was the case through the mid-1960s, then intra-European exchange rates were fixed.)

Through the 1970s, France at first engaged in a period of competitive devaluation, allowing its currency to plunge versus the Deutsche mark during the 1974–5 Great Recession and its immediate aftermath. Then as France, unlike Germany, became immersed in a Great Inflation, there was a change in the pendulum of monetary thinking amongst the French political elite. France had to get a grip on the inflation problem or the franc would become one of Europe's second-tier currencies (together with the pound and lira), whilst Germany would be in a strengthened position of monetary hegemony on the Continent. French officials engaged in intensive rounds of diplomacy towards launching a process of European monetary integration. These culminated in the European Monetary System (EMS), coming into effect in 1978, which Chancellor Schmidt defended in private session to the reluctant Bundesbankers by stressing Germany's special obligations to Europe in view of its Nazi past.

Barely three years after EMS was launched, French currency nationalism mutated from 'France in Europe and Europe in France' back to aggressive devaluation of the franc. The Mitterrand Administration, coming into power in spring 1981, effected a series of franc devaluations so as to gain the necessary monetary freedom to pursue its socialist agenda. As economic and social utopia failed to arrive, but high inflation returned, popular support for the Mitterrand Administration plunged. President Mitterrand and his advisers hit on the strategy of embracing 'Europe' as the grand aim to revive electoral fortunes. And a whole string of historical coincidences (culminating in the fall of the Berlin Wall) – together with a remarkable close relationship forged with German Chancellor Kohl – allowed this to move forward with remarkable speed.

During the series of negotiations leading up to EMU, the French advocates argued adamantly that continuing US monetary turbulence made the present Deutshe mark-based monetary order (the European Monetary System) unsatisfactory. In particular, as tidal flows of money crossed the Atlantic in either direction, powered by US monetary disequilibrium, the Deutsche mark was driven up or down against other European currencies, including in particular the French franc. And so US monetary turbulence produced strains inside the fixed exchange rate bloc centred on the Deutsche mark. This complaint also struck a chord with much business and political opinion in the Federal Republic, given that German industry had to make painful adjustment to sometimes significant rises of its currency against those of neighbouring European currencies.

The complaint was always short on substance. If the French franc were to become as attractive as the Deutsche mark to international investors, why would the tide of money flows from the US dollar concentrate any more on one currency than the other? The exchange rate between those two leading European currencies would be largely unaffected. But the French political elite never had an interest in promoting the franc as hard money to rival the Deutsche mark. Perhaps the elite just regarded this as mission impossible given German industrial might. Rather Paris had its sight on overturning German monetary hegemony by driving forward to European Monetary Union and it was hard to distinguish its promotion of 'Europe' from that of France.

In the years running up to the launch of the euro, there was significant tension between France and Germany about the form of the union to be constructed. Paris favoured a union which would extend also to 'economic governance'. Bonn, and later Berlin, was adamant that there would be no 'economic government' and that there should be no potential burden sharing. Fatally, however, the German negotiators never realized that the only real defence against monetary union turning into fiscal or transfer union was to have a clearly defined possible exit route for individual members together with effective obstacles to the European central bank bailing out governments and banks via its back door. If a member country lost the confidence of investors it would be driven out of the union by massive capital flight and no-one would come to its rescue.

It is dubious that there was ever any realization in Berlin of the extent to which a French head of the ECB could turn European Monetary Union into an instrument of French policy and with what serious results for all. M. Trichet had not even fully taken the President's Chair in autumn 2003 when he used the Dubai G-7 summit to join with the Bush Administration in demanding a break-up of the Asian dollar bloc. It had long been an aim of Paris to see a diminution in the dollar's global role with this being taken over in part by the euro. In the two years which followed the Dubai summit, Trichet used his skills as an economic diplomat to promote the mantra that the main problem in the world economy was 'global imbalances', meaning that the US had to take steps to reduce its current account deficits and Asia to reduce its surpluses. But in carping about the lack of savings in the US and the responsibility of this for the mega US current account deficit, Trichet ignored totally the true threat to the global economy – a credit bubble which was being fuelled by monetary disequilibrium worldwide with the Greenspan/Bernanke Federal Reserve the leader of the orchestra and the ECB itself not far behind!

In consequence of his flawed diagnosis of global ills based on longtime hang-ups of the French political elite, Trichet failed to see that EMU was failing in one of its main objectives – to insulate Europe against US monetary shock. In fact the ECB ended up creating a monetary shock as large if not larger as that emitted by the Greenpan/Bernanke Federal Reserve during the years 2003–6. Of course Trichet and the French political elite would never admit that. The closest to a confession about the ECB's key role (alongside the Federal Reserve) in generating the global credit bubble and bust came from the Bundesbank President, Professor Axel Weber. But one of the bizaare twists of EMU history was that he found himself let down by the German government, with Chancellor Merkel making one concession after another to Paris as the bust phase which followed the bubble intensified.

The decisive date in Chancellor Merkel's yielding to French demands (as fully supported by Trichet at the ECB) was May 2010 when Bundesbank President Weber buckled at Trichet's proposal for a further big expansion of the ECB's 'bad bank' role – specifically in the direction of unlimited further lending to Greek banks against the collateral of Greek government debt (even though this was now rated as junk by the credit agencies) and of purchases in the secondary market of weak member sovereign debt (especially Greece). In the EU summit of May 2010, though, Chancellor

Merkel effectively repudiated the Bundesbank President's position by agreeing with French President Sarkozy to a vast bail-out for Greece (a long-time close ally and armaments client of France) and for a new European institution, the EFSF, to be set up, which would borrow in global capital markets with the benefit of guarantees provided by the financially strong members and would take part in agreed lending programmes to the weak. No limit was imposed on Bad Bank operations of the ECB.

Paris viewed the EFSF as an embryo European Monetary Fund which from its start has been a key institution in the transformation of European Monetary Union into a transfer and fiscal union. In an EU summit a little over a year later (July 2011), just three months before Trichet's scheduled retirement, Paris achieved substantial further progress in its ambition to turn EMU into a deeper union spanning 'economic governance'. The role of the EFSF was to be now expanded into providing credit lines to member countries under 'payments pressures' and into re-capitalizing weak banks which otherwise could not obtain capital (Greek banks were potentially at the front of the queue given their large holdings of Greek government bonds and the looming default on these).

Trichet throughout the second phase of the Greek crisis (as the first) remained adamantly against a resolution in the form of no further bail-out – meaning most plausibly an exit of Greece from EMU. In this he was entirely in line with the French government. And in fact the view from Berlin – at least from the office of the Chancellor – was not so different. Professor Weber, despite his unhappiness in early 2010 at the direction in which Trichet was taking the ECB, culminating as one factor in his subsequent resignation (in early 2011), never advocated exits from EMU. Indeed he spoke of a 'Marshall Plan' for Greece. And so there remains some essential ambiguity about his position.

From the standpoint of winter 2011/12 it remains unclear how far EMU has journeyed into being a transfer and fiscal union with area-wide economic governance. Much will depend on how far Berlin agrees to further increases in the resources of the EFSF including its leveraging-up and how far it retards more generally the growth of that institution. Also the attitude of Berlin to further bad bank expansion at the ECB will be crucial. The clash between French monetary nationalism on the one hand and the German traditionalist vision of monetary union without economic government and transfer union seems set to continue, albeit that at the time of writing Paris has won several (but by no means all) showdowns with a remarkable weak German government. As a much bigger showdown, though, may yet lie ahead. Also likely to continue is a failure of European Monetary Union to provide any defence against US monetary instability.

It is always difficult to write history while it is writing itself. But in the new episode of US monetary instability which started with the Bernanke-ite QE-2 inflation time-bombing campaign of Autumn 2010 it seems that yet again European Monetary Union as an institution has failed to provide any insulation against US shock. Instead, the ECB, doubtless influenced by the sharp devaluation pressure on the dollar (induced by the QE-2 campaign), kept its peg for money rates at remarkably low levels (from the perspective of core EMU) during late 2010 and early 2011. Expectations that this pegging at low levels would persist (with only one or two small rises over say a year or more) as encouraged by ECB 'official-speak' contributed to longer-term risk-free market rates staying well below neutral.

In the situation of winter 2010 and spring 2011 there was no likelihood of European monetary disequilibrium creating a credit bubble within the euro-area, though there were some troublesome symptoms of asset price inflation in specific European markets – including Paris residential real estate for example. But the below neutral level of market rates in euros (and neutral is heavily influenced by the inner core countries which form say around two-third of the euro-zone in economic terms), alongside US monetary disequilibrium, contributed to the rise of temperature across a range of asset classes outside Europe and the US – in particular emerging market equities, emerging market bonds, and commodities. These high temperatures would likely go along with much mal-investment – too much investment (relative to long-run efficiency as would have prevailed if temperatures had not risen) in the emerging market world (where a significant proportion of the total was by multinationals responding to equity market bullishness in the pricing of projects here – a bullishness which corporate managers would in most cases share) and in commodity-related investment and too little robustness in capital spending in US and Europe.

In sum, the most recent past appears to demonstrate that European Monetary Union as constituted by the Treaty of Maastricht has failed to cope with two big challenges – US monetary instability and French monetary nationalism. EMU has provided less insulation both within Europe and globally against US monetary instability than did the Old World (pre-EMU) with a monetarist Bundesbank running a Deutsche mark-bloc. And that Old World had more defences against French monetary nationalism than the Maastricht monetary union, though both in the end succumbed. French monetary nationalism defeated the old Bundesbank order. It also seems to have won several battles along the way (while also losing some) to mould the Maastricht monetary union according to its vision and turning it into a transfer union. But victory (for French monetary nationalism) is far from assured. The successes at first in President

Sarkozy's strident euro-diplomacy with respect to Germany may yet end up in a 'Napoleon III moment' – a debacle where France has to accept unreservedly German terms for continuing with EMU.

The monetary menu now hanging on the wall for those European citizens interested to look – for they will not have a chance to choose from the alternatives there! – include the following possible futures.

First, European Monetary Union, as constructed at Maastricht, evolves into a full transfer union in which the French elite's vision is triumphant. The ECB continues to operate the present monetary framework – remarkably similar in many respects to the Bernanke-ite system except in the crucial respect of no QE time-bombing and no waging of currency war. Germany would not countenance that. But everything else is there – strict money rate pegging, inflation targeting, rejection of monetarism. In this first menu item, US and European monetary instability will continue to reach high crescendos mostly at the same time and inter-reacting to magnify the harmful effects both domestically and in the outside world.

Second, EMU-1 collapses, to be replaced by EMU-2. This second monetary union is founded on monetarism and on no bail-outs. The realization of EMU-2 does not have to mean the death of French monetary nationalism but an important metamorphosis would have taken place. It would not now be France in Europe and Europe in France but a dual French–German monetary order in Europe. US monetary instability, even in its present virulent Bernanke-ite forms, would most likely continue to co-exist with EMU-2, meaning sometimes violent fluctuations in the euro–dollar exchange rate. But EMU-2 would create a bulwark against US monetary instability being imported into Europe where it would become a secondary source (alongside the primary US source) of instability in the global economy. Eventually Bernanke-ism might fall and a second monetarist revolution triumph in the US. Then Europe would no longer suffer the violent exchange rate fluctuations and the world generally would enjoy a degree of monetary stability unseen since gold standard days.

Third, EMU-1 collapses, and there is no EMU-2. But all previous member countries of EMU agree on a new form of monetary cooperation. In this they all introduce monetary base control regimes designed to achieve monetary stability and exchange rates are freely floating (with the possibility of some small countries deciding to become monetary satellites of a larger country). By construction, French monetary nationalism dies under this menu item. Yes, US monetary instability might continue even including the Bernanke-ite aspect of currency warfare. But as each of the European monies would be highly attractive to international investors there would be no reason to assume that waves of capital flows in or out of the dollar would cause turbulence in intra-European exchange rates. And each independent monetary authority in allowing their currency to float up freely in response to US inflationary monetary shocks would be confident that other monetary authorities (in neighbouring European countries) would be acting similarly. Again, as for the second item in the monetary menu, this third item would be much more enjoyable if the second monetarist revolution took place and triumphed in the US.

Fourth, EMU-1 breaks down, there is no EMU-2, and French monetary nationalism undergoes metamorphosis into its previous form of currency belligerence (beggar-your-neighbour devaluation). One or more countries might adopt monetarism (monetary base control with a freely floating exchange rate). But with France ready to launch currency warfare especially during a period of economic weakness and French monetary and currency policy subservient to wider national interests as perceived by the Paris policy elite, other countries, even Germany, could decide that the adoption of monetary base control and a freely floating exchange rate would just leave them defenceless against French attack. If against this background a second monetarist revolution triumphs in the US, then life for the monetarist economies in Europe would become less harsh, though they would still have to deal with intermittent French monetary shock.

Isolated, the French elite can only be a monetary nuisance. France does not have the power on its own to set a big monetary monkey wrench in the machinery of the global economy. But Europe in France does have such power. And it is not just the monkey wrench which is troubling. It is also the use by Paris of EMU power to pursue its agenda of a special relationship with Beijing so as to promote multi-polarism and combat US monetary hegemony. The deals have been growingly blatant. Beijing supports increased resources for the IMF and its use to shore up EMU and agrees to French heads for the IMF in exchange for Paris using its best endeavours to thwart any aggressive stance by Washington in a campaign to force Beijing to play by the market rules of the global economy.

So far, under EMU, successive US Administrations have acted blind to how monetary nationalism as pursued by the French policy elite has undermined progress in the biggest economic conflict area globally – trade and currency relationships between China, now the second largest economy, where state capitalism and mercantilism remain triumphant, and the rest of the world. US Administrations have also ignored how much EMU with all its flaws has subtracted from European prosperity thereby undermining the Atlantic Alliance. Instead they have blandly supported European monetary integration and most recently approved big new contributions of the US to the IMF for the ostensible purpose of shoring up European Monetary Union (though US officials, still traumatized by the 2008 Panic, put stress on the more prosaic objective of avoiding a second 'Lehman moment').

In practice, the greatest contribution by the US to the building of monetary stability in Europe would come from a successful monetarist revolution against Bernanke-ism and Washington sharpening its direct international economic diplomacy (whilst turning its back on the IMF and vetoing further funds for this institution). Outside the US, the exit routes of Europe from monetary failure all pass through an inter-change where the Paris political elite suffers terminal setback to its ambitions for Europe in France. There is also another key interchange where both French and German public opinions come to realize the full extent to which needless and avoidable monetary instability (where this is inter-preted to include credit and asset market temperature rises and all the mal-investment which this brings) as generated by European Monetary Union in its Maastricht form is to blame for erosion in their living standards. Hopefully this volume will help towards the reaching of those interchanges on the exit route from European monetary failure as well as towards gaining sight of the route's possible end destination.

Bibliography

Aliber, R. Z. 'Client Letter', 29 April 2009.

Aliber, R. Z. and Kindleberger, C. P. 'Manias, Panics, and Crashes', Palgrave Macmillan, 2005.

Baba, McCauley, R. and Ramaswanny, S.'US Dollar Money Market Funds and non-US Banks', BIS Quarterly, March 2009.

Bank for International Settlements, Annual Report, June 2008.

Bini-Smaghi, Lorenzo 'Conventional and unconventional monetary policy', Keynote lecture at the Center for Monetary and Banking Studies, Geneva, 28 April 2009.

Blamen, Robert 'Bernanke-ism: Fraud or Menace', Paper delivered at Burton S. Blumert Conference on Gold, Freedom & Peace, LawRockwell.com.

Broaddus, J. Alfred and Goodfriend, Marvin 'Sustaining Price Level Stability' Federal Reserve Board of Richmond Economic Quarterly, Vol. 90/3, Summer 2004.

Brown, Brendan 'Bubbles in Credit and Currency', Palgrave Macmillan, 2008.

—— 'Monetary Chaos in Europe', Routledge, London, 1986.

—— 'The Euro on Trial', Palgrave Macmillan, 2004.

—— 'The Global Curse of the Federal Reserve', Palgrave Macmillan, 2011.

—— 'The Yo-Yo Yen', Palgrave Macmillan, 2002.

—— 'The Case for Negative Interest Rates', *Financial Times*, 20 November 2008.

—— 'This is not a tale of two depressions', *Financial Times*, 18 June 2009.

Brown, William Adams (1940) 'The International Gold Standard Reinterpreted 1914–31', New York, National Bureau of Economic Research.

Bruner, Robert and Carr Sean, D. 'The Panic of 1907: Lessons Learned from the Market's Pefect Storm', Wiley, New York, 2007.

Brunnermeier, Markus K. 'Deciphering the 2007–8 Liquidity and Credit Crunch', *Journal of Economic Perspectives*, 23(1), pp. 77–100, Winter 2009.

Buiter, Willem, H. 'Overcoming the zero bound on nominal interest rates with negative interest on currency: Gesell's solution', *The Economic Journal*, 113 (490), pp. 723–46, 2003.

Butler, Eamonn 'Adam Smith – A Primer', IEA, 2007.

Bank for International Settlements, Annual Report, June 2008.

Cecchetti, Stephen G. and Schoenholtz, Kermit 'How Central Bankers See It: The First Decade of ECB Policy and Beyond', NBER Working Paper 14489, November 2008.

Dimand, Roger and Geanakoplos, John 'Celebrating Irving Fisher: The Legacy of a Great Economist', Blackwell, 2005.

Eggertsson, Gauti and Woodford, Michael 'The Zero Bound on Interest Rates and Optimal Monetary Policy', Princeton University Working Paper, 26 June 2003.

Eggertson, Gauti, IMF 'How to Fight Deflation in a Liquidity Trap: Committing to be irresponsible', 1 March 2003.

Eichengreen, Barry 'Viewpoint: Stress Test for the Euro', *Finance and Development*, June 2009 (IMF).
—— 'The Gold Standard in Theory and History', Routledge, London, 1997.
Friedman, Milton 'The Optimum Quantity of Money', Aldine Transaction, London, 2006.
—— 'Essays in Positive Economics', University of Chicago, 1966.
Friedman, M. and Schwartz, A. 'A Monetary History of the United States', Princeton University, 1963.
Galati, Cabriele and Tsatsaroris, Kostas 'The Impact of the Euro on Europe's Financial markets', BIS Working Paper, No. 100, July 2001.
Gerrats, Pera M. 'ECB Credibility and Transparency', ECB Economic Papers 330, June 2008.
Gesell, Silvio 'The Natural Economic Order', Peter Owen, London, 1958.
Hayek, Freidrich A. and Salerno, Joseph T. 'Prices and Production and Other Works on Money, the Business Cycle and the Gold Standard', The Ludwig von Mises Institute, 2008.
Hayek, Freidrich A. 'Denationalization of Money: The Argument Refined', The Ludwig von Mises Institute, 2009.
—— 'New Studies in Philosophy, Politics, Economics, History of Ideas', London, Routledge, 1978.
Hetzel, R. L. 'Monetary Policy in the 2008–9 Recession', *Economic Quarterly*, Vol. 95, No. 2, pp. 201–33, 2009.
Hirsh, Michael 'Channeling Milton Friedman', *Newsweek*, 17 July 2009.
Hördahl, Peter and King, Michael 'Developments in repo markets during the financial turmoil', *BIS Quarterly*, December 2008.
Issing, Otmar 'The Birth of the Euro', Cambridge University Press, 2008.
Issing, O., Gaspar, V., Angeloni, I. and Tristani, O. 'Monetary Policy in the Euro-area', Cambridge University Press, 2001.
Jordan, Thomas 'Central Banks in Action; financial market turbulences and policy measures', Speech to the 36th General Assembly, Association of Foreign Banks in Switzerland, Geneva, 6 June 2008.
Kindleberger, C. 'The World in Depression', University of California Press, 1973.
Leaman, Jeremy 'The Bundesbank Myth', Palgrave Macmillan, 2001.
Lowenstein, Roger 'The Education of Ben Bernanke', *New York Times (Sunday Magazine)*, 20 January 2008.
Mankiw, Gregory 'It May be Time for the Fed to Go Negative', *New York Times*, 18 April 2009.
Marsh, David 'The Euro: The Politics of the New Global Currency', Yale University Press, 2009.
McGuire, Patrick and von Goetz, Peter 'US Dollar Shortage in Global Banking', *BIS Quarterly*, March 2009.
Meltzer, Alan 'A History of the Federal Reserve, 1913–51', University of Chicago Press, 2004.
Pollock, Alex 'Towards Creating a Systemic Risk Adviser', American Banker, 17 July 2009.
Rogoff, Kenneth 'Risk of Deflation', Nihon Keizai Shimbun, 17 July 2003.
Rothbard, Murray, N. 'America's Great Depression', The Ludwig von Mises Institute, 1972.
Schwartz, Anna 'Man Without a Plan', *Wall Street Journal*, 26 July 2009.

Stark, Juergen 'Economic prospects and the role of monetary policy in the current situation', Speech to the Deutsche-Luxemburgische Wirtschaftskonferenz Luxembourg, 9 March 2009.

Streit, Manfred D. and Wohlgemuth, Michael 'The Market Economy and the State: Hayekian and ordo-liber conceptions', Max-Planck-Institut zur Ergorschung and Wirtschaftsystemen, Diskussionsbeitrag, 06-97.

Taylor, John 'Getting Off Track: How Government Actions and Interventions Caused, Prolonged, and Worsened the Financial Crisis', Hoover Press, 2009.

Vanberg, Vicktor J. 'The Freiburg School: Walter Eucken and Ordoliberalism', Freiburg Discussion Papers on Constitutional Economics, 04/11.

Volcker, Paul 'Winning over the Americans', in 'Schmidt and the World, Tribute to Helmut Schmidt', 13th Annual Conference of the German–British Forum in Hamburg, October 2008.

Von Mises, Ludwig 'Human Action: A Treatise on Economics', The Ludwig von Mises Institute, 2003.

—— 'The Theory of Money and Credit', The Ludwig von Mises Institute, 1971.

White, William 'The Coming Transformation of Continental European Banking', BIS Working Paper, No. 54.

Yellen, Janet, speech, 'The Uncertain Economic Outlook and the Policy Responses' 25 March 2009, presentation to the Forecasters' Club of New York.

Index